THE
ULTIMATE
PLANTING
GUIDE

THE
ULTIMATE
PLANTING
GUIDE

NOËL KINGSBURY

ADDITIONAL RESEARCH BY SHARRON LONG

WARD LOCK

A WARD LOCK BOOK

First published in the UK 1996
by Ward Lock
Wellington House
125 Strand
LONDON
WC2R OBB

First paperback edition 1998

A Cassell Imprint
Reprinted 1997

Distributed in the United States
by Sterling Publishing Co., Inc.
387 Park Avenue South, New York, NY 10016-8810

Distributed in Canada
by Cavendish Books Inc.
Unit 5, 801 West 1st Street
North Vancouver, B.C. Canada V7P 1PH

A British Library Cataloguing in Publication Data block for this book may
be obtained from the British Library.

ISBN - 0-7063-7752-4

Designed by Grahame Dudley Associates

Printed and bound in Spain

Page 1: A campanula and a diascia make an attractive, easy
combination for a container – and one which is more subtle than traditional
pelargoniums and petunias.

Page 2: A selection of strong colours is skilfully blended
to form an harmonious whole, the effect enhanced by the glaucous foliage
of a mertensia.

CONTENTS

INTRODUCTION

WHERE DO YOU START when you want to buy plants for a garden? It can seem a bewildering business. Garden centres stock a huge range of plants, some familiar, many more unfamiliar; books are full of attractive pictures but unattractive Latin names. You may visit gardens and see things you like, but be unable to find them in either your book at home or the garden centre. Is it possible to obtain these plants? Will they grow in your garden? Then, having decided on some plants, the next problem is putting them together: will they grow well next to each other, and will the combination look good?

This book aims to guide you through the jungle of plant selection and combination – the art of finding plants that you like, that will look good in your garden and that will grow well together. The emphasis is very much on giving you the tools and the confidence to take on this process yourself, enabling you to make use of reference books and other sources of information, and to make the most of garden centres and nurseries when obtaining plants.

Each chapter features a number of planting schemes for different sites and purposes. There are ideas for family gardens that will take three toddlers and a dog in their stride, for low-maintenance gardens designed for those who want to sit and enjoy, not dig and enjoy, and for gardens with an exotic theme for those who would rather be somewhere else altogether. There are gardens for what are popularly called 'difficult' places, such as dry areas, shade and boggy spots, although a better way to think of these is as places with potential, special habitats where a different range of plants may be grown. Then there are ideas for town gardens, gardens for the disabled and gardens that incorporate herbs among the shrubs and flowers. These schemes are all designed to function for many years to come if they are planted as suggested, but they can also be used as a springboard for your own ideas.

CHOOSING PLANTS

As with shopping generally, everyone differs in the way that they buy garden plants. Some are very systematic, especially keen gardeners – they visit gardens, watch gardening programmes on television, read gardening books, and compile lists of what they want to grow. Most people are not so systematic, and the impulse buyer is found in the garden centre as much as in the supermarket – the person who picks up the plant seen flowering away by the checkout and thinks 'I'll find a space for it somewhere'. However, even the greatest impulse buyers are predictable to some extent: we all have particular tastes, likes and dislikes, and even if we have no idea of how to design a garden, our unconscious tastes will begin to create a common theme among the plants we buy.

If you are in the process of creating a new garden or replanting part of an existing one, it is useful to think about what you do and do not like. Reflect on your favourite plants in the garden and the ones you like in other people's gardens. Think also about the ones you don't like: what do they have in common? It may be that they all have brightly coloured flowers or that a particular shade keeps on cropping up – for example, I love anything with dark red or plum-coloured flowers, but tend to be very wary of bright yellow. Your preferences may also be to do with a habit of growth: neat, cushion-shaped plants may appeal, or those with elegant, arching branches. Take time to consider all these factors, because knowing what you like is a fundamental part of creating anything.

The next big question is 'How will the plant do in my garden?' Impulse buying can lead to problems at the best of times, but in the garden this is even more true. The charming little conifer in the back of the car, fresh from the garden centre, may be a 10m (30ft) monster in 20 years' time, while the honeysuckle freshly planted by the back door may take on jungle-like proportions within just three years. Impulse purchases may not even be suitable for the conditions in your garden – how many rhododendrons end up languishing in the limy soils that they hate, never flowering and the leaves turning progressively more yellow?

Then there is the question of how the plants in your garden will get on together: will that sweet little rose bush, for example, turn out to be a thug that elbows its way over the lavender hedge and the pinks? Even if the plants are delighted with each other's company, you may not be – the bright pink geranium you bought last year may well look truly hideous next to the new orange poppy. Plants have to be thought about together, not just separately, and if you are standing in the checkout queue at the garden centre, your time may be well spent considering where you are going to plant the startling orange-flowered shrub in the trolley.

Like much of life, gardening is the art of compromise, of getting the balance right between what you want and what it is possible to grow. You have to consider not only your desires, but also the plants' needs. This book aims to help you in making these difficult choices, so that you end up with a garden you are happy with and that is filled with healthy plants.

A varied selection of plants, including a pale yellow cytisus and Abutilon x suntense, *create a colourful garden in early summer. The effect is enhanced and held together by a clear overall design.*

Part One

GARDEN DESIGN

To be successful, a garden has both to satisfy the needs of the people who use it and to work within the constraints of the local environment. In this chapter we will look at how to choose a style of gardening that is appropriate for your lifestyle, and how to select plants that will grow well in your particular garden.

Chapter One

THE GARDEN ENVIRONMENT

BEFORE YOU START to think seriously about the planting areas of your garden, you will need to understand the limitations that the environment imposes on what you can do. Certain plants will grow well in some places but not in others, primarily due to differences in soil and prevailing weather conditions. Plants also vary in their tolerance of conditions that differ from what they like best. For example, it is reasonably well known that rhododendrons dislike soils containing lime, but what are less well known is their intolerance of any dryness at the roots and the need for many varieties to be grown in a position well protected from strong winds. Altogether, they are rather fussy plants, only doing well in reasonably moist climates on acid soil. A good example of the opposite type of plant is *Rosa rugosa*, which forms a large shrub with glossy green leaves and showy, fragrant flowers, and is an undemanding plant that will thrive in a wide variety of climatic and soil conditions.

SOIL

One approach to gardening is to try to change the conditions to suit the kind of plants you want to grow. You cannot do much directly about the weather, but soils can be altered by the addition of various materials, or even changed altogether, which in turn can also change the way that the weather affects plants. For example, someone who loves rhododendrons may garden on a thin, limy soil in an area of relatively low rainfall. It is possible to change the soil pH by the addition of a chemical (aluminium sulphate) so that it is more acid, and to increase its water-holding capacity by adding organic matter (vegetable compost, for instance) and hi-tech water-holding gels. In this way the soil will be changed, and its improved water-holding capacity will counteract the dryness of the local climate, thus making it possible to grow healthy rhododendrons – for a few years at any rate.

But surely, it could be argued, this is the wrong way round? We should be growing the plants that suit the place, not trying to change the place to suit the plants. The approach outlined above will keep the rhododendrons happy for a few years, but not forever. Rainwater will wash in lime particles from the surrounding soil, a very dry summer may be more than the soil modifications can cope with, and the use of hosepipes could be banned. There is also

There is a good range of colourful species that will thrive on a hot, dry bank, including magenta Gladiolus byzantinus, *mauve-flowered sage and pale yellow onosma.*

the argument that soil modification always involves environmental damage somewhere along the line – the massive destruction of bogs to supply peat for gardens being just one example.

I favour the approach of choosing plants that will naturally grow well in the garden environment without expensive, time-consuming and often temporary attempts to swim against the tide.

What gardeners often call 'problem areas' are not necessarily so. Of course we all want the lovely soft loam soil that they always seem to have on gardening programmes on television, but it is not a necessity in order to create a beautiful garden. Soft loam with perfect drainage is only one soil, one environment among many. Each natural environment has its own flora, and 'difficult' soils have some of the most attractive of all. For example, gardens with thin limestone or chalk soils are a nightmare for most gardeners, and yet the wildflowers that grow on them are among the most colourful of all, and the same plants will also thrive on crushed rubble!

I believe in making the most of the situation we have in the garden, and in seeing the potential rather than the problems of a site. To take the example of thin limestone soil again, many would bewail its ghastliness, beg sympathy from gardening friends and then start to import vast quantities of peat, compost and manure, breaking both their backs and their bank balances in the process. Instead of this, consider what will grow well: there are plenty of attractive plants from poor, dry, alkaline soils that will love these conditions – poppies, lavenders, wild herbs such as thyme, oregano and sage, and the lovely waving heads of *Stipa* grass are just a few examples.

The wall in this photograph catches the sun, enabling slightly tender plants like the blue agapanthus and scarlet Dahlia 'Bishop of Llandaff' to be grown.

CLIMATE

Before you rush out to start planting, however, you must find out about your local environment. If you are new to the area, it will take a long time to find out about all the little local climatic quirks – which direction the really cold wind blows from, just how heavy the snowfall is, how hard the first frosts can be. Your neighbours, especially any keen gardeners, can be a great help as can local nursery owners and farmers, but beware the pessimism of some old gardeners – every neighbourhood has at least one who loves to regale newcomers with horror stories of 'the winter of '86, when the ground froze for three months' or 'the wind that blew the leeks out of the ground'. They will have lots of dreadful things to tell you about the soil as well: 'Oh terrible stuff; took me 10 years and three lorryloads of good muck before I even got a decent turnip.' I'm sure you know them, but don't let them put you off!

It is fairly obvious that it will take a whole year before you have a basic idea of the vagaries of the local climate, but it can take this long to have a reasonable understanding of your soil as well. One

hole dug and a soil sample taken will give you some information, but only some. A soil that seems perfectly workable and well drained in summer may turn to liquid concrete in the winter, and only time and experience will tell you how quickly it dries out, and how wet it gets when it rains.

Soils can vary tremendously across the garden, not just for geological reasons, but because of builders. It seems to be an iron law of garden design that the exact spot you have chosen to put a pond turns out to be the one on which they buried a whole pile of broken concrete blocks. It will take

time and experience to find these places: the patch that always gets really soggy in winter or the area where the grasses begin to yellow first in a hot summer.

Talking to neighbours will teach you a lot not only about the local climate but also about which plants will grow well. Try to observe what does well in local gardens and parks, not just with a view to growing more of the same but for what it can tell you about climate and soil. Big, healthy rhododendrons are a good indicator, for example: the thought of one in your garden may fill you with

COPING WITH THE WIND

A Solid obstacles such as walls create turbulence in the lee of the wind, which can cause plant damage.

B Hedges or other barriers that are only about three-quarters impermeable, such as temporary plastic windbreak netting, offer the best resistance to the wind. They let some through, but break its force (indicated by smaller arrows).

C Most effective of all is a hedge with a chamfered top on the side of the prevailing wind, which helps to direct it up and over.

dread, but if they do well locally then you can be sure that other lovers of acid soil that are more to your taste – camellias, hydrangeas, pieris or heathers, perhaps – will thrive as well.

It is now time to look in more detail at these environmental factors, the effect they have on the selection of plants, and the feel or ambience that you can develop by using them.

THE COLD

Cold is quite rightly considered one of the greatest factors in limiting what can be grown, although the problem is more complicated than simply running off a list of plants against a temperature reading. Cold always has a context: is it the deep cold of a high-altitude, or inland winter, where the ground is frozen for months, or the capricious cold snap of a normally mild but damp maritime climate?

Plants from continental climates are used to the cold but possibly not to the damp, or the alternation of cold and wet, that they may experience in a maritime climate. Many alpines, for instance, are used to a steady cold all winter, but will suffer greatly from rotting in climates with a less predictable winter. Many plants from the Himalayas or Asia, such as magnolias and camellias, are genetically programmed to flower when the temperature rises above a certain point, but in a less predictable climate than the one they are used to, their buds can be stimulated to open by a warm spell and then badly frosted by a cold snap the following week.

It is one of the great challenges of gardening to grow plants from warmer climates than our own, bringing a touch of the exotic to the garden. Such plants can often flourish in the mild winters of a maritime climate, but in the case of woody plants

PROTECTING TENDER PLANTS

A

B

C

D

Mulching roots with natural insulating materials can make a lot of difference. A 10–15cm (4–6in) layer of straw, for example, keeps out a remarkable amount of cold, but it can blow around the garden and make a fine mess unless held down, and may also provide a splendid holiday home for slugs.

Bubble plastic is an excellent insulator but, like all plastics, makes for very humid conditions underneath. This can cause decay in stem and leaf tissues, which means that its use should be limited to short spells of cold weather. Plastics are best used for protecting the roots and underground buds of herbaceous plants; they will not save the tops of shrubby plants, although they will enable such plants to sprout again from the base if the tops are killed.

In climates where the winters are predictably cold all the way through, straw or matting may be tied around plants for protection. This is especially effective for single-stemmed plants like palms and cordylines. Bubble plastic can also be used, but only for limited periods as it may lead to stem rot.

A structure made of bubble plastic securely fixed to a wooden frame, such as an old cabbage crate, will make a miniature greenhouse for tender plants, although some ventilation should be admitted in temperatures above freezing. Such structures need to be weighted down well.

like trees and shrubs, the new growth does not ripen properly and an unexpected cold spell can do a lot of damage to soft young shoots. Species from dry summer climates can often cope with cold, but not cold and damp together. I once met someone who grew several Californian shrubs on Scotland's bitterly cold east coast; I think they survived because the winters are relatively dry and too consistently cold to stimulate unseasonal growth.

In both maritime and continental climates, wind is a factor that can exacerbate the cold, as many of us know from our own experience of winter days. Herbaceous plants, tucked away underground, are safe from winter wind chill, and deciduous trees and shrubs have considerable protection, but evergreens can suffer terribly, showing severe leaf 'burn'.

If you want to experiment with some slightly tender plants in your garden, how do you choose a suitable place? The key is to find somewhere protected from both cold winds and frost. Experience will reveal the sheltered parts of the garden, where the chill of a winter wind is reduced, but the areas that are least susceptible to frost are less easy to find. The best way is to get up early on a cold day when there is some frost, but not one that covers everything. You will be surprised how patchy it is. Cold air is heavy and flows like a liquid, filling up hollows, rolling off slopes and becoming dammed up behind walls. As the sun rises, it melts first on slopes facing the sun, then on level ground and last of all on areas in day-long shadow. Use such early morning winter strolls to find the warmest parts of the garden: these are 'the places for your tender treasures, as well as for fruit trees such as peaches, whose early flowers suffer from frosts, or those that need sun to ripen the fruit, such as vines and figs.

So much for finding the warm spots in your garden. What is it like gardening in cold areas, colder perhaps than the gardening books usually allow for? You may well be limited in the trees and shrubs you can grow, choosing hardy conifers and deciduous species from areas with a similarly cold climate, but there are plenty of herbaceous species that will tolerate winter's cold. Some of the finest are natives of continental centres, where winters plunge to many degrees below zero and growing seasons are short and sweet. Ideas for planting in cold regions are given on pages 40–41.

HEAT AND DROUGHT

Heat as such is not a problem for most plants, but the resulting drought usually is. Most gardens get pretty dry at some stage, but for those on a very sandy or stony soil the problem is chronic. It is also a major headache in regions that have hot, dry summers. The conventional response has been to water, and water again, resulting in a massive burden being placed on water resources. There are, however, two alternatives to irrigation: one is to try to improve the soil so that it holds more moisture and use a mulch so that water loss is reduced, and the other is to grow drought-tolerant plants. Gardeners in Australia and California have traditionally grown plants such as roses and rhododendrons, and tried to maintain emerald green lawns of temperate European grasses, but such unnatural gardens have been difficult to sustain as water shortages have increased. Not surprisingly, there has been a great expansion of interest in these areas in growing native plants that are tolerant of local conditions.

Opposite: Hot, dry climates offer wonderful opportunities for dramatically sculptural planting, such as the yuccas, echeverias and aeonium in this scheme.

Below: Wet ground is the perfect place for orange and yellow candelabra primulas and varieties of Iris ensata, *the Japanese iris, as well as lush foliage plants.*

Dry soils, or soils in dry areas, may be improved by the addition of copious quantities of manure, garden compost or any organic material that will decay rapidly to create water-holding humus. These will enable the soil to absorb and hang on to more moisture, as well as nutrients. Mulching also greatly reduces moisture loss from the soil surface. Lawns cannot be mulched, however, and moisture-improvement techniques such as these involve a lot of backbreaking barrowing around of bulky materials. In a bad drought they will fail anyway.

More than anything else, the selection and cultivation of drought-tolerant plants is the key to creating attractive gardens in hot, dry climates. This does not mean serried ranks of aggressively spiny cacti and agaves, although these are one option: drought-tolerant plants can be amazingly beautiful, and include the intense blue ceanothus of California, the brilliant bulbs of South Africa and the Mediterranean, and the extra-terrestrial beauty of Australia's banksias.

Drought-tolerant plants tend to be either woody – often in the form of dense, low-growing shrubs – bulbous or annuals; there are very few herbaceous perennials. The main structure of the garden will be made up from the shrubs. Nearly all are evergreen, often with attractive grey or blue foliage, and they include lavenders, cistus, acacias and melaleucas. Even before they flower, the patterns and colours made by their foliage are most attractive. In addition, their flowers are often more intensely colourful than those of shrubs from moister climes.

Bulbs and other tuberous plants tend to flower in a blaze of glory during the cooler, wetter seasons, retreating underground during the summer heat. Tulips, species gladioli, cyclamen and anemones are among the vast number of such plants that originate from regions with dry summer climates. Colourful annuals, too, play an important part in gardens and natural landscapes in such regions. A planting scheme for a hot, dry climate is given on pages 38–39.

In dry areas, ground cover can be achieved easily using a variety of low-growing evergreen shrubs, which are much more attractive and interesting than vast expanses of lawn grass, whether emerald or brown. Nevertheless, drought-tolerant varieties of grass are now available.

WET GROUND

Water is the stuff of life for gardens and it might seem rather churlish to complain of too much of it, yet many gardeners do. Poor drainage, especially when it is combined with clay soils, makes for difficult growing conditions for many garden plants, because the soil moisture will prevent their roots from breathing.

While good drainage is essential for lawns and vegetable gardens, it is not crucial for ornamental

TREES AND SHRUBS FOR DAMP GROUND

Plant	Height x spread	Flowers	Foliage (D=deciduous)
Amelanchier lamarckii	5x4m (15x12ft)	white, spring	red, yellow, orange autumn colour D
Clethra alnifolia	2x2m (6x6ft)	white, summer	D
Cornus alba 'Sibirica'	2x2m (6x6ft)	white, spring	D
Myrica gale	1x1m (3x3ft)	catkins, spring	D
Physocarpus opulifolius			
'Dart's Gold'	2x2m (6x6ft)	white/pink, spring	golden yellow D
Rhamnus frangula	2x1.5m (6x5ft)	insignificant	yellow autumn colour
Salix elaeagnos	3x5m (10x15ft)	catkins, spring	yellow autumn colour
Salix helvetica	50x50cm (20x20in)	catkins, spring	D
Salix purpurea 'Nana'	1.5x1.5m (5x5ft)	catkins, spring	D
Sambucus racemosa	3x3m (10x10ft)	yellow, spring	D
Spiraea x billiardii			
'Triumphans'	2x2m (6x6ft)	pink, summer	D
Viburnum opulus	3x2m (10x6ft)	white, summer	red, orange autumn colour D

Shade is the place to experiment with cool green foliage and subtle colours, such as the ferns and white-flowered Dicentra eximia *shown here.*

borders. There are so many lush and attractive plants that relish damp conditions that it seems pointless to put great effort and money into soil drainage in these circumstances. First, it is important to work out why it is so wet. If surrounding areas are dry, or you are on any kind of slope, the cause may be a hard pan of compacted or clay soil underground. This is often the result of builder's activities in the garden – they are fond of dumping dreadful subsoil in gardens and then covering it with a veneer of topsoil to hide their misdeeds. Compacted soil can be dug through and broken up, but clay is more problematic. Small patches can have sand or gravel mixed in to open them up; larger areas may need drainage channels dug or the addition of a deep, thick layer of imported free-draining topsoil. Laying drainage pipes in gardens is a major operation, and should be attempted only if absolutely necessary and as long as there is somewhere for the water to be drained off to.

Raised beds are a good and relatively straightforward way of improving drainage. They are ideal for vegetable beds, but are more difficult to combine with ornamental plantings; a raised bed could, perhaps, be made into a feature in itself, with railway sleepers, thick branches, bricks or stones forming the sides and plants spilling over the edges. An alternative is to create different habitats

Aspect	Soil
sun/part shade	most
part shade	acid
sun acid/neutral	
Dsun/part shade	acid/neutral
sun	most
sun	tolerates waterlogging
sun	tolerates waterlogging
sun	most
sun/part shade	most

RAISED BEDS

A raised bed is a good way of creating the soil conditions that choice woodland plants like ferns and trilliums will need in shady conditions, such as those around buildings. Fortunately, these kinds of plants are shallow rooted, so not too much soil depth is required: 30cm (12in) will be enough, but extra watering will probably be needed in summer. The house wall should be protected from damp by a layer of thick plastic.

in the garden by digging out areas and piling up the resulting soil in low mounds. The lower areas can be planted up with plants that like boggy conditions, and the higher areas with plants that need better drainage.

Far and away the easiest way to deal with bad drainage, however, is to accept it, and select a range of plants that relish wet conditions. The choice is wide and spectacular, mostly comprising herbaceous perennials such as the various colourful species of iris and primula, vigorous summer flowerers such as astilbes, and leafy rodgersias and hostas. Moisture-loving plants are often lush and vigorous, and they are thus ideal for creating a sub-tropical appearance.

Another aspect of water in the garden is its value to wildlife; even in a city, a pond will rapidly become a mini-nature reserve, while lush waterside vegetation will provide cover and food reserves for both insects and birds. Marshland is a much-threatened natural habitat and one that is vital for many animal and plant species, so creating a small area to stimulate it in your garden is a step towards redressing the balance. Some ideas are given on pages 188–9.

SHADE

Despite being welcome in hot, dry climates, shade can be a major limitation on what can be grown in less sunny regions, although it also offers tremendous possibilities. Before we look at what can be grown in shade, it is important to understand how it interacts with other factors that limit growth.

Light shade, such as where there is sunlight for

SHRUBS FOR FULL SHADE

Plant	Height x spread	Flowers	Foliage (E=evergreen D=deciduous)
Aucuba japonica			
'Crotonifolia'	3x3m (10x10ft)		green/gold E
Berberis linearifolia	2x3m (6x10ft)	orange, spring	red in autumn E
Elaeagnus pungens			
'Maculata'	3x3.5m (10x11ft)	white, autumn	green, centre yellow E
Exochorda x			
macrantha 'The Bride'	2x2m (6x6ft)	white, spring	grey-green D
Hydrangea sargentiana	2x2m (6x6ft)	pink/lilac, summer	D
Hypericum calycinum	0.3x1.5m (1x5ft)	yellow, summer	D
Mahonia x media			
'Charity'	3x2m (10x6ft)	yellow, winter	E
Prunus laurocerasus			
'Otto Luyken'	1x2m (3x6ft)	white, spring	E
Ruscus aculeatus	1x1m (3x3ft)	green, spring	E
Sarcococca hookeriana	1.5x2m (5x6ft)	white, winter	E
Skimmia japonica			
'Rubella'	1x1.5m (3x5ft)	white, spring	E
Symphoricarpos	0.5x1m (1½x3ft)	pink, summer	D

several hours a day, or dappled sunlight will limit the growth of vigorous sun-loving plants but provide favourable conditions for many attractive spring- and summer-flowering species. Deeper shade, where there is no direct sunlight, excludes many altogether, but provides a home for woodland plants. These tend to be ferns, spring-flowering bulbs, which do all their growing and reproducing before the leaves are on the trees, or evergreens able to take advantage of sunlight for 12 months of the year. An average to moist soil will provide excellent opportunities to cultivate a wide range of interesting and attractive plants; a dry soil will be more problematic, greatly restricting what can be grown. Deep shade, especially if the soil is dry – as is often the case beneath trees or at the side of buildings – is the worst kind. Few plants will thrive, ivies *(Hedera* species) and periwinkles *(Vinca* species) being among the most successful.

Most shade-loving plants grow best in the kind of humus-rich soil found in woodland, and many will only flourish in the cool, moist root-run this kind of soil provides. If you have established trees with undisturbed soil like this, then you have conditions that are perfect for growing a wonderful range of plants such as ferns, hostas, wood anemones and trilliums. However, shady conditions in small or town gardens do not often reach this ideal, especially around the house, where the soil may be full of rubble. Such conditions make it very difficult to establish many woodland plants, and you would either have to concentrate on the limited range of plants that do not mind, or improve the soil with copious quantities of rotted manure or garden compost.

Planting in shade is quite different from planting in sun, as the nature of shade-tolerant plants themselves is quite different. There are plenty of spring-flowering shrubs for light shade, including many species and varieties of rhododendron and azalea, along with camellias and witch hazels *(Hamemelis* species), but there are few for summer or for totally sunless shade where you will have to resign yourself largely to evergreens, although these can be very decorative, especially if the soil is moist, when bamboos will thrive.

The floral impact of a planting in full shade will be focused very much on the spring, making extensive use of bulbs and of perennials such as the pulmonarias, Solomon's seal *(Polygonatum* species) and primulas. The summer will have few flowers, but many interesting foliage shapes and textures; indeed, it will be easier to do interesting things with foliage in shade than in sun, at least if the soil is not too dry. Hostas, ferns and ground-cover plants, such as *Pachysandra terminalis* and ivies, can all be used to create very attractive foliage patterns. One possible approach is to create a Japanese effect, using elegant foliage plants in conjunction with bamboos around paths of gravel and stepping stones.

A planting in partial shade will be much more colourful in summer, as there are quite a few later-flowering perennials that will thrive in these conditions, including foxgloves *(Digitalis* species) and *Campanula latifolia* for midsummer, and the elegant wands of cimicifuga and the fulsome Japanese anemones for late summer.

SOIL TYPES

There are innumerable different soil types, and yet it is surprising how well the majority of plants adapt to growing in them. Each species has its preferences, though, and wise gardeners stick to those that do especially well on their soil. As mentioned earlier, looking to see what neighbours grow is always a good guide to what will flourish on the

Soil	Notes
most	male variety; very colourful
most	blue/black autumn berrie
most	may revert to all green
avoid very alkaline	avoid exposed positions
most	
most	good ground cover
most	opens out in very deep shade
most	red/black autumn berries
avoid wet	bright red autumn berries
avoid dry	highly scented flowers
acid/neutral	dark red buds in winter
most	white, red or pink berries in autumn

Woodland soils rich in humus provide perfect conditions for spring bubs like wood anemones and scillas.

local soil, but beware of getting too much inspiration from famous local gardens, unless you can be absolutely sure that they have the same geology as your garden. Not only can soils change with remarkable rapidity from one place to another, but contractors have the annoying habit of shipping in soil to fill in gardens around housing estates (usually disgusting clay), so your soil type may be different from what is common locally.

Fertile, loamy soils encourage strong-growing plants, as do clays, which are usually fairly fertile, too. Such a soil will be ideal for roses, many shrubs, fruit and vegetables and for vigorous herbaceous plants, but not for smaller, slower

A RUBBLE BANK

If your soil is full of stones or rubble left behind from building work it can be difficult and expensive to remove the problem, especially if there is no direct access from the garden to the road. An alternative is to pile up the stone interspersed with a little soil to form a low bank, and then cover this with a layer of soil and gravel which need be no more than 5cm (2in) deep. Plant up the bank with lime-loving rock-garden plants and wildflowers, which will relish the conditions. As a final decorative finish, add a surface dressing of gravel.

growing species, which may become swamped by their larger brethren. A clay soil may be very hard to work but, unless you are growing vegetables or bedding plants, both of which necessitate regular cultivation, it is probably not worth the effort of trying to change it. Vigorous plants will be able to make the most of it. Poor soils, on the other hand, favour plants that tolerate stress. Thin limestone or chalk soils, for example, create an inhospitable environment for most garden plants, yet many alpines and colourful wildflowers, as well as bearded irises and Mediterranean species, will thrive. These plants will also do well on light, sandy soils.

Poor, acid soils can be the despair of the rose or vegetable grower. While such soils may be worth 'improving' for the sake of crops, this is not the case for ornamentals that are not suited to them. Why bother with roses, when there is the huge rhododendron and heather family to play with, or vice versa on heavy clay?

Because different soils favour different kinds of plants, the style of planting that can be developed will vary from soil to soil, and this will have some effect on the overall feel of the garden. Fertile soils, which favour vigorous perennials and shrubs, will tend towards a lush feel. Herbaceous borders and cottage gardens full of such plants are a good way of making the most of these conditions. Thin limestone soils, on the other hand, do not favour lush growth, but the kind of plants that flourish on them are wonderfully colourful; a wildflower meadow or an informal planting of drought-tolerant perennials and ornamental grasses are two possibilities.

It will be difficult to get much vigorous growth on a poor, acid soil, but the use of rhododendrons and other lime-hating plants will give gardens on these soils a distinctive character; the emphasis will be on shrubs, spectacular spring and early-summer colour, interesting evergreen foliage and a final splash of red and gold in autumn. For a more open feel and year-round colour on such a soil, choose heathers and dwarf conifers.

Chapter Two

GARDEN TYPES AND STYLES

THE MOST FUNDAMENTAL questions to do with planting and design are practical ones. What is the garden going to be for? Is it primarily for show, creating a nice view from the house, or is it to be enjoyed on a more active basis? Will it be used for entertaining, barbecues and parties? Do you have small children, or (even worse for plants) large ones, or perhaps grandchildren? Do you have pets? Do you want to grow only ornamental plants, or would you like fruit and vegetables as well? Do you have special interests – alpines or roses, for example?

In most cases, a garden has to fulfil several functions, so compromises are necessary. The traditional format of lawn with borders allows space for entertaining and children's play, but also for growing attractive plants or vegetables. Conversely, those who are more interested in gardening for its own sake should perhaps consider reducing the size of the lawn or getting rid of it entirely. It is perfectly possible to plant right across a garden, with narrow paths that give access to all areas, but which are more or less invisible from the distance, creating an illusion of continuous planting.

GARDENS FOR CHILDREN

Whatever else you may want to do with a garden, if you have young children they will end up dictating the basic framework. The garden must be a safe place for them, so there should be no nasty prickles or thorns, or plants that look attractive to play with or eat but that are poisonous. However, every gardener with a family knows that the children end up doing more damage to the garden than vice versa. Their activities often end up with balls and toys being lost in borders, followed by expeditions to find them, and plantings provide inviting places to play hide-and-seek or build dens.

First and foremost, children need a lawn, and the more space they have, the less damage there is likely to be around it. If the garden is big enough, you should think about planting specifically for children's games, with bushes to hide in and narrow, winding paths that encourage the imagination. It helps to think about things at their height – a number of shrubs at adult head-height can become an exciting jungle for children. Further suggestions for a family garden are given on pages 96–7.

Gardens for families need to be flexible, with plenty of space provided for children to play, and places for entertaining as well as for relaxation.

GARDENS FOR ENTERTAINING

Gardens that are used for entertaining need plenty of lawn space for guests to move around and in which to set up barbecues or discotheques. Around the grass you will need something for guests to look at other than the fence or the neighbour's plot. A well-planted garden will not only provide a pleasant environment for entertaining but will also furnish plenty of talking points, especially if you have included some unusual plants. Planting that looks its best when you do most of your entertaining (usually summer) is important, as is scent. Most fragrant plants come into their own in the evening, which is very convenient, and can add immeasurably to a romantic party atmosphere. Plants in containers are also a good idea for those who entertain often, because they can be put on show or hidden away depending on how good they are looking.

GARDENS FOR SHOW

Most gardeners want their gardens to look good for as long as possible, to create a good impression in the neighbourhood or simply as an attractive view from the windows – or all three. It is not too difficult to bring together a selection of plants that look attractive and interesting for much of the year, but creating space to plant them in is perhaps more of a challenge.

If a constantly changing array of flowers, fruit and foliage is your priority, perhaps this is another time to challenge the supremacy of the lawn. If it is not actually going to be used, especially in a small front garden, why not dig it up and plant something more interesting instead? How about extending the border to cover the whole of the area, with narrow paths criss-crossing it? The traditional cottage garden is a bit like this (see pages 56–7), but there is no reason why any border theme cannot be developed in this way: take a look at the very formal garden based on paths, gravel and small clipped hedges on pages 48–9, or the opposite extreme of drifts of colourful perennials and grasses on page 46–7.

GARDENS FOR WILDLIFE

Gardeners who want to cater for wildlife will put a low priority on lawns, preferring wildflower meadows along with lots of shrubs and undergrowth. Making a successful nature reserve in your garden means providing both food sources and safe places for birds, amphibians and insects to breed. At the same time, the garden needs to be attractive and also open enough for you to be able to see and appreciate the wildlife it attracts, preferably from the house.

Diversity is the key to encouraging a wide variety of wildlife, so you will need to include different habitats and numerous food sources – such as thick grass, shrubs, a pool and wetland – in the garden. Birds in particular appreciate trees and shrubs at a variety of heights and thick shrubbery, which makes for safe nesting. Grass or wildflower meadows provide habitats for different species of insects, which in turn provide food for insectiverous birds. A good seasonal spread of flowering plants will supply nectar for insects both early and late in the year. Finally, a range of shrubs with berries will keep the birds interested for much of the winter. Ideas on the nitty gritty of wildlife gardening and on establishing a suitable garden can be found on pages 50–51 and 188–9.

GARDENS FOR FOOD

Apart from the lawn, the main practically orientated parts of the garden will be areas for growing fruit, vegetables and herbs. Long relegated to the rear of the plot, as if the working garden were somehow shameful, it is time to consider how edible plants can be integrated with the rest of the garden. Certain practical or aesthetic considerations may dictate their being kept separate – proximity to the compost heap and the undeniable tattiness of brussel sprouts in winter are two that come to mind – but think how beautiful red-tinged oakleaf lettuces, bulging yellow squashes and feathery carrot tops can be.

It should go without saying that herbs need to be near the kitchen door, since no cook wants to

*Colourful phlox, achilleas and ornamental cabbages contribute
to a relaxed cottage-garden atmosphere.*

traipse through the garden in a force-nine gale searching for a sprig of mint. Many herbs are quite decorative as well, so there is no problem in fitting them into borders or other plantings. Alternatively, a garden plan based on herbs is given on pages 104–105.

GARDENS FOR PLANTS

Of course the garden will have plants in it, but some gardeners are lovers of plants above all else. These people are enthusiasts and actually collect plants, so they will need need a garden that suits their hobby, designed primarily to be able to fit in lots of new acquisitions. In my experience, these gardeners often live with a partner who is interested in more mundane considerations, such as whether the garden looks nice, and such 'plantsman' gardeners must learn the art of compromise in order to accommodate their collections to the other uses of the garden. The best solution is to ensure that all members of the family are happy with a basic framework consisting of lawns, paths, a place for herbs and salad vegetables and some attractive shrubs and perennials. The enthusiast can then fill in the gaps, or perhaps have a corner of his or her own. We will look in more detail at the enthusiast gardener on page 34.

AMBIENCE

Having thought about what the garden is for, let us now discuss some aesthetic factors and think about how you want your garden to look. The architecture of your house or neighbourhood or the surrounding countryside can seem almost to dictate a certain style: 'olde worlde' charm or pastoral scenery might suggest cottage gardens full of colourful scented flowers tumbling between old-fashioned roses, or perhaps something a little more formal, yet still capturing the essence of times gone by, using clipped hedges, rectangular pools and precisely ordered planting.

But do old buildings *have* to be surrounded by this kind of planting? Isn't it a bit unoriginal, boring even, for everyone in a pretty village to have a garden that looks like something out of a historical romance? I have a friend in a picture-postcard, half-timbered house, which used to have a classically formal little garden but she has ripped

it up and replaced it with an asymmetrical series of hedges delineating rectangular beds, rather like a Mondrian painting, to create an uncompromisingly modernist effect. Yet the garden remains in keeping with its surroundings, as the hedges and border plants used here are much the same as those in the rest of the garden and are typical of the cottage-inspired style – the content is the same, only the form is different.

Often gardeners are not daring enough. Dramatic contrasts between old and new can work surprisingly well; what is important to avoid is cliché. Anything that looks suburban, for instance, can bring a whole set of inappropriate associations to mind in a country setting, while the ubiquitous tall hedge of leyland cypress (x *Cupressocyparis leylandii*) can often spoil a picturesque or natural landscape.

Just as with interior design, it is possible to create all kinds of different ambiences in the garden using both plants and objects. Some remind us instantly of a particular place or environment: bamboo – the Far East; a classical urn – Italy; large-leaved plants – the jungle; grey foliage – dry, sunny hillsides in Spain or California. Using these plants in a garden can create a very powerful sense of place. The problem is that they have such strong associations that it can be difficult to use them in other ways: bamboo could look lovely next to a thatched cottage, but when you are trying to create a traditional English garden it is like going on holiday with the wrong guidebook.

The creation of a distinct ambience is most successful when it is carried out in an enclosed garden or corner, or in surroundings to which it is appropriate. An example of the former might be a tiny courtyard, where a Japanese feel is often very successful, and of the latter a pastoral landscape, where a European-style formal garden is very much in keeping.

Creating a distinctive ambience is a challenge, but the result is most rewarding if it works, especially when carried out in cramped and hostile surroundings, such as a city backyard or roof garden with tenements and factories as neighbours. Part of the trick is to block out eyesores with creeper-covered trellis, trees or other plantings, but the real magic lies in creating a garden that so holds the attention that the eye is not tempted to stray beyond. Some of the more distinct ambiences are

*There are few sights more
satisfying than rows of
vegetables, for at the end
of the day we know we
can eat them! Sweet peas
add a touch of colour to
this productive patch.*

dealt with on pages 30–34, while on pages 110–111 consideration is given to the possibilities of creating gardens in confined urban environments.

HOW MUCH EFFORT?

In thinking about the uses of the garden, we must not neglect the very act of gardening itself – some people actually enjoy it for its own sake! A low-maintenance garden may be what many of us

want, but not everyone: a lot of people find gardening therapeutic and a relaxing and healthy break from office or indoor work. Others seek the company of plants and flowers, to have nature humming and pulsing around them. Choosing the right level of maintenance is very important for your enjoyment of the garden, and you will need to strike the correct balance between, on the one hand, being faced with too many chores to carry out, and, on the other having too little to do.

When planning a garden or even just a new planting, it is important to consider at the outset how much time and effort it will involve. This depends partly on the plants used and partly on the kind of planting. Some plants are undeniably high maintenance in any setting – hybrid tea roses, for example, always require annual pruning. Others need a lot of attention only in some contexts: for example, many of the taller, late-flowering herbaceous plants, such as rudbeckias and asters, have a reputation for being hard work since they need feeding, staking and tying up, cutting back in the winter and dividing every other year, but this is true only if you are growing them in the conventional way. In the traditional herbaceous border, plants are grown in separate clumps and fed well, resulting in much taller and weaker growth than they would make in the wild. The modern way of growing them – in poorer soil, blended with each other and with ornamental grasses – means that they stand up better, with no need for support. The style of planting can have considerable impact on how plants actually grow.

Some planting styles also require higher standards of maintenance if they are to appear attractive and well cared for. Everyone will look askance at the odd weed in a formal bedding scheme, for example, but it would be less likely to offend the eye in a cottage-garden border, and would not even be noticed in a wildflower meadow.

In considering maintenance, you will need to think not only about the time involved but also about the kind of work – a little gentle weeding is a world away from pushing around huge piles of manure in a wheelbarrow.

LOW AND HIGH MAINTENANCE

Here we consider different garden styles and how much work they involve, starting with the style that requires the hardest work and ending with the one that needs the least, together with some indication of the tasks required.

FORMAL BEDDING

This is the style beloved of parks the world over, and it is characterized by geometric arrangements of brightly coloured annuals. You either love it or hate it. Usually I hate it, but sometimes it is so well done and artistic you have to admire the achieve-

ment. France and Romania are the two countries that do it to its excessive best, to the point of using wire frameworks to support three-dimensional plant sculptures, but whatever you feel about it there is no denying that bedding out is hard work. Everything has to be planted out every year, kept rigorously weeded and watered often, and then dug up in the autumn. The ground has either to be kept bare all winter or planted up with winter bedding, such as bulbs and pansies. Replacing plants every year is expensive if they are purchased from a garden centre or nursery, and to do it yourself

Formality and informality combined make a powerful statement. The standards here are a species of privet (Ligustrum) *and* crataegus.

requires a greenhouse, a propagator and lots of time.

There is no doubt, however, that this is the style that really creates front-garden impact, and that the best practitioners of the art are usually retired people with plenty of time.

FRUIT AND VEGETABLES

These really are as much hard work as bedding out, but at least you can eat the results and you don't have to worry so much about the beds looking spick and span. If you are at all serious about being self-sufficient you will nearly always have

something to do – sowing, planting out, weeding, harvesting, watering, and digging in or spreading compost. Many people prefer to grow just a few vegetables, perhaps some salad specialities such as lettuce and spring onions that are best eaten as fresh as possible, or particular varieties that are difficult to buy in the shops, such as old-fashioned and tasty tomatoes.

ROSE BEDS

Another favourite of public parks, the traditional rose bed is usually planted with varieties that need meticulous pruning every year, and nothing else is allowed to grow around them. Weeding is then a fairly constant task, as there is nothing that weeds like more than bare ground. Roses are prone to all sorts of fungal diseases that might not matter so much in a more casual setting but tend to be very noticeable in a formal one like this, so regular spraying throughout the summer is often needed. I find this the most unsatisfactory method of growing roses, as on their own they always strike me as garish in appearance, and they look dreadfully forlorn in winter.

TRADITIONAL HERBACEOUS BORDERS

Like the old-style rose bed, the traditional herbaceous border, planted entirely with perennials in discrete clumps, demands a lot of attention. The plants require an annual cut-back in winter, and until they are back in full growth again the following summer the gaps between them will need weeding, while staking and tying the taller plants, such as delphiniums and asters, to stop them flopping about in the wind and rain are time-consuming and fiddly exercises. Having said all this,

The popular cottage-garden style depends for its success on a carefree assortment of flowers, preferably in soft colours.

however, a well-planted herbaceous border is a magnificent sight in late summer and autumn, and for many dedicated gardeners it is worth all the trouble.

FORMAL GARDENS
In this context, 'formal gardens' means the use of clipped evergreens like yew (*Taxus* species) and box (*Buxus* species) in the form of hedges and topiary. This style is not as labour intensive as you might think, unless, of course, you are the fortunate purchaser of a property where there are already sizeable hedges. Although they will need clipping only once a year, this is quite a skilled operation.

MIXED BORDERS
Very much the style of the last few decades, the mixed border combines shrubs, perennials, bulbs and annuals to give a succession of colour and interest through the year. Planting is usually fairly tight, so weeds do not get too much of a chance to insinuate themselves, but the level of maintenance involved does depend very much on the plants that are used.

COTTAGE GARDENS
A style that has also become very popular since the 1950s, the cottage garden is perhaps a middle-class fantasy of how poor country people used to garden, but it is undeniably attractive and fairly low in maintenance needs. Indeed, a certain untidiness is part of the ambience, and self-sowing is *de rigeur*. The idea is to mix 'traditional' perennials, annuals, fruit, vegetables and herbs together in an attractive jumble of soft colours and sweet fragrances. The tight planting characteristic of this style keeps weeds out, but the emphasis on herbaceous plants does mean that at least one good annual clearout of dead vegetation is vital if it is not to look distinctly abandoned. This style is ideal for those who like a little pottering, with occasional weeding, staking and seed sowing, but who do not fancy the dedication needed for the traditional herbaceous border.

LAWNS
Grass is the conventional ground-cover plant for large areas but, as any of us with anything larger than a postage stamp of grass well know, lawns can be very time consuming. All grass really needs is regular cutting throughout the summer, but a lawn to be proud of requires far more: feeding, aeration, weed control, mowing and watering can consume whole weekends of your time.

Indeed, in some areas where there are statutory limits on water use, the maintenance of a conventional verdant lawn may be virtually impossible. I think it is time to look critically at the large expanses of green that cover so much of our gardens and to consider alternatives, ones that involve reduced use of precious natural resources and less work and that, let's be honest, look more interesting.

WILDFLOWER MEADOWS AND OTHER 'NATURAL' PLANTINGS
Very much the style of the moment, 'wild' plantings are, in theory, low maintenance. The idea is to establish a community of plants that will coexist happily and flourish because they are suited to the prevailing conditions. Plant selection is therefore important, and so is careful attention while the planting is becoming established. Once this phase is past, maintenance can be reduced to a minimum, a once-a-year cut being all that is needed. Even if you are a conventionally tidy-minded gardener, there is no denying the usefulness of wild gardens in out-of-the-way or difficult-to-get-to corners.

SHRUBS AND GROUND COVER
Perhaps given a bad name by unimaginative 'landscaping' around supermarkets and motorway junctions, the use of shrubs and low-growing evergreen ground covers is a highly effective way of sealing the ground against weeds and providing some interest all year round. The species chosen should mostly be evergreens and, of course, ones that do not require fancy pruning regimes. This does not have to mean boring berberis – the range of possible species is actually very wide, but it has to be said that the emphasis on evergreens can make for monotony after a few years, especially in shady areas. Once established, however, the attention these plants need is absolutely minimal.

For open sites, a popular and very colourful variant on this theme is the combination of dwarf conifers and heathers, where maintenance is restricted to cutting back every few years.

THE ENTHUSIAST'S GARDEN

Enthusiasts are those gardeners who have a passion for growing one particular kind of plant. Their hobby could be cultivating alpines, growing vegetables or flowers for competitive showing, or just taking an interest in one plant group, such as hardy cyclamen, bamboos or old-fashioned roses.

Some of these pursuits, such as the growing of prize vegetables, are visually difficult to fit into the rest of the garden and are perhaps best given their own special area, screened off from the main part. Others can make a major contribution, but their place needs to be considered carefully if the garden is not to become simply a collection of plants. A specialist rhododendron display, for example, can be stunning for two months of the year, but jolly dull for the other ten, so subsidiary plantings should be made to create colour and interest for the rest of the year, with bulbs to make a splash in the spring and small groups of late-flowering perennials, such as golden rods *(Solidago* species) and rudbeckias, to provide colour later on.

Specialist gardening sometimes involves greenhouses, cold frames, rock gardens or raised beds. In my experience, these are often an eyesore, with no thought given to how they might fit in with the rest of the garden. However, there is no reason why this should be the case: these items are not especially attractive, but their effect can be softened by planting low shrubs or perennials around the base of greenhouses and frames, and making raised beds and rock gardens that follow the contours of the ground or echo the lines of other garden features, such as borders or paths.

COLLECTABLE PLANTS

Cacti and succulents

You either love them or hate them – especially cacti. Needing to overwinter indoors in many areas, cacti and succulents benefit greatly from standing outside in the summer, opening up all sorts of exciting bedding-out possibilities. Ideally, the plants should be planted out in their pots, up to their necks in a very free-draining material such as sand, gravel or an open soil.

Flowers for show

Flowers for showing can usually be integrated quite well into borders with other plants. They will need constant attention, though, so good access is vital. This can be achieved by growing them in narrow borders or in beds cross by paths. The same applies to plants grown to produce flowers for cutting.

Alpines

Alpines are pretty addictive, especially for those whose gardening style is cramped by a tiny garden or through disability. The plants vary greatly in their tolerance of winter weather: some will survive outside in raised beds, in containers such as sink gardens, or growing on lumps of tufa rock; others need protection from winter wet and should be covered with sheets of glass or placed in a cold frame during wet weather.

Vegetables

Even if vegetables are grown separately from other plants, the vegetable garden can still be made attractive with the addition of occasional herbs and flowers. Certain flowers, such as English marigolds (*Calendula officinalis*), also act as 'companion plants' to vegetables, discouraging pests and encouraging bees. Vegetable areas can be screened off from the rest of the garden by hedges, or by trellis covered with climbers.

Herbs

Like vegetables and flowers for cutting, herbs need good access and so should never be too far from a path. Many herbs, both culinary and medicinal, are reasonably decorative plants, but the area can be made more attractive with the addition of some purely ornamental plants. Low box hedges are a traditional feature of herb gardens but should not be allowed to get too big, as the roots are quite greedy.

A SCHEME FOR FULL SHADE

AREAS OF FULL SHADE, where there is no direct sunlight, can be surprisingly colourful in spring with the flowers of primulas, pulmonarias, bulbs and other woodland plants. Some bulbous and tuberous plants, such as anemones, trilliums and erythroniums, are summer dormant, so they disappear underground after flowering. This means that the role of foliage plants is very important for interest in the summer. Fortunately, there is a wide variety of ferns and evergreen plants for situations like this, such as the bugle (*Ajuga reptans*) so that, with imagination, a shaded part of the garden can look good for most of the year.

Shade-tolerant shrubs tend to be evergreen with glossy, dark green leaves – a rather depressing prospect in reduced-light conditions. Luckily, however, there are a few excellent and easy-to-grow variegated shrubs that will serve to light up the gloom.

MAINTENANCE – *Low*

Shade does not encourage many weeds, and shade-loving plants do not make a lot of growth, so all in all not much maintenance is required. Leaf-fall from trees in the autumn can smother plants underneath, especially evergreens, so clearing up leaves is important. Since leaf-derived humus is very beneficial for many plants from woodland environments, and shady areas in gardens are often short of it, the collected leaves should be made into compost for later use as a mulch. Alternatively, they can be shredded and applied around the plants as a mulch without composting.

SITE AND SEASON

Any reasonably fertile, well-drained soil with average moisture would be suitable for this scheme. 'Full shade' is where there is little direct sunlight, but without being dark.

Flowering will be in late spring, with foliage interest for much of the year. The pulmonarias are invaluable for their long season of interest.

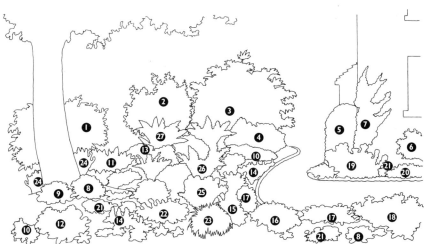

Shrubs

1 *Prunus lusitanica*
2 *Elaeagnus × ebbingei* 'Gilt Edge'
3 *Fatsia japonica*
4 *Euonymus fortunei* 'Variegatus'
5 *Buxus sempervirens*
6 *Daphne mezereum*

Climbers

7 *Hedera helix* 'Glacier'

Perennials

8 *Primula vulgaris*
9 *Viola odorata*
10 *Galium odoratum*
11 *Convallaria majalis*
12 *Pulmonaria rubra*
13 *Trillium grandiflorum*
14 *Ajuga reptans* 'Jungle Beauty'
15 *Mertensia pulmonarioides*
16 *Lamium maculatum*
17 *Asarum europaeum*
18 *Lamium argentatum*
19 *Euphorbia robbiae*
20 *Pulmonaria saccharata*

Bulbs

21 *Anemone blanda*
22 *Erythronium dens-canis*

Grasses

23 *Carex oshimensis* 'Evergold'

Ferns

24 *Asplenium scolopendrium*
25 *Athyrium felix-femina*
26 *Dryopteris affinis*
27 *Matteuccia struthiopteris*

A HOT, DRY CLIMATE

GARDENS IN CLIMATES that have hot, dry summers are often at their best in spring and autumn, many of the plants becoming more or less dormant in summer in order to conserve moisture.

Selecting plants that are drought tolerant will drastically reduce the amount of water needed for irrigation, and consequently the cost and labour involved in garden maintenance. These plants can also help to reduce the fire risk that is ever-present in these regions. Fortunately many new dry-land species are coming on to the market, a lot of them natives of California, South Africa or Australia, so the choice of plants is improving rapidly.

Most of the plants in this scheme are evergreen, often with very attractive greyish foliage; this should be made a feature, as there may be few flowers during the summer. In the very driest areas cacti and succulents, such as agaves and aloes, can be grown for contrast.

Bulbs have a special place in dry gardens, flowering during the winter and early spring, and then dying down as the sun rises to its summer height. Species tulips are among the most colourful, reliable and easily available. During the hot season, annuals are often the best bet for colour if a small area can be kept irrigated for them. Indeed, dry-land annuals give us the most intensely coloured of all flowers.

MAINTENANCE – *Low*

In hot, dry climates relatively little growth is made, and consequently the need for pruning or clearing up will be minimal. The plants selected are all drought tolerant, so irrigation is not necessary once they are established. In the early years, however, water will be needed; it should be given infrequently and in sufficient quantity to soak the soil thoroughly – 'little and often' is a recipe for disaster.

SITE AND SEASON

This scheme is suitable for a site in full sun or light shade, and any soil that is not seriously and seasonally waterlogged.

The main flowering is in late spring, although flowering times may vary greatly in different regions. Bulbs can be grown for earlier colour and annuals for later.

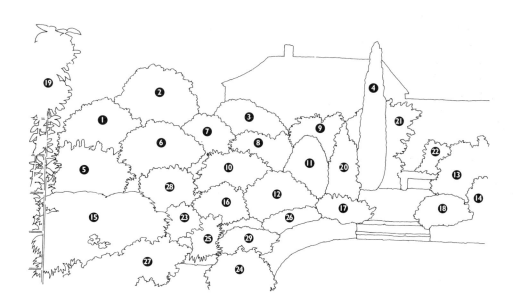

Trees
1 *Feijoa sellowiana*
2 *Arbutus unedo*
3 *Acacia dealbata*
4 *Cupressus sempervirens*

Shrubs
5 *Banksia spinulosa*
6 *Dendromecon rigida*
7 *Caesalpinia gilliesii*
8 *Banksia speciosa*
9 *Callistemon citrinus*

10 *Mahonia* 'Golden Abundance'
11 *Dodonaea viscosa* 'Purpurea'
12 *Cistus × purpureus*
13 *Nerium oleander* 'Tito Poggi'
14 *Grevillea rosmarinifolia*

Dwarf shrubs/ground cover
15 *Juniperus × media* 'Pfitzeriana'

16 *Banksia dryandroides*
17 *Banksia blechnifolia*
18 *Cistus salviifolius*

Climbers
19 *Pyrostegia venusta*
20 *Sollya heterophylla*
21 *Bougainvillea spectabilis*
22 *Plumbago auriculata*

Perennials
23 *Penstemon eatonii*
24 *Zauschneria californica*

Bulbs
25 *Freesia* 'Yellow River'
26 *Tulipa tarda*

Annuals/biennials
27 *Eschscholzia californica*
28 *Oenothera hookeri*
29 *Nemophila menziesii*

A COLD GARDEN

Not many plants will survive temperatures as low as -40°C (-4°F, US zone 3) but these will, with some to as low as -45°C (-13°F, US zone 2). As a general rule, herbaceous plants, which can retreat below ground, are hardier than woody plants, which have to take the full force of arctic winds. The perennials' high rate of growth enables them to take maximum advantage of short growing seasons, especially when the day-length is long at high latitudes. Among evergreens, only the hardier conifers will survive, others becoming hopelessly wind burned and dehydrated. When you are selecting plants for cold places it always helps to discover their region of origin, those from northern and north-eastern America and Asia being the toughest, although there are surprises, such as the oriental poppy (*Papaver orientale*) from Turkey.

In addition to these plants, many of the prairie plants given on pages 90–91 will thrive in these conditions. Annuals can also be used to provide summer colour, although many may have to be started off under cover.

MAINTENANCE – *Low to medium*

Since most of these are robust herbaceous plants, they will need only an end-of-year tidy-up. If the shrubs require pruning, this should be carried out just after flowering.

SITE AND SEASON

Plant up this border in full sun and any reasonably fertile, well-drained soil.

The main season of interest is early summer, although it should be noted that many plants flower later in cold climates. For later colour, North American prairie perennials, such as rudbeckias and golden rods, can be used as border plants for this scheme.

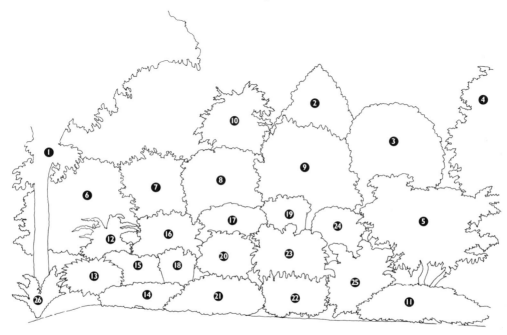

Trees
1 *Betula papyrifera*
2 *Picea glauca*
3 *Malus × schiedeckeri* 'Red Jade'
4 *Acer saccharum*
5 *Rhus typhina* 'Laciniata'

Shrubs
6 *Spiraea × vanhouttei*
7 *Cornus alba* 'Elegantissima'
8 *Rosa rugosa*
9 *Syringa vulgaris* 'Madame Antoine Buchner'

10 *Hippophae rhamnoides*
11 *Juniperus horizontalis* 'Wiltonii'

Perennials
12 *Dicentra spectabilis*
13 *Hosta plantaginea*
14 *Geranium sanguineum*
15 *Alchemilla mollis*
16 *Hemerocallis lilioasphodelus*
17 *Achillea* 'Moonshine'
18 *Allium caeruleum*

19 *Iris sibirica* 'Perry's Blue'
20 *Lysimachia clethroides*
21 *Nepeta × faassenii*
22 *Veronica incana*
23 *Paeonia lactiflora* 'Sarah Bernhardt'
24 *Saponaria officinalis*
25 *Papaver orientale* 'Turkish Delight'

Ferns
26 *Polystichium acrostichoides*

A SHELTERED SITE

WALLS THAT FACE THE SUN, are protected from cold winds and have good frost drainage are an absolute boon to gardeners. They provide the kind of warm microclimate that is ideal for tender plants, protecting them from the worst of the winter cold and enhancing the effect of summer heat. Exotic foliage plants, like the large-leaved magnolias and *Melianthus major*, are in their element and can form the basis of such a planting. Combine them with showy, free-flowering shrubs like abutilons to make a truly unusual planting. Of course, there is a risk that an unusually hard winter will kill off all your efforts, but this can be avoided to some extent if the roots and lower parts of the plants are protected by insulating materials such as straw (see page 15). Fortunately, many of the plants in this border are quick growing and are thus well able to spring up again from the base. They are also easy to propagate. Cuttings can be taken from early summer onwards and overwintered under cover. Some of these can be distributed to gardening friends, an apparently selfless activity but really a disguised way of protecting your assets, since you can always ask for cuttings in return if you lose your plants.

MAINTENANCE – Low to medium

The main tasks here are protecting the plants in winter, and pruning. Many of these are vigorous, almost rampant growers and so require frequent cutting back. This is best done after the winter, as the more growth that is left on them, the better the plants will survive inclement weather.

SITE AND SEASON

A warm and sheltered site receiving as much sun as possible is essential for this scheme. A well-drained soil is also important, but fertility is not; indeed, it could be argued that these plants will survive cold winters better on poor soil.

Most of the plants flower in early summer. Many will bloom again later in the year, and abutilons are capable of flowering all year round if the winter is mild. For colour later in the year, the bright American salvias such as the pineapple sage (*Salvia rutilans*) can be added.

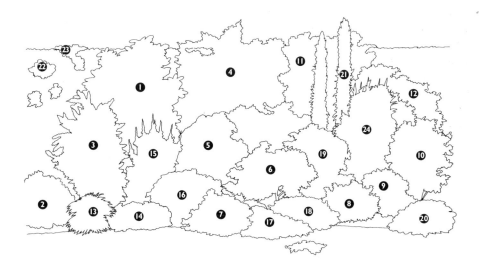

Trees
1 *Magnolia delavayi*

Shrubs
2 *Myrtus communis* ssp. *tarentina*
3 *Callistemon rigidus*
4 *Rosa banksiae* 'Lutea'
5 *Clianthus puniceus*
6 *Rhododendron* × *fragrantissimum*
7 *Convolvulus cneorum*
8 *Aloysia citriodora*
9 *Correa* 'Mannii'
10 *Abutilon* 'Canary Bird'

Climbers
11 *Solanum jasminoides* 'Album'
12 *Clematis florida* 'Sieboldii'

Perennials
13 *Fascicularia pitcairniifolia*
14 *Diascia cordata*
15 *Salvia guaranitica*
16 *Mimulus aurantiacus*
17 *Convolvulus althaeoides*
18 *Geranium palmatum*
19 *Melianthus major*
20 *Malvastrum lateritium*
21 *Echium pininana*

22 *Lampranthus spectabilis* 'Tresco Apricot'
23 *Lampranthus spectabilis* 'Tresco Red'

Grasses
24 *Arundo dona* × 'Variegata'

A COASTAL GARDEN

THE SEASIDE may be a fine place for a holiday, but it is a difficult one in which to garden – we can flee indoors from storms, but plants cannot. However, plants that are adapted to life by the coast are often very good looking, and the waxy grey leaves and stems that are their means of protection from harsh, salt-laden winds are an attractive feature. Most are also evergreen, an additional advantage. Many coastal plants, or those that come from similar harsh environments, also have a distinctive foliage form, such as the rosettes of yuccas and cordylines. Given such a range of interesting foliage, the possibilities for creating a garden are excellent, even before flowers are considered. As a general rule, most grey-leaved plants and those with leathery leaves are suitable for coastal planting.

A good windbreak is a must for any seaside garden. Behind this it is possible to make use of the relatively warm winter temperatures typical of the coast. The sycamore (*Acer pseudoplatanus*) is one of the best windbreaks, but the pine used here is better looking and also fast growing.

MAINTENANCE – *Low*

Most of these plants are shrubby and hence do not need much of an annual tidy-up. Coastal soils are often thin and the environment is very drying, so watering may have to be considered in summer, and any bare areas of soil should be mulched. *Hippophae rhamnoides* has a tendency to sucker, so an eye should be kept out for growths around it that might displace neighbouring plants. Some of the larger shrubs may need occasional pruning.

SITE AND SEASON

Any well-drained soil is suitable for this scheme, including a poor, dry, stony one. Full sun, however, is essential.

The main flowering takes place in midsummer, although the foliage in the border looks attractive all year round. Bulbs can be planted in more sheltered areas for spring colour. Small rockery plants, which also tend to be spring flowering, could also be used.

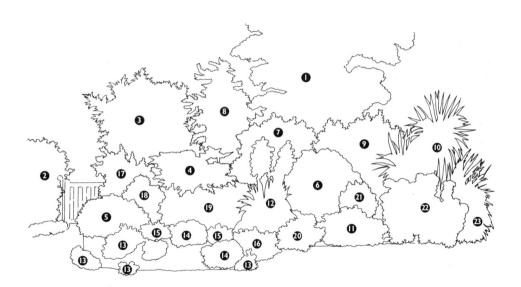

Trees
1 *Pinus radiata*

Shrubs
2 *Escallonia rubra* var. *macrantha*
3 *Tamarix ramosissima*
4 *Fuchsia magellanica* 'Riccartonii'
5 *Hebe* × *franciscana* 'Blue Gem'
6 *Rosa pimpinellifolia*

7 *Berberis darwinii*
8 *Hippophae rhamnoides*
9 *Elaeagnus commutata*
10 *Cordyline australis*
11 *Brachyglottis rotundifolia*
12 *Yucca filamentosa*

Perennials
13 *Armeria maritima*
14 *Dianthus caesius*
15 *Mertensia maritima*
16 *Gaillardia pulchella*

17 *Althaea officinalis*
18 *Eryngium planum*
19 *Limonium latifolium*
20 *Oenothera odorata* 'Sulphurea'
21 *Phygelius capensis* var. *coccineus*
22 *Euphorbia characias*

Grasses
23 *Elymus arenarius*

HEATHLAND COLOUR

CHARACTERIZED by poor, acid soil and strong winds, heathland can seem an inhospitable place for a garden. Yet heathland plants, notably the heathers (*Calluna*, *Daboecia* and *Erica* varieties), can be very colourful, and have a very long flowering season. Birches (*Betula* species) and sorbus provide some shelter and are used to create the basic structure of this garden, while the ground can be covered with a variety of heathers to flower all year long, but with perhaps the widest range of varieties blooming in late summer. The smaller 'whipcord' hebes, superficially like heathers but less attractive in flower, also thrive on heathland, although most do best in areas swept by warm, moist winds rather than cold ones, while the pernettyas have coloured berries that last well. Alternatively, dwarf rhododendrons might be combined with the heathers and allowed to spread to form a tight, weed-excluding mass of vegetation.

MAINTENANCE – *Low to very low*

Beyond clipping some of the more straggly heather growths every other year after flowering, this planting requires little maintenance. Weeds must be rigorously removed in the first few years, but after this the plants should mesh together to exclude them.

SITE AND SEASON

The soil needs to be acid and fairly well drained in order for these plants to thrive, although it can be quite poor. The planting is suitable for windswept sites in full sun, although in warmer areas *Gentiana sino-ornata* will need shade.

Flowering takes place from late summer to early autumn. Other varieties of heather, hebe and related plants may be added to create a planting that will be colourful all year long.

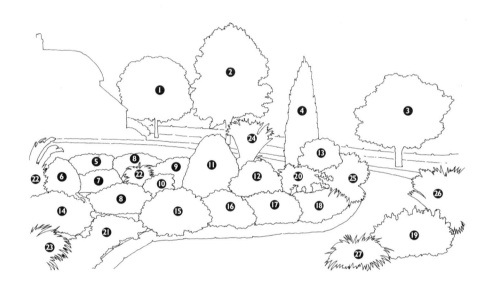

Trees
1 *Sorbus vilmorinii*
2 *Betula jacquemontii*
3 *Sorbus hupehensis*

Shrubs
4 *Juniperus scopulorum* 'Skyrocket'
5 *Calluna vulgaris* 'Multi-colour'
6 *Hebe cupressoides*
7 *Erica vagans* 'Lyonesse'
8 *Erica cinerea* 'Purple Beauty'
9 *Erica tetralix* 'Pink Star'
10 *Erica cinerea* 'Romiley'
11 *Picea glauca* var. *albertiana* 'Conica'
12 *Gaultheria mucronata* 'Bell's Seedling'
13 *Gaultheria mucronata* 'Alba'
14 *Erica tetralix* 'Alba Mollis'
15 *Hebe* 'Autumn Glory'
16 *Daboecia cantabrica* 'Bicolor'
17 *Calluna vulgaris* 'Elsie Purnell'
18 *Erica carnea* 'Springwood White'
19 *Erica vagans* 'Birch Glow'

Perennials
20 *Gentiana asclepiadea*
21 *Gentiana sino-ornata*

Grasses
22 *Carex testacea*
23 *Carex comans* bronze
24 *Molinia caerulea* 'Winterfeuer'
25 *Deschampsia cespitosa* 'Bronzeschleier'
26 *Molinia caerulea* 'Windspiel'
27 *Uncinia rubra*

CLASSICAL FORMALITY

W<small>E MAY NOT</small> be able to have the vast acres of Versailles on our doorstep, but traditional formality suits any size of garden and rarely looks out of place. The reliance on form and geometry, rather than colour, means that such gardens are largely unaffected by the seasons and have an atmosphere of calm and deliberation. They are also surprisingly low in maintenance requirements: clipping of evergreens need only be carried out once a year and there are no messy flowers to worry about! Mathematical precision is the watchword if you are serious, so careful planning is required.

Such a garden is an ideal accompaniment to almost any old house, although it can look a bit out of place in front of a humble cottage. The geometric formality also works well with modern buildings, even if the classical urns and symmetry may not.

MAINTENANCE – *Low*

Regular mowing and an annual clipping of the shrubs in late summer are all that is required to keep this garden looking trim. The lavender should be pruned in spring.

SITE AND SEASON

This garden requires sun for most of the day, and is suitable for any reasonably fertile, well-drained soil.

Flowering takes place in late summer, but one of the great things about this style of gardening is that it looks good all year round.

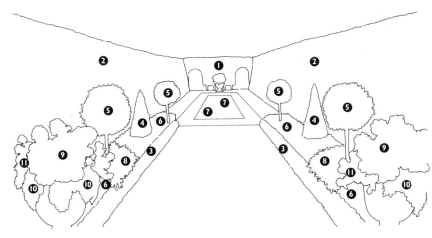

Trees
1 *Carpinus betulus*
2 *Taxus baccata*

Shrubs
3 *Buxus sempervirens* 'Suffruticosa'
4 *Laurus nobilis*

5 *Elaeagnus pungens* 'Maculata'
6 *Lavandula angustifolia* 'Munstead'

Perennials
7 *Nymphaea* 'Attraction'
8 *Penstemon* 'White Bedder'

Half-hardy
9 *Pelargonium* – red zonal variety
10 *Lobelia erinus* 'Sapphire'
11 *Verbena* 'Sissinghurst'

A GARDEN FOR WILDLIFE

I T IS IMPORTANT that locally native tree, shrub and wildflower species are predominant in wildlife-oriented gardens, so that the insects that are such a vital part of the food chain can find suitable plants on which to feed. Thus the planting here – very much a north-western European one – would have to be modified considerably in other areas. Nevertheless, the wide seasonal range of flowers will feed a very large number of nectar-sucking insects, and the berries borne by shrubs and trees such as *Amelanchier* and *Prunus* will be very popular with birds in winter time. In addition,

some annual or biennial plants such as teazel (*Dipsacus fullonum*) and sunflower (*Helianthus annuus*) will provide a larder for seed-eating birds.

Diversity is the key to a good wildlife garden, both of plant species and habitats. It is important to have lots of dense shrubbery in which birds can nest safely, and grass of various lengths for different insects. The cultivation of some species normally considered undesirable is important too; stinging nettles (*Urtica dioica*) are one of the finest food sources for certain butterfly caterpillars.

MAINTENANCE – *Low to very low*

Wildlife gardening suits the lazy gardener, as untidiness is often to the benefit of wildlife: long grass left over winter feeds birds and shelters insects, piles of dead wood provide shelter for invertebrates, and unpruned shrubs provide good nesting and roosting sites. Ideally, a wildlife garden should be managed to provide a balance between being decorative and offering good habitat diversity.

SITE AND SEASON

The species listed are nearly all sun-lovers; if the garden is big enough, some trees could be planted to give more shade. Any well-drained soil, including poor, stony ones and shallow soils over chalk, would be suitable.

The main flowering takes place in midsummer.

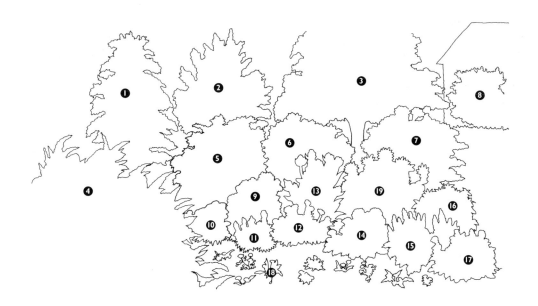

Trees

1 *Juniperus virginiana*
2 *Prunus avium*
3 *Quercus robur*

Shrubs

4 *Buddleia davidii*
5 *Amelanchier × grandiflora*
6 *Viburnum tinus*
7 *Crataegus monogyna*

Climbers

8 *Hedera helix*

Perennials

9 *Tanacetum vulgare*
10 *Knautia arvensis*
11 *Linaria vulgaris*
12 *Centaurea scabiosa*
13 *Dipsacus fullonum*
14 *Sedum spectabile*

15 *Stachys officinalis*
16 *Urtica dioica*
17 *Centranthus ruber*
18 *Hieracium pilosella*

Annuals

19 *Helianthus annuus*

A ROSE GARDEN

ROSE GARDENS are a traditional feature of parks and gardens, yet they are often gaunt and bare for much of the year and feature only modern hybrids with scentless flowers in garish pinks and oranges.

This rose garden is different. It concentrates on the old-fashioned varieties, with flowers mostly in subtle shades of pink, and nearly all have an excellent scent. Many of the older roses flower only once in the season, but the selection here will either flower continuously from early to late summer or will repeat flower in late summer after their main, early summer season.

Roses look so much better when grown in company with geraniums, artemisias and various other perennials. These not only complement the colours of the roses but also minimize weeding underneath them.

MAINTENANCE – *Medium*

Older rose varieties do not need the rigorous annual pruning that is customary for modern hybrids. In fact, if in doubt – leave alone! Pruning should really be left until the plants are becoming too big and untidy for their situation. Then it should be carried out in late winter, removing dead and unhealthy-looking stems, and any that are relatively thin and weak, crossing or overcrowded. The remaining strong stems should be cut back by one-third. Feeding and manuring need be carried out only on poor or sandy soils.

The perennials featured here need only be cut back in late autumn. However, for the first two or three years of the roses' lives the perennials should be be kept away from their bases, so that the roots can become established.

SITE AND SEASON

This garden requires a site in full sun. While deep and fertile soils are the best for roses, this selection has been chosen to do well on poorer soils than roses would normally thrive on. As much as possible should be done to enrich poor soils by mulching with well-rotted manure, or by using a combination of garden compost and feeding.

The garden will be at its peak in early summer, but most of the roses will flower off and on until early autumn, as will the pink geraniums. Bulbs can be added for spring interest.

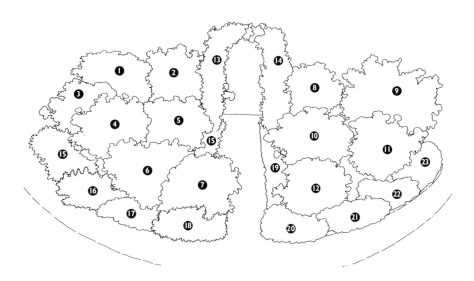

Roses
1 *Rosa rugosa* 'Alba'
2 'Gloire de Ducher'
3 'Comte de Chambord'
4 'Reine des Violettes'
5 'Charles Lefèbvre'
6 'La Reine Victoria'
7 'Louise Odier'
8 'Ferdinand Pichard'
9 'Roseraie de l'Haÿ'
10 'Jacques Cartier'
11 'Baroness Rothschild'
12 'Rose de Rescht'

Climbing Roses
13 'Souvenir de Docteur Jamain'
14 'Swan Lake'

Perennials
15 *Pulmonaria saccharata*
16 *Artemisia canescens*
17 *Geranium × oxonianum* 'Wargrave Pink'
18 *Artemisia ludoviciana*

19 *Galium odoratum*
20 *Geranium himalayense*
21 *Geranium × oxonianum* 'Winscombe'
22 *Geranium endressii*
23 *Geranium versicolor*

A FAR EASTERN LOOK

No one but the Japanese can make (or under-stand) a real Japanese garden, but we can attempt a version that suits us well enough. While most of the plants featured here are traditional in Japanese gardens, the key is to find plants that look Japanese in this kind of setting, even if they are not. *Alchemilla mollis* is one; its subtlety and elegance seem just right.

Bamboos, of course, are a must in setting the right mood, as are carefully placed stones and an overall emphasis on form and texture rather than colour. Nevertheless, colour does play a part, and can be surprisingly bright:

the year might start off with camellias and proceed to azaleas, which are among the most dazzling of all shrubs. However, the classic Japanese flowering plants are the well-known flowering cherries (*Prunus* species), and the less-often-grown *Iris ensata*.

Through its spareness and frugality, Japanese garden style is ideally suited to modern architecture. Ideally one would incorporate various props, such as lanterns and bamboo screens, into a planting such as this. They are, however, difficult to obtain and expensive. Good planting should be enough to create that distinctive oriental feel.

MAINTENANCE – *Low*

The emphasis here is on slow-growing foliage plants, which need little pruning and produce hardly any debris to clear away. Wisteria, however, takes a long time to get going and needs very careful pruning to encourage it to flower – for best results a pruning guide should be consulted.

SITE AND SEASON

Any reasonably fertile, moist soil, especially if it is acid, is suitable for this scheme. The site should be in full sun or very light shade.

The main flowering takes place in early summer. Autumn is also a good time, with the vibrant colours of the maples and ginko.

Shrubs
1 *Chamaecyparis obtusa* 'Nana'
2 *Cercidiphyllum japonicum*
3 *Cryptomeria japonica* 'Spiralis'
4 *Ginkgo biloba*
5 *Prunus* × *yedoensis*
6 *Acer palmatum* 'Osakazuki'
7 *Acer palmatum* Dissectum Atropurpureum Group

8 *Acer palmatum* 'Bloodgood'
9 *Azalea* 'Irohayama'
10 *Azalea* 'Hinomayo'
11 *Paeonia suffruticosa*

Climbers
12 *Wisteria sinensis*

Perennials
13 *Alchemilla mollis*
14 *Ophiopogon japonicus*
15 *Iris ensata*

Grasses
16 *Phyllostachys aurea*
17 *Phyllostachys nigra*
18 *Shibatea kumasasa*
19 *Semiarundinaria fastuosa*

Ferns
20 *Dryopteris erythrosora*
21 *Sasa veitchii*

A COTTAGE GARDEN IN LIGHT SHADE

THE FASHIONABLE cottage garden of today bears little resemblance to the plots that our ancestors would have had – utilitarian rows of vegetables with a few herbs and the occasional flower – but these humble origins have inspired an important garden movement of relaxed planting with a variety of shrubs, perennials and annuals. Allowing plants to self-seed, as with the foxgloves (*Digitalis purpurea*) here, is an important part of the philosophy: it lets the plants themselves participate in the design, choosing their own place in which to grow.

MAINTENANCE – *Low*

The perennials will need only an annual cutting back, either after flowering if you value a tidy garden, or at the end of the year if you are not too worried. An advantage of not cutting back the foxgloves and the campanula is that they both self-seed freely, spreading the group and sending up odd plants elsewhere, but never enough to become a nuisance. All the perennials here will live for many years with no other maintenance.

SITE AND SEASON

Any well-drained, reasonably fertile soil is suitable for this scheme, although it should preferably be slightly acid, and certainly not dry. The site should receive sun for no more than half the day, or dappled sunlight all day.

The flowering season is from early to midsummer, with some year-long foliage interest. The camellia and pulmonaria are spring flowering, while the mahonia blooms in winter.

Shrubs

1 *Camellia × williamsii* 'Donation'
2 *Hydrangea macrophylla* 'Blue Wave'
3 *Rubus* 'Benenden'
4 *Mahonia × media* 'Charity'
5 *Cornus kousa* var. *chinensis*

Climbers

6 *Lonicera periclymenum* 'Belgica'

Perennials

7 *Meconopsis cambrica*
8 *Astrantia major*
9 *Ligularia przewalskii*
10 *Campanula latifolia* var. *macrantha*
11 *Hosta sieboldiana*
12 *Polygonatum × hybridum*
13 *Primula florindae*
14 *Pulmonaria saccharata*
15 *Digitalis purpurea*
16 *Phlox paniculata*
17 *Phlox stolonifera*
18 *Geranium endressii*
19 *Pachysandra terminalis*

Bulbs

20 *Lilium martagon*

Grasses

21 *Milium effusum* 'Aureum'

Ferns

22 *Dryopteris dilatata*
23 *Polypodium vulgare*

Part Two

CHOOSING PLANTS

STANDING IN A GARDEN CENTRE with a wealth of tempting plants all around can be a bewildering experience. The aim of this section is to help you to make a sensible selection, choosing plants that will enhance your garden for years to come instead of becoming something you, or others, may regret. We will look at each different category of plant in turn and how it can be used in the garden, and then discuss how to go about selecting those that are just right for you and your garden.

Chapter Three

THE

BACKBONE

WOODY PLANTS – trees and shrubs – are always with us. Their size dominates wherever they are and changes their surroundings dramatically. Even those that lose their leaves in winter are still very much present, their branches and twigs giving permanence, structure and framework to the garden.

Trees and shrubs can be used to give height to a garden, create divisions, close off views, act as focal points and much else. While most take up a lot of space in the average garden and thus require careful selection, there are also some useful dwarf or small-growing shrubs that can create that all-important sense of permanence in smaller spaces.

TREES

Planting a tree is one of the most long-term actions that any of us is ever likely to undertake – the tiny sapling you plant today could still be there, now towering over the garden, in several hundred years' time. Needless to say, it is important to get it right: a tree in the wrong place can create all sorts of problems, providing unwanted shade or blocking off an attractive view. The most common mistake is to plant a tree too close to the house, which can result in considerable destruction if it blows over, not to mention the damage that roots can cause to foundations and drains.

Another common fault in tree planting is simply to plant too many, condemning the next owner of the house to living in a tightly packed jungle. Not only that, but it is impossible fully to appreciate trees when they are crammed close together – you need to establish a certain distance between yourself and a tree in order to make the most of it.

Not only is a tree long term, it also has an effect on the wider landscape. In the town or suburbia any tree is welcome, but in a rural district inappropriate tree planting can create eyesores, or simply look out of place. Cypresses, especially the leyland cypress (x *Cupressocyparis leylandii*), often look out of place in a rural setting, injecting a note of suburbia. Eucalyptus can also jar in settings where one expects to see deciduous trees or traditional evergreens.

Trees can play an important part in linking the garden to the wider landscape. Planting something that is to be seen in the immediate vicinity can

Trees for gardens need to combine as many attributes as possible. Acer pensylvanicum *has a good shape, autumn colour and attractive bark.*

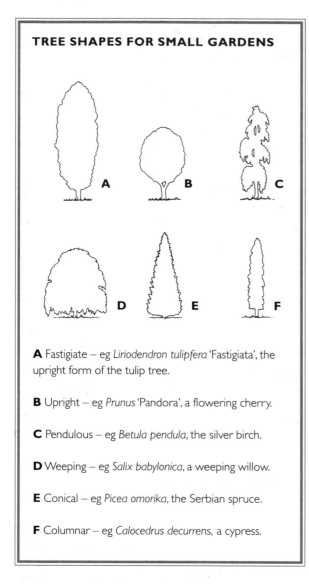

TREE SHAPES FOR SMALL GARDENS

A Fastigiate – eg *Liriodendron tulipfera* 'Fastigiata', the upright form of the tulip tree.

B Upright – eg *Prunus* 'Pandora', a flowering cherry.

C Pendulous – eg *Betula pendula*, the silver birch.

D Weeping – eg *Salix babylonica*, a weeping willow.

E Conical – eg *Picea omorika*, the Serbian spruce.

F Columnar – eg *Calocedrus decurrens*, a cypress.

task as quickly as possible, and fast-growing species will be needed. Trees for windbreaks must themselves be secure against blowing over. Suitable varieties never seem to be in the first order of desirability, but the balsam poplars, such as *Populus* x *candicans*, are very fast growing, and to be downwind of one when the leaves unfurl in spring is to experience a fragrance of extraordinary beauty. The upright-growing lombardy poplar (*Populus nigra* var. *italica*) is more suitable for small gardens.

The eventual size of a tree and its shape must be borne in mind when making a selection. You may never see it at its final stature but someone will, and you probably do not want future generations to curse your legacy. The wisest way to approach this task is to decide on the size required (taking both height and spread into account) and then be very disciplined about sticking to it, not allowing yourself to be seduced by a siren that will outgrow its space and welcome.

Narrow trees like cypresses have the advantage that they will grow tall but occupy little sideways space, thus casting only limited shade. Sometimes relatively uncommon upright forms of common trees are available; if you are determined you would like that tree, then it is worth tracking down a supplier. Weeping trees, such as the weeping ash (*Fraxinus excelsior* 'Pendula') or Persian ironwood (*Parrotia persica*), look marvellous and provide wonderful playing places for children, although it is impossible to grow anything underneath them. Most trees fall somewhere between these extremes of shape, but many also change shape as they age; ginkgos, for example, start off growing erect, but broaden out as they mature.

Shape is probably the crucial question when considering the purchase of a specimen tree – that is, one that will stand on its own in splendid isolation. Such a tree must have more than one string to its bow, however, and attractive flowers, fruit or autumn colour are all bonuses.

Trees vary not only in their size and shape but also in the type of shade that they cast. Conifers, beeches and many maples are notorious for their heavy shade, making it impossible to grow anything underneath. Other trees, such as birches, cast only a light shade. Planting a tree in a garden is a special event, so it is vital to ensure that the correct one is chosen for the prevailing conditions.

have the effect of 'tying in' the garden to the locality and making it seem larger than it is or at least blurring the distinction between garden and surroundings. Another visual trick of this kind is to ensure that the base of the tree is hidden with shrubs or perennials, or a feature such as a low wall or hedge. Hiding the base prevents the viewer from seeing precisely where the tree originates.

CHOOSING TREES

Having decided where to plant your trees, the next most important thing is to decide whether or not they are to perform some useful function, such as providing shade or acting as a windbreak. In this case you will want them to be able to perform their

Evergreens – in this case Juniperus communis 'Hibernica' –
*add structure and a sense of framework to the garden at all
times of year.*

EVERGREENS

Most evergreen trees – at least the hardy ones – are
conifers. Cypresses tend to create a suburban
atmosphere; wellingtonias (*Sequoiadendron giganteum*) and cedars give an air of country-house
grandeur; while spruces (*Picea* species) and pines
tend to make us think of mountains and colder
climes. Caution should be exercised when planting
conifers, because most cast a dense shade beneath
them in which little will grow. They can also create
a distinctly funereal atmosphere when they are
planted *en masse*, a sin committed by far too many
gardeners.

Of non-coniferous evergreens, hollies are the
best known, and they are excellent trees for small
gardens. So are the arbutuses, including the straw-
berry tree (*Arbutus unedo*) and madrona (*A. menziesii*), with their lily-of-the-valley flowers and
red-brown bark.

FLOWERING TREES

Apart from the horse chestnuts or buckeyes (*Aesculus* species), most flowering trees are relatively
small. Apples (*Malus* species) and cherries (*Prunus*
species) are the most popular. They are hardy, but
tend to suffer from a formidable list of diseases.
Some – the ornamental crab apples in particular –
have attractive fruit and are thus dual-interest
trees. *Crataegus* species, which include the familiar hawthorn (*C. monogyna*), likewise often have
attractive fruit. The finest range of berries is to be
found among the rowans (*Sorbus* species), many of
which are exactly the right size to suit small
gardens.

Magnolias are the most sumptuous trees for
spring flower, but their blooms are frost tender,
and it is advisable to make sure that the variety
you choose will be suitable for both your soil and
the climatic conditions.

TREES FOR FORM AND FOLIAGE

Most trees are grown for their attractive shape or foliage, or some combination of the two. Selecting trees of attractive form is not easy, as book illustrations are often inadequate and labels useless – only a stroll around a public garden or an arboretum to look at mature trees will really help you choose a tree with the right shape.

Trees can be selected on the basis of having attractive leaves: the maples (*Acer* species) and oaks (*Quercus* species) are popular for this reason. Some trees have leaves of a size or appearance that gives them a distinctly tropical look; *Catalpa bignonioides*, *Paulownia tomentosa* and some of the magnolias are outstanding in this respect.

Whether one likes variegated or coloured foliage is a question of personal taste. Copper beeches (*Fagus sylvatica* 'Purpurea') were well established over a century ago, but more modern varieties can look suburban and artificial. This is even more true of trees with variegated foliage, which can look as if the tree is diseased (as, in fact, it can be – some variegation is caused by viruses). In addition, as with any variegated plant, branches can revert to the normal vigorous green, in which case the whole tree may eventually revert, or the tree will become lopsided if the green branch is removed.

Many trees have wonderful autumn colour; the maples, North-American oaks and rowans are particularly noted for this, but there are many more, including plenty that are suitable for small gardens.

However, not all trees will colour up in all climates, and areas that have cool summers and mild autumns will never produce the quality of colour to be found in regions with warm summers and sudden, cold autumns.

Opposite: Cherries – this one is Prunus subhirtella *'Autumnalis' – are deservedly popular as garden trees. Choose carefully, as the colour range is wide.*

SPECIMEN TREES

Plant	Height x spread	Shape	Flowers	Foliage (E= evergreen, D=deciduous)
Arbutus unedo	8x8m (25x25ft)	spreading	white, autumn	E
Betula pendula	12x5m (40x15ft)	upright	catkins, spring	D
Catalpa bignonioides	10x10m (30x30ft)	spreading	white/purple	D
Cedrus libani	25x15m (80x50ft)	tiered	–	E
Crataegus × lavallei	6x4m (20x12ft)	rounded	white, summer	D
Fraxinus excelsior 'Pendula'	6x5m (20x15ft)	weeping	yellow, spring	D
Ginkgo biloba	18x7m (60x22ft)	upright	–	D
Gleditsia triacanthos 'Sunburst'	8x6m (25x20ft)	upright	green, summer	D
Ilex × altaclerensis	10x10m (30x30ft)	upright	–	E
Malus	7x5m (22x15ft)	rounded	white, pink, red, spring	D
Parrotia persica	8x8m (25x25ft)	spreading	crimson, spring	D
Paulownia fargesii	12x8m (40x25ft)	spreading	purple, spring	D
Picea breweriana	10x3m (30x10ft)	upright	–	E
Prunus 'Spire'	10x7m (30x22ft)	narrow	pale pink, spring	D
Pyrus salicifolia 'Pendula'	9x8m (28x25ft)	weeping	white, spring	D
Robinia pseudoacacia	16x10m (50x30ft)	upright	white, summer	D
Salix matsudana 'Tortuosa'	12x10m (40x30ft)	upright	catkins, spring	D
Sequoiadendron giganteum	50x10m (160x30ft)+	upright	–	E
Sorbus aucuparia	10x5.5m (30x18ft)	rounded	white, spring	D

Speed of growth (S=slow, M=medium, F=fast)	Aspect	Soil	Notes
M	sun/part shade	most	flowers and fruits borne together
M	sun/part shade	avoid thin chalk	good varieties include 'Youngii' and 'Dalecarlica'
M	sun	well drained	huge leaves
M	sun/part shade	avoid wet	pendant habit when young
M	sun	most	good autumn colour
S	sun	most	better for gardens than the common ash
F	sun/part shade	avoid wet	fan-shaped leaves turn golden in autumn
S	sun	most	bright yellow/green leaves; thornless variety
S	sun/part shade	most	*I. aquifolium* varieties are hardier
M	sun	most	attractive fruits in late summer
M	sun	most	autumn colour best on acid/neutral soil
F	sun	well drained	shelter from high winds
M	sun	most	hanging woody cones in autumn; many other varieties available
M	sun	most	
S	sun	most	silver/green leaves; pears inedible; many other varieties available
M	sun	most	grey-green leaves; attractive bark
M	sun	well drained	grey-green leaves; curiously twisted branches
F	sun	avoid shallow chalk	one of the largest trees
M	sun/part shade	most	many good varieties available

SHRUBS

The sale of shrubs appears to be the stock-in-trade of the garden centre business, with the result that many small gardens have become little more than dense shrubberies. Careful selection and placing of shrubs in the initial stages can save a lot of trouble later, as removing mature shrubs is a major undertaking. In addition, it is possible to plant densely at the beginning with a view to thinning out some of the shrubs as they grow, an approach that demands a ruthless streak but that does at least give you several years before making a decision that may be too difficult at the beginning.

Along with trees and buildings, shrubs form part of the framework of the garden; they are always there, giving a backbone to the rest of the planting – a role that is especially important in winter, when herbaceous plants will have died down. Shrubs can screen off one part of the garden from another and act as a backdrop for smaller plants. They also play a major role in directing the eye around the garden.

Shrubs will take many years to reach their mature size, so if you want quick results it is best to ensure that you have plenty of robust perennials as well, which will fill in the space for the first five years or so. The perennials may then be thinned or removed as the shrubs grow.

CHOOSING SHRUBS

When selecting a shrub, first check whether or not it is a lime-hater – a lot of the finest are. Next, consider whether it is the right size for the intended spot, although do bear in mind that it can always be kept pruned to a smaller size.

Overall soil fertility is not of major importance for shrubs, but good light is. There are quite a number that are tolerant of light shade but very few that will thrive in heavy shade. Soil moisture is another important factor for many shrubs, although a reasonable number of common varieties do well on wet ground and some on dry.

Most widely available shrubs are perfectly hardy, but there are many lovely ones that are not

Opposite: Azaleas and rhododendrons are a boon to those who garden on poor, acid soils, as they come in an enormous range of colours and require little attention.

SPECIMEN SHRUBS

Plant	Height x spread	Flowers	Foliage (E= evergreen, D=deciduous)
Acer palmatum Dissectum Atropurpureum Group	3×2m (10×6ft)	–	purple-red D
Aesculus parviflora	3×3m (10×10ft)	white/red, summer	D
Aralia elata	3×3m (10×10ft)	white, late summer	D
Berberis × lologensis	3×1.5m (10×5ft)	orange, spring	olive E
Buddleia alternifolia	3×3m (10×10ft)	lilac, early summer	silvery green D
Cordyline australis	4×3m (12×10ft)	white, summer	sword-like E
Cornus controversa	15×15m (50×50ft)	white, summer	D
Eucryphia × nymansensis 'Nymansay'	12×7m (40×22ft)	white, summer	glossy E
Fatsia japonica	3×3m (10×10ft)	creamy, autumn	large, glossy E
Holodiscus discolor	4×4m (12×12ft)	creamy, summer	D
Hydrangea paniculata 'Grandiflora'	3×2.5m (10×8ft)	pink/white, summer	D
Ilex aquifolium 'Silver Queen'	5×4m (15×12ft)	–	creamy margins E
Magnolia stellata	3×3m (10×10ft)	white, spring	D
Mahonia × media 'Charity'	2×1.5m (6×5ft)	yellow, autumn to midwinter	large, prickly E
Pittosporum tenuifolium 'Silver Queen'	6×3m (20×10ft)	deep purple, summer	E
Viburnum plicatum 'Mariesii'	2.5×2.5m (8×8ft)	white, spring	D
Yucca gloriosa	2×2m (6×6ft)	white, late summer	sword-like E

Speed of growth (S=slow, M=medium, F=fast)	Aspect	Soil	Notes
M	part shade	acid/neutral	shelter from wind
M	sun	most	young leaves bronze
M	sun/part shade	well drained	attractive variegated forms available
M	sun/part shade	most	purple berries in autumn
S	sun/part shade	most	weeping habit
S	sun/part shade	well drained	avoid cold areas
F	sun/part shade	most	tiered branches
M	part shade	acid/neutral	best in sheltered gardens
M	part shade	most	may need winter protection in cold areas
M	part shade	most	suckering habit
F	part/full shade	most	flowers held in cones
S	sun/part shade	most	autumn/winter berries
S	sun/part shade	most	fragrant flowers
M	sun/part shade	avoid dry	fragrant flowers
M	sun/part shade	most	silver-grey variegated leaves
M	sun/part shade	most	tiered branches
M	sun/part shade	most	avoid very cold areas

(the kinds of plants that may tempt you when on holiday in a warmer region), so make sure that your choice has a reasonable chance of survival at home before you buy.

Beyond these cultural and size factors, the choice comes down to selecting the flowering season and flower colour, and the overall form of the shrub.

EVERGREENS

We appreciate evergreen shrubs most in the winter, when any green is welcome and they will give structure to an otherwise formless scene. During the rest of the year evergreens can seem dour and funereal, most having leaves in a very uniform dark green. There are some notable exceptions, however: for example, several species and varieties of elaeagnus have silver or variegated leaves and can do wonders for cheering up gardens in winter; they also look moderately interesting for the rest of the year.

When choosing an evergreen, make very sure that you can live with it all year long and that you have a very clear idea of how big it will grow. Evergreen shrubs cast a very dense shade, which can make growing other plants around or underneath them problematical. As with evergreen trees, their shade is likely to be least welcome in the winter, when light is at a premium.

FLOWERING SHRUBS

Most shrubs are grown for their flowers and, along with bulbs, these are usually the main source of colour and fragrance in the garden in spring. They are, however, relatively limited in their colour range, and there are very few that bear blue or scarlet flowers.

One problem with flowering shrubs is their bulk. Forsythia is a classic example: a blaze of welcome, sunny yellow for a few weeks in late winter becomes a nondescript and scruffy-looking lump for the rest of the year. Dual-season shrubs are a boon to the small garden; the snowy mespilus (*Amelanchier* species), for example, has spring flowers as well as good autumn colour, and berries to boot.

In a small garden, the best strategy is probably to work out how much space you want to give to shrubs and then distribute your selection across the flowering seasons, one for early spring, one for late spring and so on. Imagine, too, what effect each shrub will have on the garden when it is not in flower – how much matt green do you really want for the majority of the growing season? It is important also to be clear about how much space you want in the garden for plants other than shrubs – an important point to bear in mind as you stroll around the garden centre being tempted by neat little flowering shrublets. If your aim is to surround your shrubs with herbaceous plants to give colour once the shrubs have finished, these too will require space.

The gardener on poor, acid soil is in a different league when it comes to shrubs. Roses and herbaceous plants may languish but the mighty rhododendron tribe will flourish in these conditions, giving ample opportunity for colour in the first half of the year. Gardeners in an area where rhododendrons do well may want to hand over more space to shrubs than they otherwise might. Opportunities for interest later in the year are more limited, but there are some exciting possibilities – hydrangeas, for example, usually do well in rhododendron country.

SHRUBS FOR AUTUMN COLOUR

While the selection of autumn-colouring shrubs is nothing like as wide as for trees, there are some good ones – amelanchiers, some viburnums and the smaller maples, to name just a few. Perhaps more important than those with russet leaves, however, are the large number that bear brightly coloured berries. Red and orange are the usual colours, but there are shrubs with berries that are yellow, white, blue and even mauve. Sooner or later the birds will eat them, but these garden visitors are a source of interest in themselves.

SPECIMEN SHRUBS

A plant is usually grown as a specimen because its shape is so fine and distinctive that it deserves to be appreciated on its own. It has to be said that

No matter how wild the rest of the garden, formal hedges and clipped shapes will always add dignity and form to a garden, which is especially useful in winter.

THE ULTIMATE PLANTING GUIDE

few shrubs fall into this category. There are some – such as *Fatsia japonica*, *Aralia elata* and the mahonias – that have splendid foliage and an architectural form, but most shrubs are rather amorphous in shape and look best combined with other plants. In addition to this, the majority of shrubs are a bit on the dull side when they are not in flower, and they are thus not worth turning into a feature.

However, there are sometimes places in the garden that are simply too small for a tree, but where something free-standing is required. A classic position is on the front lawn, which has to be kept open but needs a point of interest – a focus of attention if nothing else, or a feature to make your house stand out from the rest. A shrub for this kind of position will need to be of interest for as much of the year as possible, and be neat and attractive in shape as well.

HEDGES

Hedges are a lot more than just a barrier or an alternative to a fence. They can be used to separate different parts of the garden from one another, or to provide backdrops for borders or other plantings. They play an essential part in creating a feeling of intimacy or seclusion in the garden, but are also very useful in a practical sense for sheltering the garden from the wind, which is filtered much more effectively by a hedge than by a solid fence or wall (see page 14).

FORMAL HEDGES

Essential for a garden with any pretence to formality or grandeur, hedges are traditionally made from yew (*Taxus* species) or box (*Buxus* species), or Italian cypress (*Cupressus sempervirens*) in warmer climes. These three can be kept clipped with geometric precision, and their dark good

PLANTS FOR HEDGING

Plant	Speed of growth (S=slow, M=medium, F=fast)	Aspect	Soil
Berberis × *stenophylla*	M	sun	most
Buxus sempervirens (box)	S	shade	most
Camellia × *williamsii*	S	shade	acid/neutral
Carpinus betulus (hornbeam)	M	sun	most
Chamaecyparis lawsoniana	F	sun	most
Crataegus monogyna (hawthorn)	M	sun	most
× *Cupressocyparis leylandii*	F	sun	most
Cupressus sempervirens (Italian cypress)	F	sun	most
Elaeagnus × *ebbingei*	S	sun	avoid chalk
Escallonia macrantha	F	sun	most
Fagus sylvatica (beech)	M	sun	avoid clay
Griselinia littorialis	M	sun	most
Ilex aquifolium (holly)	S	shade	most
Lavandula spica (lavender)	S	sun	most
Lonicera nitida	F	shade	most
Poncirus trifoliata	M	sun	well drained
Prunus laurocerasus	M	shade	most
Pyracantha rogersiana	M	shade	most
Rosa rugosa	F	sun	most
Taxus baccata (yew)	S	sun/shade	most
Thuja plicata	M	sun	most
Viburnum tinus	M	shade	most

looks make a superb background for borders, gravel paths and traditional architecture. Yew and box have a reputation for being slow growing, which is not the case; once established, and if fed well, they can make respectable progress. Lawson's cypress (*Chamaecyparis lawsoniana*) or *Thuja plicata* give quicker results, and if you are impatient but love clipping so much that you will happily do it several times a year, then leyland cypress (x *Cupressocyparis leylandii*) can be used.

Deciduous formal hedges can be made using beech (*Fagus sylvatica*) or hornbeam (*Carpinus betulus*). An old technique that has enjoyed a recent revival is pleaching, where gaps are left between the bare trunks, the hedge starting at a height of at least 1.5m (5ft) above ground. Limes (*Tilia* species) are very popular for this, although the branches will need to be trained by tying them in the right direction.

INFORMAL HEDGES

The majority of trees and shrubs cannot be kept clipped in the disciplined fashion of the species mentioned above. In any case, informal hedges involve a lot less work, there being very little clipping to do. Hedges of camellias, pyracanthas, berberis or some of the rose varieties will flower and bear attractive berries, while the variegated foliage of plants such as *Elaeagnus* x *ebbingei* 'Limelight' will create a hedge that will remain cheerful all year long.

If security is a concern, there are two traditional answers: hawthorn (*Crataegus monogyna*) for cool climates and *Poncirus trifoliata* for warmer ones. Both have spines that make crossing a close-cut hedge an unpleasant experience. Hawthorn also makes an excellent barrier against wind.

Lavender hedges do not create a major barrier in the garden but they can be used to create a psychological one, a bit like the traditional low box hedging. This is very appropriate for cottage and Mediterranean-style gardens. Other possibilities for such low 'step-over' hedges are *Lonicera nitida* and dwarf forms of *Berberis thunbergii*.

MIXED HEDGES

There is no reason whatsoever why a hedge should be composed of only one species. A traditional country hedge of hawthorn mixed with other shrubs native to the locality creates a rustic feel as well as being physically strong, especially if it is grown two plants thick and professionally cut and laid. Suitable shrubs for blending with the hawthorn are *Cornus mas*, guelder rose (*Viburnum opulus*), wayfaring tree (*Viburnum lantana*), beech, holly (*Ilex aquifolium*), and field maple (*Acer campestre*), but there is no reason why you should not be adventurous and include an even wider variety, combining garden and country shrubs to make an individual blend.

Such a mixed hedge can play an important part in the wildlife garden, as a variety of shrubs will play host to a rich fauna of insects and birds. To complete the countryside feel, climbers such as honeysuckle and wild roses can be added. The latter will also increase the physical strength of the hedge. Once the hedge is established, wildflowers can be planted along the bottom to complete the picture.

Foliage (D=deciduous, E=evergreen)	Notes
E	flowers and berries
E	good for topiary
E	flowers in spring
D	retains dead leaves through winter
E	best as a formal hedge
D	white flowers in spring
E	very fast; best as a windbreak
E	grey, rounded cones; best in warm climates
E	leaves damaged by cold winds
E	flowers in spring
D	retains dead leaves through winter
E	good for seaside gardens; semi-tender
E	berries in autumn and winter
E	flowers in summer; low hedge only
E	shrubby; low hedge only
D	flowers and berries; best in warm climates
E	white flowers in spring
E	flowers and berries
D	flowers and hips
E	poisonous
E	best as a hedge in winter
E	flowers

Chapter Four

COVERING
SURFACES

C LIMBERS, WALL SHRUBS and ground covers are plants of great practical use, enabling us to cover areas that are crying out for some attractive surface, be it a bare wall, a trellis around an eyesore like an oil tank, or an area of garden that is unimportant but still needs something. Ground covers, among which can be included many climbers allowed to trail, can be used to decorative effect as well as being functional.

CLIMBERS

Every garden has vertical spaces or opportunities for climbing plants. In the case of small town gardens, especially those surrounded by high walls, there may be more vertical space than horizontal; climbers and other vertically growing plants become very important in such a context. Even in a larger garden, there is a need for the vertical dimension. In fact, a garden that lacks such a dimension will feel dull and bleak. This is the problem faced by many new garden owners lucky enough to start off with a clean slate, as it will be many years before their new trees, shrubs and hedges are tall enough to make much of an impact.

Given appropriate support, climbers can do much to fill vertical space and create interest in a garden quickly. Given a few more years, they will add a patina of maturity to a still young garden. Since most of them have a definite tendency towards being unkempt, with vigorous shoots arching out into the breeze and swags of flower tumbling down, they may not look that appropriate in a formal context, but they are tailor made for the wildly romantic garden.

Many climbers are vigorous, and these are the ones that can go a bit wild – fine for the cottage garden, but not quite what one wants sprawling over the smart front of a Georgian town house, nor, for that matter, in a small back garden.

EVERGREEN CLIMBERS

Unfortunately, evergreen climbers are few and far between, although there is a wider range of evergreen wall shrubs (see page 75). Ivies (*Hedera* species) are number one here, and are available in a bewildering number of varieties. Ivies vary in their leaf size, and the larger the leaf the more likely it is to be damaged by cold winds. The foliage colour also varies, from dark green through

Not enough gardeners allow climbers to do what they do in nature – climb up trees and shrubs. Here a wisteria rambles over a lilac (Syringa).

SUPPORTING CLIMBERS

Climbers climb because it is a good way for a plant to grow in order to reach the light in a forest environment, without the trouble of growing a woody trunk like a tree. Instead, they use trees for support.

Climbers have a variety of physical mechanisms for climbing, which the gardener needs to understand in order to make effective use of them.

Twining
Twining is the technique used by honeysuckles and Russian vine: the stems of the plant simply wrap around a support to haul themselves up.

These climbers need a combination of vertical and horizontal supports – trellis or wires are ideal. Once they reach the top of the wall or tree, they will trail along it.

Tendrils
Passion flowers (*Passiflora* species), cobaeas and vines climb by wrapping fine but strong tendrils around anything within their reach. Clematis use a variation of this technique, with tendrils formed from the leaf bases. To be effective, supports for these plants must be thin enough for the tendrils to reach around – wire or trellis is ideal.

Thorns and sprawlers
Some climbers simply lean on a support and sprawl rather untidily upwards. In a refinement of this technique, some use thorns to hang on to their support – roses are the best example. These are the most troublesome climbers to train as they have shoots that, initially at any rate, have to be pointed in the right direction and that periodically thereafter have to be tied on to a support. On fences and walls, horizontal wires are the best solution, and shoots can be poked behind them. Roses on trees will need to be tied in until they reach the branches, when they will look after themselves.

Self-clinging plants
Ivies and virginia creepers climb by means of self-clinging tendrils or aerial roots and therefore need no support. This makes them especially useful for running up high walls.

cream to gold and silver variegation, but it is worth bearing in mind that this colouring is likely to be lost partially in shady places.

Other evergreen climbers include *Hydrangea petiolaris*, dead slow to establish but fantastic for shady walls, and the rapid-growing, tropical-looking *Clematis armandii*, potentially a very useful plant but susceptible to wind damage. The Japanese honeysuckle (*Lonicera japonica*) is evergreen in all but hard winters; it is also vigorous and hardy, and has a good scent.

FLOWERING CLIMBERS

Climbers that flower well are invaluable for romantic gardens, or for bringing beauty to barren walls and fences. A major use of climbers is to hide unsightly objects – the garage you need but that looks dreadful, for instance. For this you need something that will romp away and hide the eyesore quickly such as Russian vine, *Clematis montana*, honeysuckle (*Lonicera* species) or a vigorous rose.

Small archways and fences need something more restrained, since large climbers are heavy and quite capable of pulling down a weak structure. Most clematis, many climbing roses and indeed most flowering climbers come into this more manageable category. Be careful with 'rambler' roses, some of which are among the largest of all hardy climbers. Most climbers flower in early to midsummer, but there are also some lovely late flowers. These include the increasingly popular *Clematis viticella* varieties, the 'lemon peel' clematises (*C. orientalis* and *C. tangutica*) and, for a cool site only, the stunning scarlet *Tropaeolum speciosum*.

CLIMBERS FOR FOLIAGE

A number of climbers have insignificant flowers but attractive foliage, and some are spectacular in the autumn. The vines (*Vitis* species) are among the most popular and are moderately vigorous, although *Vitis coignetiae*, which turns a fiery red in the autumn, is one of the strongest growing of all climbers. The kiwi fruit (*Actinidia chinensis*) is another strong grower, with large leaves that give it a very tropical appearance.

Climbers for house walls need to be chosen carefully. With the exception of country cottages, most houses look best when the climbers grow very close to the wall. Ivies and the virginia creepers (*Parthenocissus* species) are among the favourites; being self-clinging, they hold themselves very tightly against the wall, and the latter produce dramatic autumn colour.

WALL SHRUBS

Wall shrubs are by nature free standing, not climbers, but are a little on the tender side, so are frequently grown against walls to protect them from the wind and to allow them to benefit from the warmth that is radiated from the wall. Generally, walls that face the sun are used and these can, of course, include house walls, which are usually warmer than those surrounding the garden.

As many of these shrubs are vigorous, note must be taken of their eventual size, and they must be kept trained against the wall behind them – many is the ceanothus (a beautiful blue-flowered shrub from California) that has been planted against a wall only to lean away from it, overshadowing the border at its feet and throwing unwieldy branches over the windows.

GROUND COVER

The use of effective ground cover is a vital part of the modern low-maintenance approach to gardening, sealing the ground against weeds and soil erosion. At its best, it is attractive all year round; at its worst, it is a dull green carpet that reminds you of the banal 'landscaping' around an office block.

When choosing ground covers, it is important to decide whether you are doing it for looks or practicality. If the former, then you may choose plants that need some maintenance, such as occasional clipping or weeding, but are worth it because of their attractive appearance. If the latter, then minimal maintenance or speed of growth are the most important factors.

Visually, ground covers can make exciting alternatives to grass; they are often a practical alternative, too, as they do not need mowing. However, with the exception of the traditional camomile lawn, they cannot be walked on.

A major factor in selecting ground covers is expense, since buying enough plants to cover a large area can be expensive. The best choices are trailers that cover the ground quickly once a few original plants are established, such as ivies and

Virginia creeper (Parthenocissus quinque-folia) is one of the best climbers for buildings as it is self clinging. Its foliage is attractive at all times.

Clematis x *jouiniana.* If you have time rather than money, some plants can be propagated after a few years to produce more plants; hardy geraniums, and bugle (*Ajuga reptans*).

GROUND COVER FOR SHADE

Shade is often the most difficult place in which to grow anything, especially grass. This is an obvious site for the use of ground cover. Bugle is excellent for damp shade, as are ferns, if they can be bought cheaply enough. For average conditions, the evergreen epimediums and lamiums are a good choice. Dry conditions present more of a problem; ivies and periwinkles (*Vinca* species) are the best bet. In fact, ivy is the best choice in the most difficult of deeply shaded conditions.

THE BEST GROUND COVER PLANTS

Plant	Height x spread	Foliage (E=evergreen)	Flowers
Agapanthus africanus	100x50cm (40x20in)	green, clumps	deep blue, late summer
Ajuga reptans	10x20cm (4x8in)	variegated E	blue, summer
Alchemilla vulgaris	45x45cm (18x18in)	grey-green	lime-green, summer
Buglossoides purpurocaerulea	20x100cm (8x40in)	green	blue, spring
Calluna vulgaris	45x45cm (18x18in)	many colours E	pink, white, red, autumn
Clematis x jouiniana	1x3m (3x10ft)	green	lilac, white, late summer
Cotoneaster horizontalis	50x150cm (20x60in)	dark green	pink/white, summer
Gaultheria procumbens	10x100cm (4x40in)	red in winter E	pink/white, summer
Geranium	60x60cm (24x24in)	green	blue, pink, purple, summer
Hedera helix	10x5m (30x15ft)	varies	–
Hypericum calycinum	30x150cm (12x60in)	dark green E	yellow, summer
Juniperus horizontalis	50x150cm (20x60in)	blue-green E	–
Lamium maculatum	15x30cm (6x12in)	green/silver, mats	pink-purple, spring
Ophiopogon japonicus	30x100cm (12x40in)	green, mats	lilac, summer
Pachysandra terminalis	10x20cm (4x8in)	glossy E	white, spring
Rubus tricolor	60x200cm (24x72in)	green	white, summer
Sedum spurium	10x30cm (4x12in)	E	pink, summer
Thymus serpyllum	5x30cm (2x12in)	grey E	red, pink, white, summer
Vinca	30x120cm (12x48in)	green E	blue, white, deep red, spring

GROUND COVER FOR SUN

In sunny conditions, ground covers are an appropriate alternative to grass. This is especially so on banks that are difficult to reach with a mower. Dry banks can be covered with lavenders, cistus, thymes or even the dwarf succulent sedums. Unstable banks where the physical activity of planting may assist soil erosion can be covered with trailers such as *Hypericum calycinum* or *Rubus tricolor*. Ground-cover roses such as 'Nozomi' are also popular for this .

MIXING GROUND COVERS

It is a dogma of the landscape architect that ground covers should not be mixed, maintaining the purity of texture inherent in unblended plants. Interesting effects can then be created by swirling separate masses of ground covers together – a kind of modernist and permanent carpet bedding.

Despite the purists, it is also possible to mix ground covers. The effect will be less tidy but more natural looking, although in time some species may succeed at the expense of others. It is the creation of such low-maintenance blends of ground-cover plants that has been behind many of the most exciting developments in horticulture.

Ground-cover plants such as this Lamium maculatum *variety are invaluable for covering areas of bare ground and reducing maintenance.*

Aspect	Soil	Notes
sun	well drained	half hardy, warm climates only
sun/shade	moist	bronze and purple forms available
sun/part shade	most	self seeds
part/full shade	most	
sun	acid/neutral	colours best in the sun
sun/part shade	well drained	roots require shade
sun	not wet	red berries in autumn
part shade	acid	red berries in autumn
sun/part shade	most	cut back the old flowers for second flush
part/full shade	most	many attractive cultivars
sun/part shade	most	semi-evergreen in cold areas
sun	dry	
sun/shade	not wet	semi-evergreen
sun/part shade	well drained	half hardy, warm climates only
shade	most	variegated form is attractive
sun	well drained	edible raspberry-like fruits
sun	well drained	good for dry areas
sun	well drained	trim after flowering
part shade	well drained	trim after flowering

Chapter Five

THE BODY

HERBACEOUS PERENNIALS – those plants that die down in winter, to reappear the following spring – bulbs, annuals, alpines and half-hardy plants lack the permanent quality of woody plants. Their seasonal appearance and disappearance is, however, vital for that sense of the rhythm of nature that so many gardeners value. On a more practical level, the size of these plants means that they will be the most important elements in the smaller garden. Indeed, one of the greatest mistakes that those new to gardening can make is to plant too many woody plants and not enough perennials. Together with bulbs and annuals, it is perennials that provide most of the colour and scent that are the main reasons why people garden. While the woody plants may give us the essential structure, it is these more ephemeral elements that are the real body.

HERBACEOUS PERENNIALS

Herbaceous perennials are plants that die back every autumn and resprout in the spring, so that all their above-ground growth is renewed annually. This means that many of them are rapid growing,

and results are achieved quickly. The impatient gardener, or someone planting up an empty garden, will obtain an attractive result in the first year, and by the second year it may be difficult to tell how long the plants have been there – a very different story from shrubs or trees. Because herbaceous plants retreat underground to escape the winter's cold they are very useful for gardeners in cold areas, especially those regions where a hard winter and short growing season limit the range of shrubs that can be grown.

The speed of growth of herbaceous perennials has its disadvantages, however. It means that their growth is not physically strong, which makes the cultivation of tall varieties in windy areas inadvisable, unless meticulous staking is a passion. Their lifecycle also means that the majority flower during the summer and autumn, with only a very limited number looking colourful for spring – but then, there are lots of bulbs for this time of year, so that is no great loss.

Herbaceous plants were a mainstay of traditional borders and cottage gardens, but then went out of fashion for many years. Interest in them is now on the increase once again, and many new

Why do some gardeners complain that late summer is dull?
Herbaceous perennials such as Thunbergia alata *and asters*
are at their best at this time of year.

varieties are coming on to the market. One reason for this is that they fit into small gardens much better than shrubs and often have a longer flowering season.

CHOOSING HERBACEOUS PERENNIALS

The criteria for choosing herbaceous perennials are somewhat different from those involved in selecting shrubs. Picking varieties of the right size is of crucial importance, as they cannot be pruned to size, while soil fertility is a much more important factor than with shrubs: many traditional perennials, such as delphiniums, must have a very fertile soil in order to do well. Such plants also need a lot of maintenance, including staking and re-propagating every few years. Perennial species, as opposed to varieties and cultivars, are often more tolerant of poor soil, however, and some, such as bearded irises, do very well in infertile, stony conditions and require little attention. Soil moisture likewise affects the growth and survival rate of herbaceous plants, and it is important that the varieties chosen are appropriate to the moisture level of your soil. Most perennials do best on limy (alkaline), neutral or only very slightly acid soils, although their failure to thrive on many of the latter has more to do with soil poverty than acidity. Very few are lime-haters in the way that many shrubs are.

Herbaceous perennials are clearly divided into groups that like full sun, light shade or full shade, with plenty of choice within each category. Unlike shrubs, the number of tender varieties available is limited, albeit increasing rapidly. Although this is a factor to be wary of when buying, it is easier to protect the plants through the winter than it is with shrubs.

Once these size and cultural factors have been noted, it is down to you to choose the colours and habit of growth that you want.

WINTER AND SPRING

The early part of the season is for bulbs and shrubs, but there are some evergreen flowering perennials that no garden should be without. Hellebores, pulmonarias and euphorbias are the most important. They flower from midwinter through to early or mid-spring in some climates – a good four months. Their foliage is attractive and, in the case of some stately hellebores, silver-splashed pulmonarias and grey-leaved euphorbias, it is a major feature. Small primula and lamium varieties should not be forgotten either. They are especially useful for filling in the bare gaps in the border between dormant herbaceous plants and leafless shrubs.

EARLY SUMMER

While the selection of varieties is still relatively limited, some very important groups of perennials are at their best in early summer, including peonies, irises, primulas and geraniums. The last is potentially one of the most important groups for the gardener, since they are amazingly tough and tolerant, as well as being very colourful. They are especially useful for underplanting roses and other shrubs, their colours complementing those of the roses particularly well.

Pink, white and blue are very much the domininant colours at this time, with few yellows or reds. Most of this season's perennials are small or medium sized, few being more than 60cm (24in) in height, which makes them ideal for underplanting shrubs, for the front of the traditional border or for dotting around in modern 'drift' plantings between the rapidly growing clumps of later-flowering perennials.

HIGH SUMMER AND AUTUMN

High summer really is the festive season for the herbaceous plant world, and the variety and potential is quite bewildering. The daisy family – *Heleniums, Heliopsis, Rudbeckias* and so on – reigns supreme, with yellows, orange and reds predominant. Phloxes glow in shades of pink and lavender, campanulas and delphiniums in blue, and day lilies (*Hemerocallis* varieties) begin to get into their stride in a range of yellows, burnt oranges, soft pinks and russet-browns.

As the season advances, the pinks and blues tend to die away, leaving the yellows and reds of the innumerable daisies. Crocosmias in yellow, red and orange become more dominant, and, in a final and spectacular burst of violet, purple and lavender, the asters provide the swansong of the year. It is not surprising that shrubs hardly get a look in, especially given that a lot of the later-flowering herbaceous plants are tall.

Choosing plants for this period can be hard,

Late winter bulbs – like these Cyclamen coum, *snowdrops and crocus – help to remind us that spring is only just around the corner.*

there being so much temptation. Choosing varieties of a suitable size is a priority: there are small counterparts to many of the larger species, so this is not usually a problem. Apart from a liking for sun, these later-flowering perennials are not fussy. There truly is something for everybody.

BULBS

Spring would not be the same without bulbs. Whether it is drifts of daffodils artlessly scattered under trees, massed ranks of bright tulips, or tiny species iris and crocus emerging on the rock garden, bulbs are a remarkably easy and instant form of gardening. But they are not plants for spring alone, as witnessed by the lilies and gladioli that adorn so many gardens in summer, or the wild cyclamen, colchicums and autumn crocuses that emerge at the end of the year.

Although the planting of bulbs and their enjoyment the next spring seems almost as fixed as

night following day, it is not necessarily the case as the years move on and it becomes apparent that some are better survivors than others, increasing in number while others vanish or do not flower after the first year. Choosing the right bulbs for your garden conditions, and knowing which are steadfast and which fleeting, is essential in order to get the most out of this valuable group of plants.

SPRING BULBS

Bulbs are invaluable for bringing early colour to parts of the garden whose main season of interest depends on summer-flowering herbaceous plants, shrubs or annuals. Bulbs can easily be put in among other plants, and their leaves will have disappeared by the time the main actors in the planting have begun to perform. Early snowdrops and crocuses are both ideal for this purpose, with daffodils later on. However, tulips used in this way do not flower well a second time because, being natives of hot, dry climates, they need a summer's

NATURALIZING BULBS

Bulbs 'naturalized' in grass or under trees should look as if nature planted them, so straight lines or geometric blocks must be avoided.

The best way of making natural-looking plantings is to scatter the bulbs by throwing, so that the distances between them are irregular. Scattered individuals should be placed around the main mass so that there is no clear border to the edge of the planting, much as wildflowers are naturally distributed in grass.

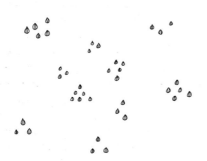

Larger areas can be planted more economically if the bulbs are distributed in odd-numbered groups, again with the groups at irregular intervals and some at a distance, blurring the boundaries of the planting.

plants and which is angled towards the sun is perfect for the regular flowering of species tulips, fritillaries and many others.

The naturalizing of daffodils, crocuses and snowdrops (*Galanthus* species) in grass is one of the most beautiful and informal ways of growing these bulbs. Most varieties will increase steadily over the years to form substantial clumps. The foliage of daffodils can present a problem in that, as with all other bulbs, it must not be cut off, as this will prevent flowering the following year. This means leaving clumps of uncut grass until late spring – not a problem in a wild garden or the outer reaches of a large plot, but a mess in a conventionally tidy or intimate setting. What is worse, when the grass is finally cut it will look dry and yellow for several weeks afterwards. All I can say is that such is the price of all that early beauty!

Apart from those bulbs that require a hot site in which to 'bake' over the summer, most are quite easy-going about site and soil, doing well anywhere that is reasonably fertile and well drained. Selecting varieties is thus mainly a question of colour, style and size. Bulbs vary a lot in their suitability for different kinds of planting scheme: tall tulip hybrids that stand to attention are fine in formal gardens, but can be completely out of place in a more relaxed context, while small narcissi, shorter tulips and fritillaries are more appropriate for informal and naturalistic settings.

The growing of spring-flowering bulbs in containers is very popular, but they need to be matched to the size and style of the container; tall daffodils, for example, might look out of place in a small pot. Many bulbs actually look a lot better if they have some non-bulbous companions in the container – polyanthus, pansies and other violas, lamiums and pulmonarias are all possibilities.

SUMMER BULBS

Bulbs play a less important part in the summer garden, but the presence of lilies is an integral feature in many gardens, gladioli in others. Most lilies are hardy; in a suitable place they will live for many years and even start to spread. Gladioli, however, are not, and will need to be lifted for the winter. In addition, there are many other less well-known summer bulbs which can be obtained from specialist suppliers. Perhaps the most exciting, and increasingly popular, are the ornamental onions

baking to ripen their bulbs in order to flower the following year. This will not happen in cool, damp regions, or if the soil in which the bulbs are growing is shaded during the summer. The answer is either to buy and plant up new bulbs every year, or to lift and store them in a warm, dry place over the summer.

Some of the most charming bulbs are very small growers, making them ideal rock-garden plants, which also suits the lifecycle of those that need a summer baking. A free-draining site where not all the ground is covered by the foliage of other

Nemesias, marigolds, lobelia and ageratum – traditional annuals always arouse strong feelings. What some call beautiful, others call garish...

(*Allium* species), notably those like *A. aflatunense* and *A. giganteum* that bear mauve 'drumstick' flowerheads on tall stalks. These plants are colourful and immensely statuesque, enhancing wild garden settings as they tower neatly above their more unkempt companions. Even so, it is in formal settings that they look their best, the verticals of their stems echoing the geometric lines of clipped hedges and paths.

AUTUMN BULBS

Bulbs come back into their own a little more in the autumn. The dwarf cyclamen that skirt charmingly around the bases of trees and the showy nerines that splash bright pink along the bottoms of walls are two highly distinctive plants. In addition, there are autumn crocuses, much like their spring relatives, and the colchicums that resemble larger versions of crocuses.

ANNUALS AND BEDDING PLANTS

Currently out of fashion with the trendsetters but stubbornly popular with many gardeners, annuals and bedding plants are undeniably easy to grow and colourful. Our nineteenth-century forebears used temporary plants such as these on a massive scale, and the way they have been employed in the garden has altered little since, although this is set to change. New species of hardy annual are being

experimented with, a whole new race of 'patio plants' has taken the garden centres by storm, and designers are arranging old favourites in new ways.

Hardy annuals are those species that are sown outside where they are to flower. Many have strong associations with the old cottage-gardening tradition, such as love-in-the-mist (*Nigella damascena*), larkspur (*Consolida ambigua*) and English marigolds (*Calendula officinalis*). These are colourful plants, but not intensely so, and have an informal feel to them. The half-hardy plants that are normally used for bedding are much brighter and more highly bred, often to the point of having lost all sense of proportion or natural elegance. They are being joined by an increasing number of somewhat larger plants known as 'patio plants', among them marguerites (*Argyranthemum* varieties) and *Osteospermums*, both members of the daisy family, and Mexican salvias. Most are very colourful plants, but bushier than traditional bedding and with a more natural appearance. Unlike the majority of bedding, they are perennials by nature, and can either be disposed of at the end of the year in the same way as bedding, or overwintered indoors.

The chief use of these temporary plants is to make gardens as colourful as possible in a short period of time, and for this they are invaluable. Set against this massive advantage is the amount of work involved in raising and replacing them every year or, in the case of patio plants, lifting them in the autumn and cosseting them in a cold frame, greenhouse or conservatory. However, for people who relish the activity and who like to ring the changes every year, this is effort well spent.

Most of these plants are lovers of sun and fertile soil, but they are otherwise easy to please and will thrive in most gardens. Selecting varieties is a matter of choosing colours that you like and a style of plant that is appropriate for the planting scheme you have in mind. Lovers of the traditional bright bedding will go for French marigolds (*Tagetes* varieties), red salvias, blue lobelias and pink, white or scarlet pelargoniums, all of which offer maximum colour all summer long. The dwarf habit of many of these plants makes them appropriate for Victorian-style geometric fantasies; the looser habit of patio plants and hardy annuals make these more suitable for informal plantings.

ANNUALS AND BEDDING IN MIXED PLANTINGS

However carefully planned a border may be, there often comes a time in summer when the shrubs and perennials go through a lull. Annuals can help to tide over the garden during such a time. I feel that hardy annuals and patio plants do the job best; their habit will match that of their companions much better than squat conventional bedding plants, which always look out of place when not in massed and serried ranks. Others think differently – I once met an American gardening writer who had busy lizzies (*Impatiens* hybrids – the most shade-tolerant bedding plants, by the way) dotted around her woodland garden to give some colour after the spring-flowering plants had finished. I would never do that, but I saw her point.

Rather than using such plants simply as gap fillers, how about a bigger and more positive role for them in the border, as equal players alongside the perennials, or even the shrubs? It is possible to create some very dramatic effects like this, especially in late summer, when everything has had a chance to grow really big and lush. The relatively intense colour of annuals and patio plants can be set alongside the more refined habit and/or foliage

of herbaceous perennials, one stunning example of this being deep pink annual cosmos sprawling around the dramatic grey-leaved perennial *Melianthus major*.

MASSED ANNUALS

It may be hard work, but the great advantage of a planting scheme made up entirely of annuals is that it gives you the chance to do something completely different every year. At one extreme, bedding plants can be arranged in geometric shapes in the manner of a public park display; at the other, romantic drifts of hardy annuals or soft-coloured marguerites worthy of a Monet painting can be created.

Pots and windowboxes full of annuals of one or two types or colours are very eyecatching, and are quick and easy to make up and establish. Hardy annuals have a role to play in the vegetable garden too, for not only will an edging of annuals make the area a lot more interesting to look at, but it also attracts bees and other pollinating insects.

HALF-HARDY PLANTS

By definition, these are plants that cannot be left outside through the winter. The growing of half-hardy plants may seem slightly perverse when there is such a tremendous variety of hardy plants available, but these inhabitants of warmer climes are cultivated because they have special qualities that hardy plants do not possess, such as exotic flowers, brightness, a long flowering season, or tropical-looking foliage. Consequently, they have a great ability to transform a garden, making it look more exotic and colourful, and imbuing it with a party mood.

The plants do not need to be replaced every year, although this is only a feasible option with small, cheap and easily replaced species. Other, more valuable plants can be kept inside over the winter, or in milder areas given some sort of winter cover (see page 15).

HALF-HARDY PLANTS IN BORDERS

Gladioli, cannas and dahlias are three well-known plants that die back to convenient bulbs or tubers,

Half-hardy plants add a touch of the exotic to the garden.
Ensete ventricosum is an ornamental banana which will need
to be brought under cover for the winter.

HALF-HARDY PERENNIALS IN THE BORDER

Half-hardy plants may be planted out to grow alongside hardy perennials and shrubs during the summer, to be dug up and brought under cover for the winter.

1 *Phygelius aequalis* 'Yellow Trumpet'
2 *Cephalaria gigantea*
3 *Solidago* 'Goldenmosa'
4 *Anthemis tinctoria* 'E.C. Buxton'
5 *Felicia amelloides* 'Santa Anita'
6 *Argyranthemum* 'Jamaica Primrose'
7 *Hemerocallis lilio-asphodelus*
8 *Diascia* 'Apricot'

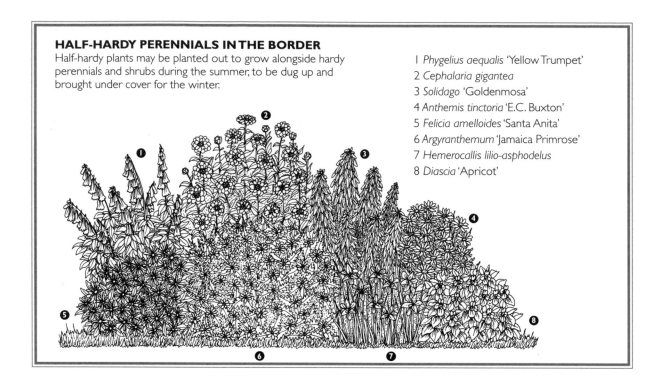

PATIO PLANTS

Key to hardiness H=fully hardy F=hardy in climates with frequent light frosts L=withstands light frosts T=minimal hardiness

Plant	Height x spread	Flowers/Foliage	Hardiness
Alonsoa	40×30cm (16×12in)	scarlet, apricot	L
Anisodonta × hypomadarum	150×50cm (60×20in)	pale pink	F/L
Argyranthemum frutescens	100×100cm (40×40in)	white, pink, yellow	L
Bidens ferulifolia	50×20cm (20×8in)	yellow	T
Brachycome iberidifolia	30×45cm (12×18in)	blue	L
Convolvulus sabatius	10×40cm (4×16in)	blue	F
Cosmos atrosanguineus	60×50cm (24×20in)	dark red	L
Diascia	30×50cm (12×20in)	pink, apriccot	F
Felicia	40×40cm (16×16in)	blue	L
Glechoma hederacea 'Variegata'	10×50cm (4×20in)	variegated foliage	H
Helichrysum	30×30cm (12×32in)	silver foliage	L
Lotus	20×60cm (8×24in)	silver foliage	T
Osteospermum	varieties vary considerably	white, pink, yellow	L– F
Penstemon	60×60cm (24×24in	white, red, pink, purple	F
Rhodochiton atrosanguineum	200×40cm (72×16in)	deep purple	T
Salvia coccinea	60×50cm (24×20in)	scarlet	T
Salvia greggii	60×50cm (24×20in)	red/apricot	F
Salvia patens	60×50cm (24×20in)	clear blue	L
Scaevola aemula	20×40cm (8×16in)	mauve-blue	T
Tropaeolum majus	30×30cm (12×12in)	red, orange, yellow	L
Verbena × hybrida	30×40cm (12×16in)	ink, white, mauve	L

which can then be lifted for winter storage inside. All three have experienced the swings and round-abouts of fashion, and tend to attract either love or hatred, with few emotions in between. Their value lies in providing colour and a showy touch to the garden from midsummer to early autumn. Although it may surprise some gardeners, dahlias are actually quite traditional garden flowers and can be fitted happily into cottage-garden schemes. Likewise gladioli, and cannas as well, but the latter have such a tropical air that they beg to be included in more exotic planting schemes (see pages 100–101). Opinions are divided on the place of such showy plants, some gardeners feeling that they are altogether too vivacious for temperate climates, inappropriate in the quieter garden and that they overpower most hardy plants growing alongside them.

Many of the traditional bedding plants are half-hardy but are normally discarded at the year's end, although most gardeners make more effort with pelargoniums. The recently fashionable patio

---

Notes

best re-propagated annually

–

many varieties, including some compact

–

–

sprawling habit

chocolate scent

many varieties, which vary in hardiness

several species

trailing habit

several species of varying size

trailing habit

many varieties, of varying size; smaller ones hardier

vast number of hybrids; need re-propagating every other year

climber; lifespan about 18 months; propagate from seed

best treated as annual

several varieties; shrubby habit

dies down to a tuber over winter

re-propagate every year

annual; many varieties

many varieties

---

plants, such as marguerites (*Argyranthemum* varieties) and salvias, are larger and more informal in feel. Marguerites in particular are superb gap fillers for the summer, vigorously filling spaces with an apparently endless succession of flowers. The salvias are somewhat less so, being taller and a bit leggy, so they need to be fitted in with shorter plants around them. They are, however, unrivalled for the intensity of the scarlets, blues and pinks of their flowers. The patio plants are joined by plants like penstemons and osteospermums, which are hardy in sheltered areas but not in others; in either case, they will benefit from being replaced or re-propagated every two or three years. These, and the patio plants, can be regarded as more exuberant versions of hardy plants, and they consequently fit in better with them than some of the showier half-hardies.

On the other hand, for those who want the full-blown exotic look and have a greenhouse, nothing beats the planting out of plants such as palms in borders over the summer.

HALF-HARDY PLANTS IN CONTAINERS

Many half-hardy plants look fine in containers, especially when they are dotted around a patio area: *Argyranthemum frutescens* is particularly splendid when trained as a standard, its white daisies spilling down from grey foliage. Pelargoniums, though, must be the world's most popular pot plants, available in apparently endless different varieties that genuinely thrive on container culture.

The larger and taller half-hardy plants are not so appropriate for containers, not simply because they are out of proportion but also because their vigorous growth means that they starve rapidly with a restricted root run; these plants flourish much better in the border. Some of the more vigorous daisies, such as the osteospermums and the popular *Argyranthemum* 'Jamaica Primrose', fall into this category.

While many gardeners may not be so keen on mixing tropical-looking plants with hardy plants in the border, the atmosphere of a patio or terrace is different and more conducive to horticultural showmanship. Many conservatory and greenhouse plants, not to mention houseplants, benefit from a spell outside in the fresh air in the summer. Not only is their growth firmer and better shaped as a

An abutilon, pelargoniums and a variegated felicia make an attractive container planting which complements its rather grand setting.

result, but they suffer less from pests and diseases. Pots of such plants as palms, daturas, abutilons and citrus can be combined with pelargoniums and patio plants to make wonderfully exotic arrangements in a paved seating area, the perfect accompaniment to alfresco eating.

ALPINES

Before discussing this group of plants, we need to define exactly what an 'alpine' is. Originally the word meant any plant that grew at an altitude above the tree line; now it has been redefined by the garden centres to mean pretty well any plant that grows to less than 30cm (12in) high and can be sold in a temptingly cheap size. Many so-called 'alpines' have never seen an alp in their lives and

would rapidly perish on one; it is possible to distinguish several different groups of plants that are commonly sold as 'alpines', including true mountain plants, plants from other harsh, usually dry, environments, and smaller versions of normally large species.

Whatever quibbles there may be over naming, there is no doubt that alpines can be extremely useful plants in the garden, ideal for tiny plots as well as for filling awkward gaps in larger ones. They are plants to grow in paving, out of walls, in containers with spring bulbs and in permanent windowboxes – all these are possibilities, even before purpose-built environments such as rock gardens and raised beds are considered. Alpines are also ideal for the wheelchair-bound gardener, as they can be grown in raised beds or in small, easy-to-handle pots (see pages 102–103).

CHOOSING ALPINES

With so many different backgrounds and habits, it is important to make sure that the right plants are chosen. Some alpines are real specialist's plants: small, slow-growing and something of a challenge. Others sold under the name are rampageous creepers that can smother neighbouring plants with thuggish glee. It is important to know whether you want them for growing on a large scale such as on a large rock garden, or in paving, walls or gravel, where small but vigorous, tough plants are needed, or on a small scale, in a trough, container garden or intimate rockery.

Specialist nurseries cater for the connoisseur alpine grower, who may select plants from a large range of fascinating species. Many of these are suitable for the average gardener but some are not, so it is as well to ensure that the plants you fancy will survive outdoors in your area with no special problems. Damp winters, especially those with alternating periods of cold and mild weather, are the main problem in growing the more fussy alpines.

VIGOROUS ALPINES

These are the sorts of plants that are suitable for the larger rock garden or one to which you do not want to have to give too much attention. They include many that are commonly available: *Alyssum saxatile*, aubrietas, campanulas, iberis and so on. Many of them, like aubrieta, form

This rockery bed provides the good drainage that alpines and dwarf shrubs need, but its sinuous shape integrates it into the garden as a whole.

a solid, weed-excluding cushion; others, like *Cerastium tomentosum* (which is capable of smothering almost everything in its path) form large carpets; others still, like *Campanula poscharskyana*, send out subterranean runners which pop up over a wide area.

Many of these plants are also suitable for growing in walls or paving. They can withstand drought and have far-questing root systems that will draw moisture and nutrients from the most unpromising of sources.

The vast majority of these vigorous alpines flower in spring or early summer; they can be mixed in with bulbs such as crocuses, dwarf irises and snowdrops, which will give an earlier start to the season, as well as with spring-flowering bulbs. They will also coexist happily with small annuals, such as *Limnanthes douglasii*, which can be used to lengthen the period of colour well into the summer.

SLOWER ALPINES

Most of the smaller and slower alpines are the 'real' ones; that is, they really do come from mountain areas. There are plenty of tricky ones for the specialist, but also many for the ordinary gardener. These plants are easily swamped by their larger brethren or by weeds, and so the conventional rock garden is not necessarily the best place for them; only plant them there if you can be sure they will receive all the attention they need.

Raised beds are an excellent way in which to grow the slower alpines (see pages 20 and 119). On a smaller scale, troughs, pots and windowboxes are also good places – even a small container can be home to a fair number.

ALPINES IN WINDOWBOXES

Windowsills can be cold, draughty places in winter and hot, dry ones in summer – in other words, a bit like the side of a mountain – and carefully chosen alpines are ideal yet underrated plants for such a situation. Choosing the right ones is important, as conditions are harsh. The spectacular lewisias, for example, will flourish in a dry windowbox in a sunny position, whereas early-flowering saxifrages, such as *Saxifraga* 'Jenkinsiae', will shrivel up, needing sunlight for only half the day.

Good drainage is vital, so ensure that there are

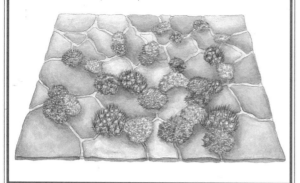

ALPINES IN PAVING

Low-growing, spreading alpines will fill the gaps between paving stones relatively quickly, denying access to the weeds that would normally colonize here, while at the same time adding a whole new decorative dimension to the path or patio.

plenty of holes in the bottom of the container and plant in a gritty, well-drained, soil-based compost, not a peat-based one. Grit spread around the plants' necks will help to drain water fast from the stem area. The other vital thing is to ensure that the plants never dry out during the growing season – a windowbox does not have the reserves of moisture of even the most barren-looking mountain-side.

ALPINES IN PAVING

Very low-growing and spreading plants, such as creeping thymes, acaenas and thrifts (*Armeria* species) can be grown between paving stones, bringing a whole new dimension to a patio – and in the case of thyme, a scented one as well. As long as they are not constantly trodden on, these plants will spread between the gaps with remarkable speed, denying them to the weeds that usually thrive there. Of course, it is important that there is some sort of soil beneath the paving, as almost nothing will grow in solid concrete.

WILDFLOWERS

Many of our most popular garden plants are wildflowers in all but name, being identical to their wild ancestors. Many other wild plants, not formerly grown in gardens, are becoming popular with the rise of 'wild' or 'wildlife gardening'. Such plants can be used to create gardens that are designed either as miniature nature reserves (see pages 188–9), or as part of a labour-saving scheme such as a wildflower meadow. Alternatively, they can be grown in a more conventional way in beds and borders, alongside the regular perennials. In addition to using wildflowers to bring an atmosphere of rural softness and informality to the garden, certain perennials that seed themselves can also be used, and often feature in the cottage-garden style.

GROWING WILDFLOWERS IN BORDERS

There is no reason why wildflower enthusiasts or those who want to grow plants to feed butterflies should not use such plants in the borders. The results will not look as orderly as a conventional border, but can certainly be colourful and attractive. You should realize, though, that wildflowers cultivated in borders usually grow larger and more vigorously than they do in the wild, where they are cheek-by-jowl with many competitors; this means that they may need staking. Some wildflowers also have a tendency to run riot in a border, with roots that engulf neighbouring plants. If this threatens, then they should be removed before too much damage is done.

WILD GARDENS

Wild gardens and meadows, where wildflowers and other perennials are grown in grass, need little maintenance once established, but they do require a lot of work at the beginning to ensure that unattractive or highly competitive weeds are excluded. The key to sucessful wild gardening is to choose plants that will grow well naturally in the soil, light and other conditions prevailing in your garden. Ironically, the most difficult situation in which to grow wildflowers is one with a fertile soil, where grasses and weeds will grow at the expense of less vigorous plants. In this situation you should restrict your selection to very strong growers, like geraniums, or to really big perennials, like inula. Such plants will coexist happily with vigorous grasses and consequently reduce maintenance needs to an annual cutting back, making a wild garden an attractive proposition on a site where access is difficult or the time for gardening limited.

The most colourful wildflower and wild gardens are achieved on poor soils, where competitive weeds have little opportunity to grow, and only stress-tolerant but attractive plants flourish. Two examples of this type of wild planting are limestone or chalk wildflower meadows (pages 50–51) and prairie gardens (see pages 190–191).

SELF-SEEDING PERENNIALS

Some common garden perennials have a tendency to seed themselves around so that new plants pop up in unexpected places – a feature that most gardeners welcome, seeing this as a sign that the plant is genuinely happy in its environment. If overdone, however, it can be a problem, so that what was once a favourite plant becomes a hated weed. Usually such overproduction can be prevented by the removal of dead flowers, so that the plant cannot set seed. With perennials that self-seed only moderately, a little 'creative weeding' is all that is required.

NATIVE OR NON-NATIVE

If your main aim in growing wildflowers in the garden is to encourage bees, butterflies, birds and other wildlife, it is important to grow plants that are predominantly native to your area, as local insect species will be used to feeding on them. Locally native plants also have the advantage that you can be sure they will thrive in your conditions. However, if your native plants are a bit on the dull side, then the addition of non-natives is essential to provide some added colour.

WILDFLOWER GARDENING AND CONSERVATION

In times past large numbers of wildflowers were dug up for cultivation in the garden, resulting in massive losses to wild populations and sometimes even in local extinctions. There is no excuse for removal of plants from the wild, and in many countries it is now illegal to do so.

On the other hand, collecting small amounts of

Why should vegetables always be shut away from the rest of the garden? Many are extremely decorative and deserve to be looked at as well as eaten.

seed from wild plants has a minimal effect on their populations, although it should not be done if a plant is locally rare or protected by law.

FRUIT, VEGETABLES AND HERBS

The first gardens were made for growing produce to eat, the cultivation of plants for ornamental purposes being a luxury restricted to the wealthier strata of society. Since the development of gardens

---

USEFUL SELF-SEEDERS

Alchemilla mollis	*Euphorbia lathyrius*	*Polemonium caeruleum*
Aquilegia vulgaris	*Lunaria annua*	*Silene armeria*
Dipsacus fullonum	*Lychnis coronaria*	*Verbascum olympicum*
Eryngium giganteum	*Malva sylvestris mauritiana*	*Verbena bonariensis*

FRUIT VARIETIES FOR THE GARDEN

Plant	Variety	Yield	Notes
Apple	'Discovery'	moderate	early crop; needs a pollinator
	'James Grieve'	high	mid-season crop; good for cooking and eating; needs a pollinator
			Apple rootstocks: eventual height of any variety
			M27 1.2–1.8m (4–6ft)
			M9 1.8–3m (6–10ft)
			M26 3–3.6m (10–11ft)
			MM106 3.6–4.8m (11–14ft)
Pear	'Conference'	high	self-fertile but better with a pollinator
	'Doyenne du Comice'	moderate	needs a warm position and a pollinator
			Pear rootstocks: eventual height of any variety
			Quince C 2.4–3m (8–10ft)
			Quince A 2.4–3.6m (8–11ft)
Cherry	'Morello'	high	self-fertile; eventual height 3.0–3.5m (10–11ft) on Colt rootstock
	'Stella'	high	self-fertile; eventual height 4.2–4.8m (12–15ft) on Colt rootstock
Plum	'Czar'	high	self-fertile; eventual height 2.4–3m (8–10ft) on Pixy rootstock, 3.6–4.8m (11–15ft) on St Julien A
	'Victoria'	high	self-fertile; heights as 'Czar'
Blackcurrant	'Ben Lomond'	high	good for cold areas
	'Ben Sarek'	high	good for cold areas
Raspberry	'Autumn Bliss'	moderate	crops throughout autumn
	'Malling Admiral'	moderate	crops in summer
Strawberry	'Aromel'	high	perpetual variety, cropping midsummer to frosts
	'Pegasus'	high	maincrop, cropping early summer onwards

as places to grow primarily decorative plants, however, the growing of food has been rather hidden from the rest of the garden, shunted off into the 'vegetable patch' as if it were something inherently unattractive. But should this be the case? Many gardeners are now looking at vegetables in a new light, as potentially decorative plants in their own right. Herb gardens have become fashionably decorative, as have potagers, where fruit and vegetables are combined in an ornamental way.

CHOOSING FRUIT AND VEGETABLES
Selecting vegetable varieties from the enormous number available can seem daunting, but once you start to look more closely it becomes apparent that some will suit you much better than others. Many vegetables will have early, mid-season and late varieties, so to ensure a good crop right across the season you need to make sure that you have a few of each. Also, some varieties crop all at once, which is particularly annoying unless you do a lot of freezing, so making sure that a variety crops over a long period is important. Some varieties do better in particular soils or districts than others, and this can mean the difference between a bumper harvest and a frustrating pile of greenery fit only for the compost heap. This is especially true of tropical crops, such as tomatoes and peppers, where there is a difference between those varieties bred for growing in a greenhouse and those for growing outside.

Choosing fruit varieties is a very taxing business, as they take several years to bear a decent crop, so making the right decision first time is vital. As with vegetables, some varieties do much better in particular soil types and areas than others. Many fruit trees need others of a different variety nearby to pollinate them, and it is essential to ensure that you select appropriate varieties to do this. It is also important to make sure you get varieties that you like, since one of the advantages of growing your own is to have fruit that it is impossible to buy in the shops – rare or old-fashioned apple varieties, for instance.

With fruit trees, choosing the right rootstock is important for controlling the eventual size and vigour of the tree. An apple variety on an M111 rootstock, for example, will grow vigorously and fill up a small garden before too long. A dwarfing M27 rootstock, on the other hand, will always stay small. Garden centres offer only a limited range of fruit, while specialist mail-order nurseries will stock a much wider selection.

DECORATIVE FRUIT AND VEGETABLES

Most fruit trees bear attractive flowers, so integrating them into the garden is no problem; indeed, an orchard with widely spaced trees and plenty of room for later plantings of flowers and vegetables is a traditional, productive and most attractive style of garden seen throughout Europe, in towns as well as in the countryside.

Herbs – most being perennial and good-looking plants in their own right – are easy to place in borders with strictly ornamental plants. Most need sun, and all should be planted somewhere near the kitchen door for easy access.

Vegetables differ greatly in their attractiveness, but some are quite spectacular; ruby chard, for instance, has rich red stems and makes a bold addition to the border, as well as a good substitute for spinach. Many lettuce varieties, especially those with reddish leaves, can be appropriate in a border, and are among the most worthwhile and popular salad vegetables to grow. Other good-looking crops include runner beans, and squashes, which can be used very decoratively as both trailers and climbers. A full-blown allotment of cabbages and potatoes can be a bit more difficult to integrate into a garden, although these plants will not look out of place in a traditional cottage plot.

DECORATIVE VEGETABLES

Plant	Decorative Varieties	Season	Appearance
Asparagus	all varieties	spring	wonderfully feathery foliage all summer
Beetroot	all varieties	summer/ autumn	red foliage
Globe artichoke	'Green Globe', 'Purple Globe'	summer	large, architectual
Cauliflower	'Violet Queen'	summer/ autumn	purple heads
Chicory	'Rossa di Veron'	autumn	red foliage
Courgette	'Jemmy' F1	summer/autumn	yellow fruit
Endive	crispy varieties, including 'Moss Curled', 'Riccia Pancaleir'	summer/autumn	crispy foliage
Leaf beet	'Swiss Chard', 'Ruby Chard'*	summer/autumn	white stems, *bright red stems
Lettuce	'Little Leprechaun' (cos type), 'Lolla Rossa', 'Red Salad Bowl' (loose leaf)	spring/summer/ autumn	red foliage
Mizuna (Japanese greens)		all year	divided foliage
Pepper/chilli	all varieties, 'Arianne' F1*	summer/autumn summer/autumn	red fruit *orange fruit
Rhubarb	all varieties	spring/ summer	red stems/foliage
Runner bean	all varieties	summer	scarlet, white, bicoloured flowers
Tomato	all varieties 'Red Alert'*, 'Golden Sunrise' **, 'Golden Tomboy' F1**	summer/autumn	red fruit

* especially good for confined spaces ** bright yellow fruit

RHODODENDRON GLORY

O N A N A C I D S O I L , especially a sandy one, rhododendrons, heathers and other related plants thrive. This is just as well, as many other popular garden plants do not do well on these rather poor soils. There is a terrific range of these plants; in the case of rhododendrons, you can have varieties in flower from late winter to midsummer, and heathers all year round.

Selecting the right variety of rhododendron needs care, as many grow far too large for a small or medium-sized garden. Fortunately there are many excellent smaller varieties, and a good

number of dwarf species and hybrids that combine well with heathers.

It is not a good idea to rely totally on rhododendrons for colour in the garden, because they finish flowering by midsummer and then tend to look very dark and dull for the rest of the year. Hydrangeas and other acid-tolerant shrubs combine well with them, as do heathers and certain grasses, and will extend the season of interest. Both rhododendrons and heathers have a rather uniform appearance, and the light, airy growth of grasses and sedges can be very welcome among them.

MAINTENANCE – *Very low*

Heathers require a clip back after flowering every other year, but that is about it. Dry years might see some need for watering, and if drought is a problem, mulching areas of bare earth with chipped bark is advisable.

SITE AND SEASON

Any soil on the acid side of neutral is suitable, especially those that are peaty or sandy. This planting requires full sun, with the exception of the plants on the far right, which prefer a little shade. The rhododendrons are all tolerant of some light shade, but the heathers are not.

The flowering season for this scheme is from late spring to early summer.

Trees

1 *Parrotia persica*
2 *Nyssa sylvatica*

Shrubs

3 *Erica arborea* var. *alpina*
4 *Rhododendron* 'Pink Pearl'
5 *Kalmia latifolia*
6 *Rhododendron augustinii*
7 *Rhododendron* 'Sappho'
8 *Fothergilla gardenii*
Monticola Group
9 *Rhododendron* 'Palestrina'
10 *Rhododendron* Elizabeth
Group

11 *Rhododendron yakushi-manum*
12 *Rhododendron luteum*
13 *Rhododendron* 'Unique'
14 *Erica × veitchii* 'Exeter'
15 *Genista pilosa* 'Procumbens'
16 *Calluna vulgaris* 'Boskoop'
17 *Phyllodoce empetriformis*
18 *Andromeda polifolia*

Bulbs

19 *Hyacinthoides non-scriptus*

Grasses

20 *Festuca ovina* 'Glauca'
21 *Carex buchananii*
22 *Molinia caerulea* 'Variegata'
23 *Deschampsia flexuosa* 'Tatra Gold'

A FOOLPROOF FAMILY GARDEN

HAVEN'T GOT TIME? Hate gardening? This is the planting scheme for you. The selection of plants is designed to provide as much colour and interest through the year as possible, without looking too much like a supermarket car park landscaping; to be as tolerant of a wide range of conditions as it reasonable to ask of plants; and to need as little care as possible. There are cheerful golden-variegated evergreens for the dark depths of winter and long-flowering shrubs and herbaceous plants for the summer. Butterflies will be drawn to the buddleia, providing an extra dimension to the garden and something of interest for children, too. The plants here are all widely available, so there is no need to search out obscure nurseries in order to obtain them.

MAINTENANCE – *Low*

The shrubs, especially the buddleia and lavatera, might need to be cut back if they outgrow their welcome. This should be done straight after flowering and not, as many people do, in the winter. The clematis will flower better if it is cut back by about one-third in late winter. The perennials will need an end-of-year tidy-up.

SITE AND SEASON

This border can be planted in any reasonably fertile soil that receives some sun.

The main flowering season is early summer, although many of the plants will continue to bloom for much longer. For spring interest, bulbs can be planted so that they bloom around and underneath the shrubs.

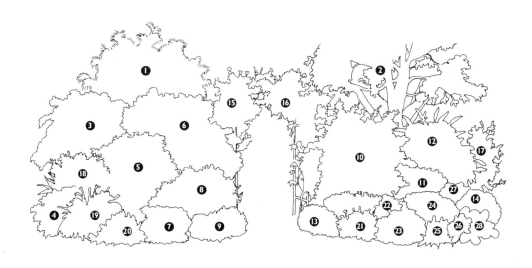

Trees
1 *Sorbus commixta* 'Embley'
2 *Betula jacquemontii*

Shrubs
3 *Genista aetnensis*
4 *Euonymus fortunei* 'Emerald 'n' Gold'
5 *Elaeagnus pungens* 'Maculata'
6 *Corylus avellana* 'Contorta'
7 *Santolina chamaecyparissus*
8 *Hypericum* 'Hidcote'
9 *Erica carnea* 'Westwood Yellow'

10 *Lavatera olbia* 'Rosea'
11 *Potentilla fruticosa* 'Abbotswood'
12 *Buddleia davidii*
13 *Helianthemum* 'Wisley Pink'
14 *Hebe* 'Carl Teschner'

Climbers
15 *Lonicera periclymenum* 'Belgica'
16 *Clematis* 'The President'
17 *Hedera canariensis* 'Gloire de Marengo'

Perennials
18 *Iris sibirica*
19 *Hemerocallis* 'Corky'
20 *Heuchera var. diversifolia* 'Palace Purple'
21 *Geum* 'Borisii'
22 *Knautia macedonica*
23 *Geranium* 'Johnson's Blue'
24 *Geranium* 'Claridge Druce'
25 *Stachys byzantina*
26 *Euphorbia dulcis* 'Chameleon'
27 *Achillea millefolium* Summer Pastels Group
28 *Bergenia* 'Silberlicht'

A TOWN GARDEN

SMALL TOWN GARDENS present a real challenge, especially to keen gardeners anxious to grow as wide a range of plants as possible. While there are undoubtedly problems – such as poor, rubble-filled soil and draughts – there are compensations, like the warmth of urban environments and the different microclimates offered by the walls: a warm, sunny wall with a selection of tender species may be only a few metres (yards) away from a shady wall sheltering cool-loving woodlanders. Where soil is thin or non-existent, containers can be used to provide extra planting space, or, as here, to create a miniature pond planted with a pygmy water lily. In a garden with high walls and fences, there may be more vertical than horizontal space; this is ideal for a rich variety of climbers, which will do much to engender the feeling of a green island in the urban desert.

MAINTENANCE – *Low*

None of these plants needs much attention; simply clear up dead stems and leaves in the winter, and prune shrubs after flowering if they begin to exceed the limits of their space (as ceanothus is often wont to do). The roses, if they need pruning, should be cut back by no more than one-third in late winter.

Given that urban soils are often impoverished by the activities of builders, feeding and humus-building are often advisable. An annual application of an organic plant food, plus bucketfuls of compost or manure, can work wonders.

SITE AND SEASON

The house wall in the plan faces the sun, with the bed on each side receiving sun for about half the day. Any reasonably fertile and well-drained soil will do.

The main flowering is in early summer, with continued interest for much of the rest of the year. Bulbs and container-grown half-hardy plants and annuals can be used to extend the season.

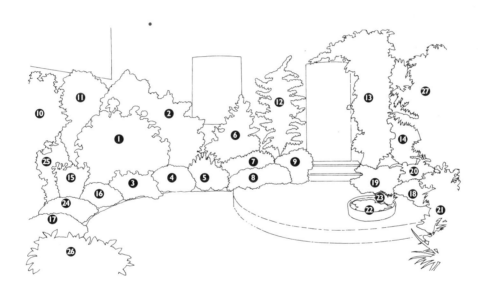

Shrubs

1 *Rosa* 'Louise Odier'
2 *Ceanothus impressus*
3 *Cistus* 'Silver Pink'
4 *Hebe* 'Red Edge'
5 *Rosmarinus officinalis* 'Tuscan Blue'
6 *Leptospermum scoparium* 'Jubilee'
7 *Lavandula stoechas* sp. *pedunculata*
8 *Helianthemum* 'Wisley Primrose'
9 *Euonymus fortunei* 'Silver Queen'

Climbers

10 *Clematis* 'Richard Pennell'
11 *Jasminum* x *stephanense*
12 *Abutilon megapotamicum*
13 *Rosa* 'Gloire de Dijon'
14 *Lathyrus latifolius*

Perennials

15 *Campanula persicifolia*
16 *Geranium* x *oxonianum* 'Winscombe'
17 *Campanula lactiflora* 'Pouffe'
18 *Alchemilla conjuncta*
19 *Campanula garganica*
20 *Dicentra spectabilis*
21 *Hemerocallis* 'Corky'
22 *Nymphaea* 'Pygmaea Alba'
23 *Acorus gramineus* 'Variegatus'
24 *Potentilla recta* 'Warrenii'

Annuals

25 *Lathyrus odoratus* 'Red Ensign'

Grasses

26 *Shibataea kumasasa*
27 *Sinarundinaria nitida*

A SHOWY SUMMER PLANTING

I OFTEN HEAR GARDENERS complaining about mid- to late summer as being a boring time in the garden. Here is just one of many possible plantings for this season. In fact, it is a potentially exciting time of year as there are lots of hardy perennials in flower, and plenty of more exotic half-hardy plants that are just getting into

their stride; annuals and bedding plants are likewise coming to maturity.

This planting scheme is based on pinks and blues. It includes a lot of strong foliage shapes and some interesting and rather stylishly shaped flowers. The overall effect is rather exotic, and ideal for enhancing your enjoyment of hot weather.

MAINTENANCE – Medium

While the core of the varieties here are hardy, requiring only an annual clearing away of dead stems, some of the planting's panache comes from half-hardy species that either need lifting or protecting for the winter. Among the hardies, *Dahlia merckii* might suffer in cold regions and should be protected with straw or bubble plastic. The half-hardies will need to be stored in a frost-free greenhouse for the winter in most areas. the cannas and *Salvia patens* die down to tubers, making for easy storage. Among the annuals, the nemophila is a hardy one which can be sown outside in spring. The others will need to be raised from seed in a greenhouse and planted out after the last frost.

SITE AND SEASON

Any reasonably fertile soil is suitable, but preferably one that does not dry out too quickly. This planting needs a warm position to do well, and certainly somewhere that receives sun for most of the day.

The flowering season is mid- to late summer.

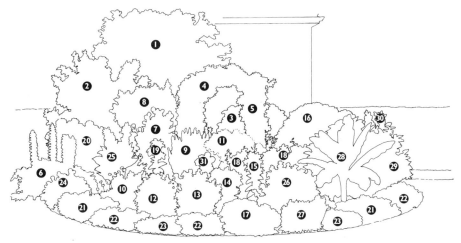

Trees

1 *Hoheria lyallii*

Shrubs

2 *Hibiscus syriacus* 'Woodbridge'
3 *Hydrangea quercifolia*

Climbers

4 *Passiflora caerulea*
5 *Clematis* 'Etoile Violette'

Perennials

6 *Acanthus spinosus*
7 *Echinops* 'Nivalis'
8 *Macleaya microcarpa* 'Kelway's Coral Plume'
9 *Lythrum salicaria*
10 *Dahlia merckii*
11 *Artemisia lactiflora*
12 *Penstemon* 'Sour Grapes'
13 *Penstemon* 'Garnet'
14 *Penstemon* 'Blackbird'
15 *Verbena patagonica*
16 *Romneya coulteri*
17 *Limonium latifolium*

Bulbs

18 *Lilium* 'Journey's End'
19 *Lilium* 'Sterling Silver'

Annuals/biennials

20 *Cleome hassleriana*
21 *Brachyscombe iberidifolia*
22 *Impatiens* hybrids
23 *Nemophila menziesii*

Half-hardy

24 *Pelargonium quercifolium*
25 *Canna* 'Orchid'
26 *Salvia involucrata* 'Bethellii'
27 *Salvia patens*
28 *Musa basjoo*
29 *Datura arborea*
30 *Canna* 'Wyoming'
31 *Dahlia* 'White Klankstad'

A GARDEN FOR A WHEELCHAIR USER

Raised beds, sinks, troughs and plants in pots on shelves bring the garden to a height at which it is possible for the wheelchair-bound to enjoy them. Alpines, dwarf conifers, dwarf bulbs and other small plants are eminently suitable for this kind of gardening, and have the advantage that a lot of variety can be packed into a small space. Gardening in containers and raised beds also means that close attention can be given to catering for the needs of individual plants, and different composts can be used. Raised beds and containers for lime-loving and lime-hating plants will have to be planned carefully so that they are all within reach from the wheelchair.

MAINTENANCE – *Medium*

The level of maintenance can be geared closely to the needs of the individual. Most of the plants require little care, although weeding of alpines has to be rigorous. The keen disabled gardener will probably want plenty to do, in which case the more challenging alpines, such as the auriculas, will provide plenty of interest. Alternatively, space in a raised bed with at least 30cm (12in) of root depth could be given over to the cultivation of annuals and vegetables, such as salad crops.

SITE AND SEASON

This garden requires full sun for as much of the day as possible, although the lime-hating plants in the raised bed on the left will appreciate some shade for a few hours each day. These are also very intolerant of drying out, and need a humus-rich, lime-free soil. The other plants require a free-draining, gritty soil.

The main flowering is in mid-spring. Further dwarf bulbs can be added for earlier interest, and other alpines used for colour until autumn.

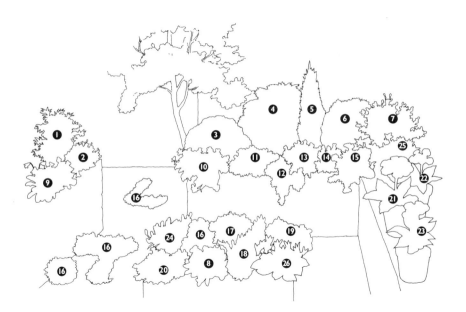

Dwarf trees and shrubs
1 *Andromeda polifolia* 'Compacta'
2 *Cassiope* 'Edinburgh'
3 *Picea mariana* 'Nana'
4 *Chamaecyparis pisifera* 'Filifera Aurea'
5 *Juniperus communis* 'Hibernica'
6 *Pinus heldreichii* 'Schmidtii'
7 *Salix helvetica*
8 *Salix reticulata*

Perennials
9 *Shortia galacifolia*
10 *Viola* 'Jackanapes'
11 *Armeria juniperifolia*
12 *Saxifraga* 'Tumbling Waters'
13 *Tanacetum densum* sp. *amani*
14 *Saxifraga sempervivum*
15 *Euphorbia myrsinites*
16 *Primula hirsuta*
17 *Erinus alpinus*
18 *Helichrysum coralloides*

19 *Saxifraga oppositifolia*
20 *Gentiana verna*
21 *Primula auricula* 'Chloe'
22 *Primula auricula* 'Janie Hill'
23 *Primula auricula* 'Mark'

Bulbs
24 *Muscari aucheri*
25 *Tulipa tarda*
26 *Cyclamen repandum*

A HERB GARDEN

I T   I S   C O N V E N I E N T for the cook to have herbs growing together in one place, and preferably near to the kitchen door. Most herbs are reasonably attractive plants, so a herb garden can be quite ornamental in its own right. It can be further enhanced by interspersing the herbs with some purely decorative cottage-garden flowers and old-fashioned roses. Access to the herbs needs to be easy, so paths are always an important feature of herb gardens.

The planting of low box hedges is a fashionable part of making a herb garden, but is inadvisable in small spaces because of the tendency of the questing box roots to take moisture and nutrients away from the herbs. A good alternative to box is dwarf lavender.

MAINTENANCE – *Medium to high*

Most herbs are perennial, needing only an autumn cut back if they become untidy. Others are either annual (basil) or biennial (parsley) and so will need to be sown afresh from seed every year.

Since herb plants are being constantly cropped, it will be necessary to feed the soil, either with an annual application of manure in the autumn or fertilizer in spring.

Some herbs – mints are especially notorious – have very invasive roots that can lead to them becoming weeds. One way of constricting the roots is to plant them in a half-barrel with the bottom knocked out, which is buried in the soil to a depth of about 30cm (12in).

SITE AND SEASON

This herb garden requires sun for most of the day. Any reasonably fertile and well-drained soil would be suitable.

Most of the herbs flower in midsummer. Bulbs and cottage-garden annuals can be added for earlier and later colour.

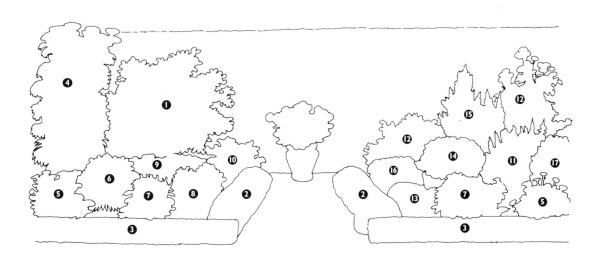

Shrubs
1 *Rosa* 'Ispahan'
2 *Lavandula angustifolia* 'Munstead'
3 *Buxus sempervirens* 'Suffruticosa'

Herbs
4 Fennel (*Foeniculum vulgare*)
5 English marigold (*Calendula officinalis*)
6 Chives (*Allium schoenoprasum*)
7 Sweet basil (*Ocimum basilicum*)
8 Sweet marjorum (*Origanum majorana*)
9 Parsley 'Champion Moss Curled' (*Petroselinum crispum*)
10 Chervil (*Anthriscus cerefolium*)
11 Sage (*Salvia officinalis*)
12 Lovage (*Levisticum officinale*)
13 Thyme (*Thymus vulgaris*)
14 Peppermint (*Mentha × piperita*)
15 Rosemary (*Rosmarinus officinalis*)
16 Purple sage (*Salvia officinalis* 'Purpurascens')
17 Summer savory (*Satureia hortensis*)

Part Three

COMBINING PLANTS

*C*OMBINING PLANTS *involves thinking imaginatively about how they can be used in the garden to provide interest and colour, either all year round or at the times when the garden is used most. It also means thinking about growing plants together to create colour schemes, or combinations based on foliage or form. In this section we look at all these factors, and at how to make final decisions about plant selection and planning.*

Chapter Six

A PLANT FOR EVERY PLACE

FEW OF US START OFF with a blank space to plant up from scratch. When we move into a new house we usually find that a basic structure of beds and borders has already been established in the garden. However, there is no need to accept what is there; one of the keys to good garden design is an ability to see new possibilities among pre-existing structures.

The vast majority of plants in gardens are grown in company with others, in borders that hug the boundary – be it fence, hedge or wall – or the side of the house, or in beds, such as island beds. The idea of the traditional border or bed may, however, be expanded to encompass a much wider stretch – perhaps even the whole garden, thus doing away with grass entirely.

Different countries tend to have different traditions about where planting takes place; the Americans have open gardens without boundaries and 'foundation planting' around the house, the British mostly have lawns with borders along the boundaries, while the Dutch generally have small front gardens that tend to be planted up completely. Being adventurous in terms of planting and garden design may mean breaking with a national tradition.

SPECIMEN PLANTS

These are plants – usually trees but often shrubs or even particularly statuesque perennials – that stand on their own, usually in grass. They can make all the difference to a space, especially an open one, but they need to be in proportion to the house and the area they occupy: many is the cedar that not only overshadows the neighbour's garden but also overpowers the house.

A good specimen plant is well shaped above all else, its form being apparent and pleasing at all times of the year. Vast lawns may support the extravagantly asymmetrical tiered branches of a cedar of Lebanon (*Cedrus libani*), but most of us only have space for something much smaller. Trees that make good specimens for small gardens are generally those with upward-sweeping branches, like the ornamental apple *Malus tschonoskii*. Some trees and shrubs that make good specimens are described on pages 64–5 and 66–7.

Fine architectural perennials may also be used as specimen plants, the pampas grass (*Cortaderia selloana*) being the most commonly seen example. An alternative would be to use any of the miscanthus grasses, which are still imposing but which are more delicate. There is also plenty of

Annual lavatera and cosmos frame and complement – but do not overwhelm – a garden statue.

APPROACHES TO PLANTING

A Open front lawns in suburban settings may require only one specimen tree, the majority of the planting being around the house. Be adventurous, and don't restrict yourself to traditional evergreens – try some shrubs that will benefit from the protection of the wall, such as ceanothus. Use perennials, bulbs and annuals to enliven the border in front of the shrubs.

B A variation on the open suburban theme is to have island beds in the lawn, in this case incorporating a small specimen tree. It is important that the size of the beds is in proportion to the area of lawn: too often beds are made too small and look rather ridiculous.

C Where a garden has well-defined boundaries, the traditional approach is for the borders to follow them, with a lawn in the middle and maybe a specimen tree or shrub in the lawn. This makes for shallow borders, ideal for traditional bedding plants and annuals, or plants that need either constant attention or easy access, such as cut flowers, herbs or vegetables. It also maximizes the lawn area.

D Borders around the outside of the garden can be made deeper to allow more plants to be grown. This approach can be taken in any plot; it helps to create a sense of privacy in a garden with an open aspect, but is especially appropriate and successful in gardens which are already surrounded by a high fence or wall. This style suits those who want a romantic retreat or who like a varied collection of plants.

E In this garden, the lawn has been dispensed with entirely and the space given over to low-growing perennials and shrubs, around which paths meander. With careful selection of low-maintenance plants this kind of planting can involve less work than a lawn. It is ideal for those who wish to grow a wide variety of plants, would like to incorporate a naturalistic pond or want to create a garden for wildlife.

A

B

scope for the imaginative use of other large perennials, such as the imposing silvery cardoon plant (*Cynara cardunculus*) or the giant hogweed (*Heracleum mantegazzianum*) – note that the latter can give a nasty rash to some people. One potential advantage of using herbaceous perennials as specimen plants is that they are seasonal rather than permanent features of the garden.

BORDERS

If a plant is not grown on its own as a specimen, it is usually grown in a border. 'Border' means an edge, and that is just what most garden plantings are – a strip along a boundary, fence, hedge or wall. It seems to be a fundamental part of human nature to want to adorn those places where the vertical meets the horizontal. It is as if we have a deep need to fill the corner, to round it off with greenery.

Such places do offer a lot to the gardener – a vertical surface for climbers and a backdrop for taller perennials and shrubs, which in turn set the stage for smaller perennials, bulbs and annuals, and the exploitation of all the possibilities on offer is part of what makes an adventurous gardener. Borders are also convenient places for planting, which will not get in the way of whatever takes up the body of the garden, tea parties, ball games or the view from the house, but this convenience should not blind us to the scope offered by planting elsewhere in the body of the garden.

Borders have gone through many incarnations in the history of gardening. From tree and shrub borders on large estates and the grand herbaceous border of the earlier part of this century, today the 'mixed' border – a pragmatic blend of shrubs, perennials, annuals and climbers, and perhaps the odd vegetable or fruit bush – reigns supreme.

Borders are relatively easy to plant. You only have to see one side of a plant, and you can hide the unattractive 'bare legs' that many flowering perennials or shrubs develop behind shorter plants.

PLANTING AROUND FEATURES

Most gardens have more to them than plants. There may be a patio or terrace, a summerhouse, statues or other garden ornaments. All these features need to be integrated into the garden, so that they become a relevant part of it, and this can be done

with appropriate planting. On the other hand, there are 'features' that one might want to do without – that factory across the road, for example – and where screening will be needed (see page 121).

Desirable garden features should not be hidden, or put in the shade, by something that steals all the attention. Statues, sundials or other free-standing ornaments can be enhanced subtly around the base with planting, which should be neutral in tone but nevertheless attractive. Most sculpture needs to be unencumbered to be appreciated, but I have seen works that benefit from being partially hidden, seen behind greenery or at the back of a border.

Luxuriant and striking foliage is often a feature of waterside planting. The pale orange highlight is provided by Euphorbia griffithii, *which will thrive in many different soils.*

Some ornaments require a context that plants can help to provide; an oriental piece, for example, may well benefit from the company of bamboo or other plants associated with the East. A classical sculpture or urn likewise needs a summer planting of pelargoniums and a setting involving some formal clipped yew or box.

Sitting places, such as summerhouses and terraces, are crucial. Here people linger and have time to appreciate the garden, but also to notice if things are not quite right. Plenty of colour and interest are essential for the season during which the area will be used and this is why bedding and patio plants are so popular, as they generally flower all summer long.

Scent is important too, and not only scented flowers but aromatic foliage as well. This can create quite a talking point as guests try the different leaves in turn. The scented-leaved pelargoniums are invaluable on this account, and eminently collectable. Such a situation is also ideal for plants that are not fully hardy, including all sorts of conservatory and greenhouse exotica that are brought out for the frost-free months such as daturas, with their fabulously scented trumpets, oleanders, bougainvilleas, palms and cacti.

PLANTING AROUND WATER

Small ponds are very popular, but to be effective they need to be sited carefully to avoid appearing out of place. They look best when treated with either total formality or total informality – nothing inbetween ever seems to work. A formal pool, rectangular in shape and with paved surrounds, is uncompromisingly formal and is therefore accepted as such, but an informal pond has to look as if it could be natural to work at all visually. No pool should ever be made on a slope: they just do not occur like that in nature and always look absurd.

Formal pools should have only sparse planting around them – perhaps some architectural plants with grand foliage (*Hosta sieboldiana* is rightly a classic). Containers can also be used to give a Mediterranean feel. Planting in the pool itself should be restricted to a few water lilies (*Nymphaea* and *Nuphar* species) and perhaps an iris at the edge; anything more and it will begin to look cluttered.

An informal pool should not have the edge, let alone the liner, showing at all. Lush and leafy plants leaning over the edge and marginals such as irises reaching out of the water will help to give it a natural feel, blending the pool with the rest of the garden. Ideally, there should be a ledge at the side of the pool where moisture-loving plants can be grown, and the whole should be backed by tall perennials, grasses or shrubs and trees like willows (*Salix* species), which we automatically associate with the waterside. If there is no ledge for marginal planting, select some large perennials that will look reasonably lush but that thrive in normal soil – the rhubarbs (*Rheum* species) are a good example.

Most water plants grow large and lush and can overwhelm a small pool, necessitating constant cutting back and dredging, which can disrupt pondlife. It is essential that plants are chosen that suit the size of the pool: less vigorous relatives of classic water plants are available, including pygmy water lilies and dwarf reedmace (*Typha minima*).

WATERSIDE VEGETATION, FROM DRY LAND TO OPEN WATER

1 Moisture-loving plants create the right context for a pool and most will grow well enough in ordinary garden conditions. Examples include *Lythrum salicaria*, *Iris sibirica*, *Lobelia cardinalis* and *Primula japonica*.

2 Marginal plants for wet soil and shallow water should be planted in soil on a ledge of the pond liner. Examples include *Iris pseudacorus*, *Butomus umbellatus* and *Acorus gramineus*.

3 Submerged aquatics such as *Myriophyllum spicatum* may not contribute much to the ornamental character of the pond, but they benefit pond life and help to suppress algae.

4 Water lilies (*Nymphaea* and *Nuphar* species) grow in soil at the base of the pond, producing their leaves and flowers at the surface. Nearly all these plants need sun in order to flower.

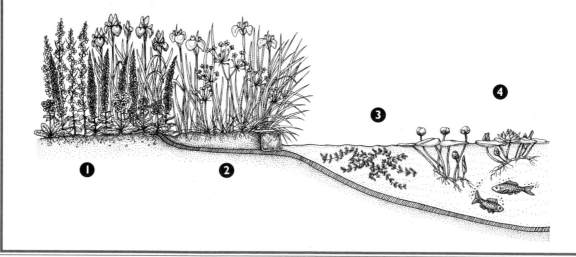

PLANTING AN ISLAND BED

These two cross-sections through island beds illustrate how the taller plants are placed in the centre and the shortest around the outside.

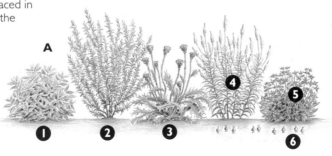

A Late summer on a dry soil. *Papaver orientale* 'Perry's White' has finished flowering, but the gap it leaves has been filled by *Linaria purpurea* 'Canon Went'. Crocuses flower in spring beneath the still-dormant origanum.

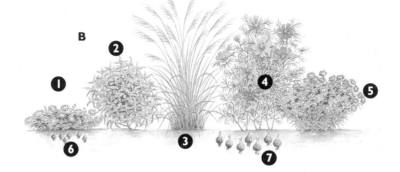

B Late summer on an average soil. The felicia on the left is a temporary half-hardy plant for the summer only; crocuses will flower on its site in the spring. The cosmos is a half-hardy annual; daffodils will flower in its position in spring.

C Early summer on a slightly moist soil. This cross-section illustrates an island bed in which the plants are not graded by height. Instead, it consists of a low drift of perennials. The *Geranium endressii* will flower on and off throughout the summer; the snowdrops flower in late winter around the still-dormant *Polemonium caeruleum*.

A
1 *Salvia officinalis* 'Pur-purascens'
2 *Rosmarinus officinalis*
3 *Papaver orientale* 'Perry's White'
4 *Linaria purpurea* 'Canon Went'
5 *Origanum laevigatum* 'Herrenhausen'
6 Crocus bulbs

B
1 *Felicia bergeriana*
2 *Spiraea japonica* 'Little Princess'
3 *Miscanthus sinensis* 'Silberfeder'
4 *Cosmos bipinnatus* 'King George'
5 *Aster amellus* 'King George'
6 Crocus bulbs

7 Narcissus bulbs

C
1 *Geranium endressii*
2 *Filipendula ulmaria*
3 *Lychnis coronaria*
4 *Geranium* 'Spinners'
5 *Geranium* endressii
6 *Polemonium caeruleum*
7 Snowdrop (*Galanthus*) bulbs

A PLANTING FOR INFERTILE, STONY SOIL

In addition to the plants on the plan, small bulbs such as crocuses and species tulips may be planted, especially in areas that may not be covered with foliage later in the season. Potentially, they can provide colour from late winter until the first herbaceous perennials flower.

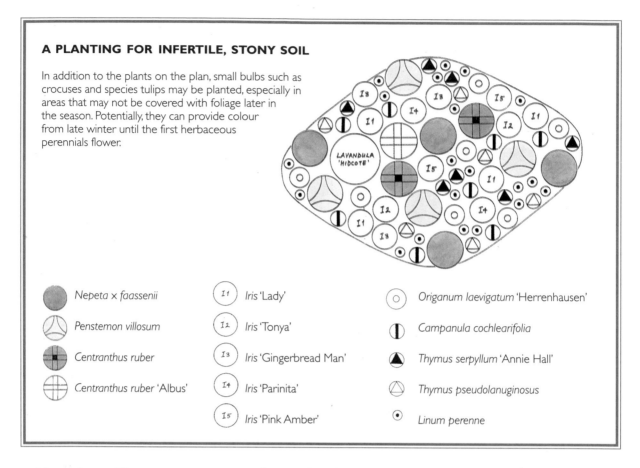

⬤ Nepeta x faassenii	(I¹) Iris 'Lady'	◉ Origanum laevigatum 'Herrenhausen'
Penstemon villosum	(I²) Iris 'Tonya'	Campanula cochlearifolia
Centranthus ruber	(I³) Iris 'Gingerbread Man'	▲ Thymus serpyllum 'Annie Hall'
Centranthus ruber 'Albus'	(I⁴) Iris 'Parinita'	△ Thymus pseudolanuginosus
	(I⁵) Iris 'Pink Amber'	◉ Linum perenne

Most of us will not want to surround a pool completely with vegetation; at least one side can be kept open to lawn or paving, with room for sitting by the pool and watching for pondlife. This open side should face the sun, so that the water receives good light. Full sun all day is not good for fish and other pond creatures, so shade at one end, or the shade of large-leaved plants, is beneficial.

ISLAND BEDS

Island beds free perennials and shrubs from the need for a backdrop of fence, hedge or wall. They are a useful way of breaking up wide expanses of lawn or, on a smaller scale, paving or gravel. To be successful, they need to be in proportion to the size of the area; beds that are too large overwhelm the surrounding space, while conversely those that are too small are themselves overwhelmed. This applies not only to the size of the bed but also to the plants in it – all too frequently a nice little shrub from the garden centre turns into a monster that occupies

the entire bed and towers over its surroundings.

Island beds are a good way in which to display plants, especially lower growing ones, as you can walk all around them. This arrangement is also quite demanding of your planting skills, as more is on display than with a conventional border. There is no space, for instance, in which to hide the bare stems of leggy shrubs.

There are two approaches to island beds. The first is to mix taller shrubs with shorter ones and perennials to create a planting carefully graded by height, with the tallest in the middle and the shortest on the outside. This is a useful approach if you need some height to use the bed for screening or to break up an area visually. Such a planting can be combined with a small tree, but choose one with an erect habit of growth or it will shade out the rest of the bed. Another way of adding height is to incorporate a climber on a free-standing support.

If a tall island bed does not seem appropriate, a lower planting using perennials and low-growing shrubs is possible. Taller perennials and grasses can

*A carefully chosen selection of strong-growing perennials,
including pink* Persicaria bistorta, *will reduce maintenance
requirements dramatically.*

be used to create seasonal height, but will be cut down in winter. Plants can either be grouped so as to create eye-catching blocks of colour, or blended more naturalistically (see pages 168–70). Extending the concept of blended perennials in an island bed leads us 'beyond the border'.

BEYOND THE BORDER

Traditionally borders have been one-sided affairs, hugging a backdrop such as a wall or fence. Island beds at least liberated planting from being largely two dimensional, but modern European garden design is becoming more radical still, developing a planting style that involves creating wide drifts of colour using perennials and grasses, a bit like a wildflower meadow. This style undoubtedly looks best when carried out on a large scale, but I have seen many smaller gardens where it also works well. The great advantage of this style for the keen gardener is that it gives extra scope for growing more herbaceous plants and for giving them more

space than in a conventional border. When an appropriate choice of plants is made, it is also easier to have a long season of interest and to reduce the maintenance that is necessary.

The key to the new style is to choose a selection of plants that look good together, and then scatter them in drifts across the planting area. The idea is to achieve rhythm through repetition, rather than planting one or two of everything, which just ends up looking messy. One way of doing this is to compose a planting made up of several groups of varieties that all flower at the same time and look attractive together, so that as the year progresses one group replaces another in succession. Early in the year the non-flowering groups are merely low clumps of green; later on those that have finished flowering are largely hidden by the group that is currently putting on its show.

Another important aspect of the new style is the way in which plants are grouped. Certain plants are by nature bold and imposing, miscanthus grasses for example, and with relatively wide spacing will

PLANTS FOR GROWING IN WALLS

For shady walls	**For sunny walls**	**For very sunny, dry walls**
Arenaria	*Alyssum saxatile*	*Cheiranthus* varieties
Asplenium and *Ceterach* species (ferns)	*Armeria* species	*Dianthus deltoides* and other small,
Haberlea rhodopensis	*Erinus alpinus*	cushion-forming dianthus
Ramonda myconi	*Erysimum alpinum*	*Helianthemum serpyllifolium*
	Gypsophila repens	*Lewisia cotyledon* hybrids
	Linaria alpina	*Phlox subulata*
	Saponaria ocymoides	
	Saxifraga species	
	Sedum species	
	Sempervivum species	

---

dominate a planting. Others, such as foxgloves (*Digitalis* species), need to be placed in loose groups or clumps to have much impact. Still others, generally the low-growing species, look best when grown as a continuous low carpet, either on their own or blended with other ground-hugging varieties.

PLANTING IN TUNE WITH NATURE

A vital part of the new movement in perennial planting is the stress put on choosing the right plants for a given environment. This will reduce the need for maintenance, as the plants will form a relatively stable community. For example, a fertile, moist soil would be planted up with robust perennials such as purple loosestrife (*Lythrum salicaria*) and geraniums, and their strong growth will make it difficult for weeds to compete. A poor, stony soil on the other hand is not an attractive environment for either weeds or robust garden plants, but it is ideal for species adapted to stressful situations, such as bearded irises, valerian (*Centranthus ruber*) and nepetas.

For the gardener who is interested in low maintenance and is quite open-minded about what to grow, this is an ideal approach, but for those with more time and a list of specific plants that they would like in the garden, it will be unsatisfactory. Such gardeners can certainly employ drift plantings, but they will have a greater task either in removing weeds from among the non-competitive plants or in soil modification to suit the kinds of plant they want to grow.

ROCK GARDENS AND RAISED BEDS

Rockeries are not my favourite garden feature. Usually they look awful, and just like what they are: piles of rock plonked where you would not expect a pile of rock. A well-made rock garden, however, is a delight, but it is one of the most difficult things to achieve. The key to success is to make it look as natural as possible, and good planting is part of the answer – too often a rock garden is planted with a couple of dwarf conifers, some heathers and aubrieta, and that is it. Yet the potential is enormous, because there are so many plants that thrive in the well-drained conditions that a well-constructed rock garden provides.

A good rockery should have plenty of variety. Its slopes can provide many different microclimates: a sunny side where dwarf thymes, oreganos and wild tulips can soak up the sun, a shady side for mossy saxifrages and ferns, and a partly shaded side for many other alpines.

Because of their small size, alpines cannot be combined easily with other garden plants and, by themselves, they make little impact on the garden as a whole. This may be one reason why a rockery so rarely looks appropriate in a garden. Raised beds offer an alternative method of growing alpines, as

Valerian, thrift (Armeria) *and a campanula spill out of a retaining wall, creating a splash of midsummer colour.*

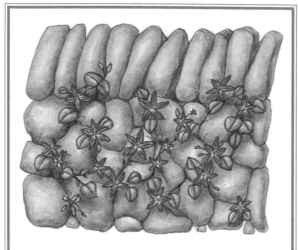

GROWING ALPINES IN A WALL

Some campanulas, especially *Campanula poscharskyana* (as here) and *C. portenschlagiana*, will penetrate the tiniest crack and throw out flowering stems over a wide area.

well as other plants that like good drainage, and are much easier to fit visually into the garden. They can be constructed so that the alpines grow out of the walls as well as in the bed in the top, thus allowing the hard surface of the stone to be softened. They are also a good means of creating divisions in a garden and, since they are raised, will add elevation.

Alpines can be grown so that they present a landscape in miniature – the very first rockeries had toy mountain goats on them!– and in a tiny garden this can be a very creative way of increasing the psychological and visual space. In any garden these plants, and their accompanying raised bed or rockery, will look a lot better if thought is given to providing some sort of appropriate context. A small conifer – a spruce, pine or juniper, such as one might find on a mountainside – makes an appropriate backdrop.

GROWING IN WALLS

One of the most adventurous ways of growing alpines is in walls. Old walls with crumbling mortar and plenty of holes are ideal in this context, and can provide homes for a large number of plants. Newer walls present a less hospitable environment, but if

bricks or stones are removed here and there, new walls too can offer planting places. One possible way of getting plants to grow in holes that are too narrow to take them, is to mix seed of appropriate species into balls of earth and stuff the balls into the cracks.

PLANTING VERTICALLY

A vertical dimension may be present in a garden in the form of existing walls, or it can be added by means of various structures. The pergola, that rather Edwardian garden feature where climbers (mostly roses) are grown over a path, is a somewhat grandiose example. Archways have become popular of late, and they are rather more appropriate for the smaller garden. Then there are the clematis-draped obelisks that started to sprout in fashionable gardens not so long ago. All these devices enable climbing plants to be grown independently of walls and fences, and they play an important part in many successful gardens.

Most climbers have a character that fits best with romantic, old-fashioned gardens and those with pastel colour schemes. Walls with tumbling honeysuckles and roses are the vital backdrop to a cottage-style garden, and an archway covered with climbers makes an appropriate exit and entry from one part of the garden to another. Obelisks or other free-standing plant supports are a very useful way of introducing climbers into borders, where their flowers or foliage can play an integral part in the planting scheme, and a can take on more central role than perhaps they would simply planted on a wall or fence.

Some climbers look magnificent growing on houses; indeed, we automatically associate *Clematis montana* with country cottages and wisteria with the Georgian style of architecture. Roses and honeysuckle are great favourites, and nothing beats their fragrance wafting in through an open window on a sunny day. In my opinion, the possibilities for using climbers on houses are not generally explored enough. Growing several climbers together is particularly effective; an early honeysuckle can be combined with a late-flowering clematis, for example, creating a longer season of flower colour.

A freer use of climbers is to grow them as nature intended, scrambling over other plants. Roses

Left: Climbers can be used to wonderfully romantic effect on gateposts. This is Vitis coignetiae *in autumn.*

Above: Pyracantha is ideal for training neatly against walls, making a fiery spectacle with its winter berries.

growing up old apple trees in cottage gardens can be seen fairly frequently, but there is no reason why we should not be more adventurous. I have seen summer-flowering clematis used over spring-flowering shrubs, and even trailing over winter-flowering heathers. Such situations demand varieties that can be cut back over the winter to allow the earlier-flowering plant beneath to perform unencumbered.

PLANTING TO DIRECT THE VIEW

When we look at a garden, our eyes do not sweep uniformly over it. We are attracted by particular things, so that our attention is focused on some parts of the scene at the expense of others. By clever manipulation of the planting and the use of features such as archways, pergolas and garden ornaments, it is possible to control the viewer's gaze. Most fundamentally, it is important to be able to hide eyesores – the garage, a neighbour's extension or the gasworks over the road.

Eyesores can generally be hidden by planting a screen in front of them or, in the case of buildings on your own land, with climbers. Usually it is not important that the plants you use are especially beautiful in their own right, but rather that they are fast growing. Since an eyesore is an eyesore, whether it is winter or summer, evergreens are preferable, although in the case of climbers the choice is unfortuantely very limited. The rapid-growing leyland cypress (x *Cupressocyparis leylandii*) might seem an attractive option for screening, but given that it sucks moisture and nutrients out of the soil and casts a dour shade, it can become a problem in its own right. The ideal screening tree is narrow in shape and light in aspect; tree of heaven (*Ailanthus altissima*) is a good deciduous option, *Prunus avium* – an attractive large cherry – another, and willows a third. Good evergreens that do not grow too wide are eucalyptus and (in warm climates) acacias.

As well as hiding unwanted features, it is good to be able to enhance desirable ones and to direct the gaze to other parts of the garden, without making it all visible at once. Arches and gateways hung with climbers not only draw the eye, they also focus it on what can be seen through them. A particularly interesting specimen or planting can also draw the eye to it, and thence onward to something not so immediately visible: a distant view, perhaps, or another part of the garden. However, the effect can be spoilt if the 'eyecatcher' is so effective that it leaps forward, shortening the perspective in the garden. A classic example of this is the magenta azalea that is planted on the far side of the garden but that is so bright that it almost yells for attention, to the detriment of everything else.

CONTAINERS

Containers are ideal for temporary plantings to liven up the area around the house or other high-profile areas, but they are also valuable for more permanent schemes where soil is limited, such as in backyards and on roof gardens and balconies. In some countries they are virtually *de rigeur* – the windowboxes that drip scarlet pelargoniums in Austria and Switzerland, for example. Elsewhere, containers are growing in popularity and

inventiveness in planting them is ever increasing.

Whether a container is for permanent or seasonal planting, it is important that the plants are in keeping with it, especially if the container is rather fine. Proportion is very important: plants that are tall or top-heavy will make the whole

composition look unbalanced (they may make it physically unstable as well), but if they are too low, the container will dominate completely. These rules can be relaxed a bit when several containers are put together, as a very tall plant can be put at the back and balanced visually by others.

Drifts of herbaceous plants, including creamy Artemisia lactiflora, *border a patch which leads the eye on into the rest of the garden.*

PLANTING IN CONTAINERS

A plant does not have the resources in a container that it does in the ground, and consequently both watering and feeding need to be regular. Hi-tech solutions have made life somewhat easier, with water-holding gels and slow-release, long-life fertilizers now widely available.

Holes in the bottom of containers are an absolute must to allow excess water to drain away, otherwise root rot will set in rapidly. Compost in a container heats up and cools down more rapidly than soil in a border. During the winter, bubble plastic or another insulating material can be wrapped around the pots to help prevent freezing, or the pots can be brought indoors when deep frost threatens.

A blend of colour can be very pleasing, and the most successful plantings often involve one flower that echoes the colour of the container. It is not a good idea to cram very ornate pots with a number of contrasting plants or plants with small and intricate foliage – a simple, bold statement made by one or two large-leaved plants will always be much more appropriate.

SEASONAL PLANTINGS

The vast majority of container plantings are for the summer season. Colourful exuberance is achieved with long-flowering pelargoniums, lobelias, petunias and other bedding plants, but increasingly gardeners are experimenting with other more subtle but equally long-lasting plant combinations, using herbs, plants with coloured foliage, grasses and even vegetables in their containers.

Plants for seasonal colour need to be quick growing in order to show results, but not so

Above: An agave, pelargoniums, marguerites and succulent echeverias form an attractive pastel composition for a summer patio.

vigorous that they will behave like cuckoos in the nest and starve the other plants. Ideally, they should not be moisture-lovers; it is a hot, and often dry, life in a pot all summer. Containers usually look better if they are planted with a limited number of plants in a tight colour scheme, than if a thousand and one varieties are stuffed in together.

While summer is the main time of year for container plants, spring schemes are an excellent way of bringing the season a little nearer to the house, which is especially valuable for those with limited garden space or even none at all. Bulbs, polyanthus and other spring flowers make excellent container plants, and they can all be planted out in the garden when they have finished flowering. If this is not possible, keep them in a light but cool place for the summer. Winter containers can be surprisingly colourful if planted with pansies, winter heathers, dwarf hebes and grasses with attractive winter leaves.

PERMANENT PLANTINGS

Permanently planted containers are the answer if you have no garden. It is vital that the plants chosen are not so vigorous that they will outgrow their container in one season and then starve. Since they are permanent, they will need to be attractive for as much of the year as possible. It is not surprising that evergreens, especially those with coloured or variegated foliage, are so popular for this purpose. In Mediterranean countries there is also a great tradition of growing evergreen topiary in containers, often in imaginative and extravagant shapes. Herbs are also successful and attractive in pots, and very practical.

The best permanent plants for containers are those that are relatively slow growing, which eliminates most herbaceous perennials. Slow- and low-growing shrubs are generally the most successful, particularly if they are shallow rooted, like camellias and rhododendrons.

BEDDING-OUT CONTAINER PLANTS

Very popular in Victorian times, and now due for a revival, is the practice of planting out tender plants in pots for the summer, immersing them in the soil to allow them to merge with the surrounding plants. In times gone by, whole borders would be filled with palms, bananas and other exotica surrounded by bedding, whereas today's practitioners like to combine their plants with hardy species.

Over the summer there is a great tendency for the roots of the plants to run through the holes in the pot and into the soil of the border, which can result in considerable damage to the plants when they are taken up in the autumn. This can be avoided to some extent by ensuring that they are potted on before planting out, or by taking them out of their pots for the summer and repotting on lifting in the autumn.

This technique can be extended by using pots full of greenhouse- or conservatory-raised flowering plants as temporary gap fillers in summer borders, sometimes for only a few weeks – an especially useful trick early in the season. It is amazing how many people are fooled by this ploy, thinking that the plants are actually growing in the ground.

'Hot' colours make the most of summer. Here, pots of variegated abutilon, lantana and soft orange Mimulus aurantiacus *share paving space.*

Chapter Seven

PLANTING PRINCIPLES

PLANTING PRINCIPLES are all about achieving interest and harmony in the garden, considering plant form and foliage as well as flower colour, to create a picture that looks good not only during the main flowering times but both before and after.

HEIGHT, FORM AND HABIT

Height is a crucial element in good planting. It is all too easy for a few tall plants to dominate a garden, or even the house. Shrubs, and particularly trees, need to be in proportion to the scale of the house, enhancing rather than overshadowing it. In borders and other plantings, the height of the tallest elements needs to be carefully planned for, otherwise the planting can look lopsided or a few large plants end up making it impossible to appreciate the rest properly.

The visual effect of height is closely linked to the width, overall form and colour of a plant. It is fairly obvious that the wider a variety will grow the greater its overall bulk will become, which is the problem with many commonly available shrubs. With trees this can be crucially important; there is

a world of difference between a 15m (50ft) oak or maple that is say, 8m (25ft) across, and a cypress of the same height that is only 3m (10ft) wide. With very narrow trees it is possible to introduce an element of the vertical into the very smallest of gardens without sacrificing much ground space and without casting deep shade. This is the special magic of the Italian cypress (*Cupressus sempervirens*), whose dark green spires are such an essential part of the landscape in many Mediterranean countries.

The form of a plant has a bearing on how much effect its height will have; an elegant shape, graceful stems or decorative foliage can all affect the impact. This is why bamboos are such useful garden plants: their upright nature means that they can be fitted into comparatively tight spaces and allow room around them for other planting, but at the same time the upward thrust of their whole personality and the delicacy of their pattern of growth and leaf shapes gives them less apparent 'bulk' than shrubs that occupy the same amount of space.

Colour is important, too. Generally, the lighter the foliage, the less impact height makes and the

Calamagrostis x acutiflora 'Karl Foerster' is a very useful grass
for adding a vertical element to the border, here with
Rudbeckia 'Goldsturm'.

A well-balanced border often consists of a mixture of plants of varied habit. Here, upright delphiniums consort with purple sage, dianthus and a penstemon.

less the overall visual bulk of the plant. Evergreens usually have relatively dark leaves and can seem sombre, especially in winter, quite apart from the fact that the shade of a tall evergreen tree may not be welcome in the darker months. Compare a spruce with a dawn redwood *(Metasequoia gly-postroboides)*: both have a roughly similar shape, but the fresh lightness of the leaves of the latter makes it an infinitely more graceful tree.

HEIGHT IN PLANTINGS

The owner of one of the finest borders I know is very proud of the fact that he can stand at one end of it and measure the angle of the planting with a protractor. Such precision is a masterpiece of the traditional way that heights are graded in borders, with the tallest at the back and the shortest at the front. It certainly allows everything in the border to be seen without anything else getting in the way.

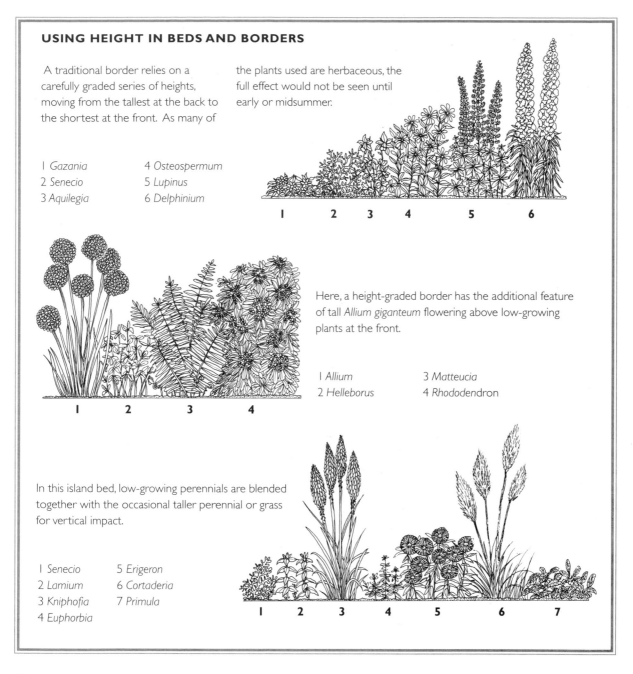

USING HEIGHT IN BEDS AND BORDERS

A traditional border relies on a carefully graded series of heights, moving from the tallest at the back to the shortest at the front. As many of the plants used are herbaceous, the full effect would not be seen until early or midsummer.

1 *Gazania*   4 *Osteospermum*
2 *Senecio*   5 *Lupinus*
3 *Aquilegia*   6 *Delphinium*

Here, a height-graded border has the additional feature of tall *Allium giganteum* flowering above low-growing plants at the front.

1 *Allium*   3 *Matteucia*
2 *Helleborus*   4 *Rhododendron*

In this island bed, low-growing perennials are blended together with the occasional taller perennial or grass for vertical impact.

1 *Senecio*   5 *Erigeron*
2 *Lamium*   6 *Cortaderia*
3 *Kniphofia*   7 *Primula*
4 *Euphorbia*

The planting in an island bed can be similarly organized, so that the tallest plants are in the middle. However, by presenting such an even plane to the world this precise grading can make borders rather flat and dull.

Even very carefully height-graded borders benefit from a little controlled dissent, and the occasional perennial, grass or clipped shrub that rears up tall from near the front of the border is a particularly useful device for livening up the scene. Such borders also benefit from including a certain number of plants that provide height with minimum bulk. The ornamental onions such as *Allium aflatunense* and *A. giganteum* are very useful in this way in early summer, and the violet-flowered *Verbena bonariensis* performs a similar trick later in the season, its flowers almost hovering above the border on hazily thin stems.

Globe artichoke is one of those perennials whose form adds a remarkable presence to the border. The blue-green grass is Elymus arenarius.

While the primary purpose of a careful selection of plant height is to ensure that everything can be seen, sometimes it is desirable to achieve the opposite. A key aim of garden design is to conceal a certain amount, so that the garden is gradually revealed as you walk round it. The occasional tall shrub or piece of hedging can be used to great effect in this way, drawing the visitor on to discover what is on the other side. Visual barriers of woody plants are permanent, but seasonal ones – of grasses and large perennials – can also be used. Tall, bulky plants, such as the grass *Miscanthus sinensis* and the late-summer flowering Joe Pye weed (*Eupatorium purpureum*), are invaluable for this purpose.

Cottage gardens rely for part of their charm on the apparently carefree nature of their planting, in which the mixing together of plants of varying heights plays an important part, as it does in naturalistic planting, where the overall effect is of meadow-like drifts of plants of roughly similar height with the occasional taller item. These taller plants are best scattered about the planting, with the occasional very loose grouping, but never so that they block the view. A classic for this purpose is the very vertical grass *Calamagrostis* x *acutiflora* 'Karl Foerster'.

The height of the tallest plant in a bed or border, or for that matter in the whole garden, is important, as a tall and bulky tree may overpower a small garden completely, as can a tall and wide shrub in a border. Island beds with shrub planting are especially prone to looking unbalanced when they feature shrubs that are out of proportion to their size. Thought must be given to the rule that the tallest plant in a bed should be no more than one-and-a-half times the length of the bed. Where tall and bulky shrubs are concerned, this rule usually works, but it may be broken for shrubs or trees that are tall and narrow.

FORM

It would be possible to create an extremely attractive garden simply on the basis of combining plant habit and form, such is the degree of variety available. Indeed, combining plants of different shapes is crucial to creating an interesting garden; there are single-colour gardens, and gardens where leaf

TREES WITH A NARROW, UPRIGHT FORM

Acer rubrum 'Scanlon'	*Gingko biloba* 'Tremonia'	*P. lusitanica* 'Myrtifolia',
Calocedrus decurrens	*Juniperus scopulorum*	*P.* 'Pandora', *P.* 'Spire'
Carpinus betulus 'Frans	'Skyrocket'	*Pyrus calleryana* 'Chanticleer'
Fontaine'	*Liriodendron tulipifera* 'Fastigiata'	*Quercus robur* 'Fastigiata
Chamaecyparis lawsoniana	*Picea omorika*	Purpurea'
'Kilmacurragh'	*Pinus sylvestris* 'Fastigiata'	*Sorbus aucuparia* 'Sheerwater
Cupressus sempervirens	*Populus nigra* var. *italica*	Seedling'
Fagus sylvatica 'Dawyck'	*Prunus* 'Amanogawa',	

shape is consistent (although this can be a bit dull), but a garden where every plant is of the same form is almost inconceivable.

Form is most apparent as a quality in winter, when there are few other distractions, and maybe this is the time of year to plan it into a garden. Size interacts crucially with form, so an awareness of how tall and wide a plant is going to grow is vital to the successful combining of shapes.

Plants vary an awful lot in how distinct their form is. Most perennials and shrubs are rather shapeless, so that a garden can be beautifully colour schemed but still look a little dull. The addition of only a few specimens with a distinctive shape can make all the difference. Cottage-style gardens, for example, attractive though they are, are often pretty formless, which is why many leading designers have adapted the genre to include formal elements, such as clipped box and yew. The resulting combination of strict formality and burgeoning borders is an extremely successful one.

UPRIGHT GROWERS

We have already seen how useful upright- growing trees are in the garden. Any tall tree makes us look up, but tall and narrow trees especially so – they have a unique ability to connect heaven and earth. In the tropics, palms perform this function exceptionally well, and in cooler climes the remarkably hardy palm *Trachycarpus fortunei* can be grown, although it has to be said that it is rather scruffy. The Italian cypress is also supremely effective at making eyes soar skyward. This tree is much hardier than is commonly supposed and deserves to be planted far more frequently; so narrow a shape is rare among deciduous trees. *Acer rubrum*

'Scanlon' is one of the best there is, and has spectacular autumn colour. Many common trees have upright, or 'fastigiate', forms; these are not always widely available, but are worth seeking out.

On a smaller scale, vertical emphasis is very useful in borders. Many shrubs, herbaceous perennials and grasses can provide it, but usually at the expense of a great deal of sideways space; this is why clipped yew is such a popular element in garden design, for it is a good upright grower which can be clipped into shape to make narrow pyramids, cylinders or columns. Another traditional element designers have recently rediscovered is the training of climbers on tall, narrow frames. Roses, clematis and many other climbers can be tied to these, allowing them to be grown independently of walls and fences.

For those who do not like the formal look of clipped yew and obelisks, the upright-growing *Juniperus scopulorum* 'Skyrocket' is invaluable as an exclamation mark, being rather like a miniature – and extremely hardy – version of the Italian cypress. While it is naturally columnar, branches can get bent out of shape by snow; this can be prevented by tying cotton thread around the plant.

CLIPPED SHRUBS AND TOPIARY

The use of shrubs or trees clipped and trained into plant sculptures has a long history, and seems much more prevalent in some countries than others. It is an essential part of formal gardens and, in this context, looks especially good with many historical architectural styles. One of the great innovations of garden design this century has been the combination of clipped formality with

CLIPPING SHRUBS

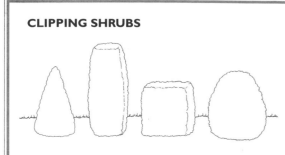

Most shrubs which have a reasonably dense habit of branching can be clipped to shape, adding a formal or sculptural touch to a planting. The denser the growth, the more intricate the clipping can be; very dense shrubs like box (*Buxus* species) and holly (*Ilex* species) can be cut into quite sharp angles, allowing them to be maintained as geometric shapes. Large-leaved shrubs like laurels are not suitable, as the cut leaves look unattractive. Clipping reduces the quantity of bloom on flowering shrubs, although this loss can be limited if clipping is carried out immediately after flowering.

Keeping a single box bush clipped requires very little work, yet its presence can contribute a sense of the definite to a planting.

TRAINING A STANDARD

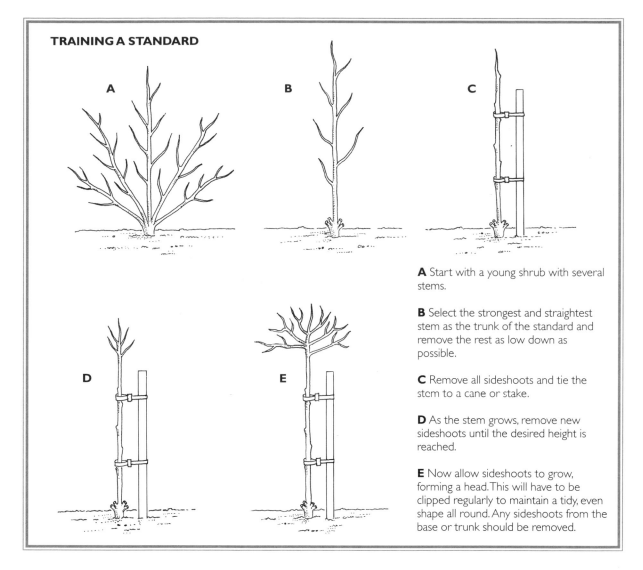

A Start with a young shrub with several stems.

B Select the strongest and straightest stem as the trunk of the standard and remove the rest as low down as possible.

C Remove all sideshoots and tie the stem to a cane or stake.

D As the stem grows, remove new sideshoots until the desired height is reached.

E Now allow sideshoots to grow, forming a head. This will have to be clipped regularly to maintain a tidy, even shape all round. Any sideshoots from the base or trunk should be removed.

loose, informal planting, where the use of hedges and topiary creates a basic structure within which the wildest planting can take place. The formal structure has the advantage that it is permanent, and is especially valuable for giving interest to the garden in the winter.

While it is possible to buy ready-formed topiary, it is much cheaper to grow your own, starting with young plants of yew and box. Both will grow reasonably vigorously in a fertile soil, and can be formed into simple shapes easily by clipping every month or so during the growing season. Simple cubes, pyramids and other shapes can be achieved in just a few years. Once you have gained some confidence, you will be able to let your imagination rip and start to sculpt more complex shapes,

including the peacocks and other figures seen in many older gardens.

The training of shrubs into standards is a craft much practised with a wide range of plants in Italy and France, but comparatively little used elsewhere. Standards are useful not only for introducing a certain level of formality into a garden, but also for providing a note of the vertical. In addition, this is a convenient way of giving shape and geometry to shrubs that would otherwise be rather shapeless or too wide spreading for a small garden.

The key to making a standard is to train one stem upwards to form the trunk and then ruthlessly remove all sideshoots. Once a head has been formed, it is kept to a tidy shape by regular clipping – annually in the case of slow-growing shrubs,

USING TRAILERS

The soil at the top of a retaining wall can be planted with rockery-type plants that tumble or, if it is a high one, with climbers grown as trailers. If the wall faces the sun it will be ideal for heat-lovers such as zauchnerias, *Convolvulus sabatius* and *helianthemums*. if shady, periwinkles (*Vinca* species) and ivies (*Hedera* species) will thrive.

An island bed with a low-growing spreading plant, such as *Rosa* 'Nozomi', and a few upright growers, such as *Betula jacquemontii*, can look very effective, again especially around modern architecture.

Climbers grown in containers on a balcony look spectacular when they are allowed to spill over the edge. This style is especially suited to modern buildings.

every month of so for faster ones. Roses, and a few other shrubs, are made into standards by grafting, although most shrubs can be tried using the training and clipping technique. It is also possible to form climbers with strong stems, such as wisteria and honeysuckle, into standards by tying one stem to a support and clipping the top growth.

Standards and topiary look best when there are identical specimens scattered at regular intervals through a garden, contributing to a sense of rhythmn and formality. The mixing of different topiary shapes can be highly effective, although only in a cottage-garden context, not a strictly formal atmosphere.

ROUNDED SHAPES

The majority of shrubs have a roughly rounded outline, which gives an informal feel to a garden in contrast to the formal atmosphere engendered by the geometry of clipped specimens. However, a garden where all the plants approximate to this shape might seem rather boring, with no variation on the basic theme. This is why upright and geometric shapes are so useful for combining with the more common rounded ones.

Some shrubs have an especially neat, rounded shape which can be particularly effective, especially in winter and early spring when they can be appreciated in splendid isolation. Several of the smaller leaved hebes, such as *Hebe subalpina*, are good examples, with mounds of fresh-looking foliage even in the depths of winter. Rounded shapes are vital in the front of borders in order to balance the more upright habit of many taller perennials, and to hide the bare or untidy stems that many develop.

SPREADING SHAPES

Plants with a spreading shape or habit are especially useful on slopes or as ground cover, or for areas where it is important to have low planting. Low-growing evergreens, such as junipers and cotoneasters, are much used by landscapers which has perhaps given them a bad name, but this should not blind us to their virtues and possibilities. Many people may not want a garden with too much height, perhaps because they wish to preserve a view from the house, or they may live in the kind of modern estate where low planting is expected. In such cases, a selection of spreading plants can be an attractive and low-maintenance alternative to grass.

Trailing plants are those that have comparatively weak stems and can be used as ground cover or in the front of borders; they also look good tumbling over retaining walls or rockeries, or spilling from containers on balconies. Many climbers, such as clematis and honeysuckle, can be used in this way, either to trail loose or as ground cover.

Gardeners with small gardens or those who like a lot of variety, will not have much room for too many spreaders. However, those who are more interested in visual effect may like to consider the dramatic impact which can be created by combining low-growing plants with upright ones, with no intermediate-sized plants inbetween. This level of contrast can be highly effective – think of upright junipers among heathers, for instance, or palms rising above silver-leaved helichrysums.

FOLIAGE

Foliage is a greatly underestimated feature of plants, although its season is much longer than that of flowers, making it especially important in smaller gardens. Leaves come in a variety of different colours, and these will be considered later on; here we will concentrate solely on leaf form.

The variation in leaf shape and size is enormous and it is possible to create wonderful plantings based only on foliage. Too much variation in leaf shape, especially if many plants with dramatic foliage are included, can be overstimulating; too little, and even the most beautifully colour-schemed border can be dull. This can be tested by taking a black-and-white photograph: if all the foliage in the border is similar in shape and size, especially where it is relatively fine, the result can look really uninteresting.

A border planting using relatively common shrubs and perennials may achieve quite a lot of interest simply through a careful blending of different shapes, with the occasional use of the upright sword-like leaves of irises, feathery artemesias, clumps of narrow-leaved grasses and the glossy, hand-like leaves of hellebores. Foliage can also be used in a much more dramatic way: for example, large-leaved perennials, such as rheums and rodgersias, may be combined with bamboos and other large grasses, like *Arundo*

Half-hardy or tender exotics can have particularly dramatic foliage. Here, Melianthus major *is complemented by a red caster-oil plant.*

donax and *Miscanthus sacchariflorus*, to create an exotic ambience.

The leaf shape of plants is closely linked to their habitat. Large-leaved perennials usually inhabit sheltered, damp places, and so will be most successful in a similar position in the garden. Denizens of dry or windswept environments often have small or needle-shaped leaves; heathers and many conifers are good examples and plantings based on these will have to rely on foliage colour and plant form to offset the similarity of the leaf size. Many plants native to dry and warm regions have spiky foliage (yuccas, for instance), succulent leaves or grey and leathery foliage. These attributes can be put to good use in a planting on a hot, dry site, with a dramatic selection of spiky leaves set amid softer grey ones.

Some of the most effective plantings based on foliage can be made in shady situations. This is rather convenient for the gardener, as the selection of colourful flowers for shade is rather limited, especially in the summer, and many of the best foliage plants are evergreen: bamboos might be combined with hellebores, and polystichum ferns with deciduous plants like hostas and Solomon's seal (*Polygonatum species*). Japanese gardens rely for a lot of their impact on the use of effective foliage plants, and a distinctly oriental feel can be introduced by combining plants like bamboos with the oriental elegance of Japanese maples.

USING FOLIAGE IN THE BORDER

A border or other planting will be greatly enhanced by a good selection of interesting leaf shapes and plant forms. Flowers will come first for most, but choosing and juxtaposing contrasting plants on the basis of their foliage will add extra interest, especially during those times when flowering is reduced. Plantings that rely on herbaceous perennials do not present too much of a problem; the key is to ensure that there is a good distribution of those varieties that have distinctive foliage or

LARGE-LEAVED PLANTS

Trees
Acer macrophyllum
Catalpa bignonioides
Magnolia grandiflora, M. delavayi
Paulownia tomentosa
Populus lasiocarpa

Shrubs
Fatsia japonica
Hydrangea aspera, H. quercifolia,
H. sargentiana
Mahonia species
Rhododendron falconeri, R. grande and
related species
Rhus species

Salix fargesii
Salix magnifica
Viburnum rhytidophyllum

Perennials
Acanthus species
Astilbe rivularis
Brunnera macrophylla
Crambe cordifolia
Gunnera manicata
Helleborus species
Hosta species
Ligularia species
Lysichiton species
Macleaya species

Peltiphyllum peltatum
Podophyllum species
Rheum species
Rodgersia species
Zantedeschia aethiopica

Perennials with linear leaves
Crocosmia
Dierama species
Grasses and species
Hemerocallis species
Iris species

PLANTS WITH INTERESTING FOLIAGE FORM

Trees
Acacia species
Acer nikoense, A. palmatum,
A. saccharinum, A. saccharum and
many others
Aesculus species
Arbutus species
Carya species
Cercidiphyllum japonicum
Eucalyptus species
Liriodendron tulipifera
Platanus species
Pterocarya species
Quercus species
Robinia pseudoacacia
Tilia oliveri
Araucaria araucana
Podocarpus species
Pinus wallichiana, P. montezumae
Gingko biloba

Shrubs
Aralia species
Ballota pseudodictamnus
Camellia species
Cytisus battandieri
Drimys species
Feijoa sellowiana
Griselinia littoralis
Hebe species
Ilex species
Laurus nobilis
Lomatia species
Nandina domestica
Paeonia, 'tree' species
Phlomis species
Pittosporum species
Sambucus species
Sorbaria species
Teucrium species
Viburnum, many species

Perennials
Alchemilla species
Aruncus species
Baptisia species
Bergenia species
Canna species
Dicentra species
Epimedium species
Ferns
Foeniculum vulgare
Heuchera species
Kirengeshoma palmata
Paeonia species
Polygonatum species
Sanguinaria canadensis
Smilacina racemosa
Thalictrum species
Euphorbia myrsinites
Melianthus major

which are a bit different to the majority of the plants in the border. Usually this means those with linear leaves such as irises, hemerocallis or crocosmias. These rarely look good together and are much better distributed among plants with a more rounded habit and leaf shape.

The selection of shrubs with distinctive foliage is rather more limited, especially if alkaline soil prevents the growing of rhododendrons, some of which have the most splendid foliage of all hardy plants. However, it is perhaps helpful to think of bamboos as shrubs, as they occupy a similar volume.

RELATING FORM AND FOLIAGE TO ATMOSPHERE

The way in which plants of different sizes and forms are used can have a major effect on a number of aspects of the garden, such as its overall 'feel' and how large it looks.

The fact that plant foliage and form is closely linked to habitat means that we have to accept certain limitations. Woodland plants are always going to look reasonably lush, while those that thrive in the harsher conditions of a dry bank or windswept heathland will never look as lush as the shade-lovers. Nevertheless, appropriate planting can alter the emotional feel of garden environments. A warm, dry bank can be planted with large-flowered varieties of cistus, the rather exotic-looking *Romneya coulteri*, which resembles a very tall poppy, and a selection of colourful hardy annuals. The result will be reminiscent of a colourful Mediterranean garden, with grey foliage setting off bright colour, especially if a seating area with a few pelargoniums and citrus fruit in tubs can be located nearby. On the other hand, you may want to accentuate the feeling of dryness and heat, in which case spiky plants, such as yuccas and eryngiums, which evoke a desert habitat can be used, alongside grey-leaved shrubs such as sage (*Salvia officinalis*) and tussocky grasses like *Stipa* and *Pennisetum* species.

Plants with a very distinctive form, like yuccas, are known as 'architectural' plants, and can play a vital role in plantings, adding both a strong sense of form and an element of surprise. The use of contrasting sculptural forms can result in a planting with an exciting and dynamic feel – this is the

effect achieved by many houseplant displays found in modern office environments. You may, however, find all this contrast a bit too exciting and the result may be a sense of clutter, particularly in an enclosed area. Architectural plants that are especially effective are large, stylish perennials

such as macleayas, the globe artichoke (*Cynara cardunculus*) and ligularias. Just one of these can make all the difference to even quite a good-sized border. The best place for dramatic plants like these, and for anything with large foliage, is near the main viewpoint, the house or terrace perhaps,

Hosta sieboldiana, *bamboos and astilbes look spectacular next to water, where they enjoy the ideal conditions for lush growth.*

with smaller foliage furthest away. This will create a sense of distance, whereas having large leaves at the far end will tend to shorten the perspective.

Less demanding on the visual sense, but still very sculptural, are the old formalities of clipped hedges, topiary and shrubs grown as standards. Despite what might appear to be rigidity, this style actually seems to suit a wide range of environments. It creates an atmosphere of tidiness, order and discipline. If the emphasis is on topiary the effect will be more 'olde worlde', and you can get quite adventurous – or even humorous – by clipping rough animal shapes around the garden. A more classical feel can be created with neatly clipped and geometrical hedges, while France and the Mediterranean can be summed up effectively with standard-trained shrubs.

In contrast to the dynamism of spiky foliage and dramatic form, the use of rounded forms and soft, feathery foliage has quite a different effect. We tend to interpret them as being comfortable and homely. The relaxed feel can be carried further with plants that have a lax habit of growth and are, to a conventional eye, somewhat untidy. Examples are many of the herbaceous plants and hardy annuals that are a distinctive feature of the cottage-garden genre. Towards the end of the season they can create a rich, if slightly chaotic, mixture of colours and textures from the combined effect of stems, seedheads and flowers.

SEASONAL PLANTING

Most gardeners want gardens that are good to look at for as long as possible. The garden may be used far more in the summer – indeed, your only view of it in winter may be safely through double glazing – but it will be a much more rewarding place for looking good in the winter months as well. Consequently, we have to think about plants not only when they are at their best, but also before and after their turn in the spotlight.

If your garden is large, or you particularly like one season more than others, it is possible to concentrate a lot of interest in a small area, and have separate spring and summer borders. The results will be magnificent, because everything there will be looking good at more or less the same time, but it can be pretty dreary for the rest of the year. A planting for all seasons will be a compromise, as there will always be certain plants not at their best. A *Rubus thibetanus* 'Silver Fern', for instance, will look a bit dull in summer, but in winter it will redeem itself with stunning white stems etched out by slanting sunlight, while summer's wondrous perennials lie sleeping out of sight.

THE ALL-YEAR BORDER

Larger gardens may be able to afford single-season schemes, but most are too small for such luxury, and the need is to pack as much seasonal interest into as small a space as possible. Plants that look

---

ARCHITECTURAL PLANTS
The plants in this list are evergreen unless otherwise stated.

Plants with spiky or sword-like foliage
Aciphylla species
Agave species (frost tender)
Astelia species
Chamaerops humilis (hardy dwarf palm)
Cordyline australis
Kniphofia species
Phormium species
Trachycarpus fortunei (very hardy palm)
Yucca species

Very large perennials (all deciduous)
Angelica archangelica
Bupthalium species
Cynara cardunculus
Eupatorium fistulosum,
E. purpureum
Fallopia sacchalinensis (invasive)
Hieracleum mantegazzianum (biennial, causes allergic reactions in some people)
Ligularia species
Macleaya species

Petasites japonicus var. *giganteus* (sideways rather than up and very invasive)

Very large grasses
Arundo donax
Cortaderia sellowiana (Pampas grass)
Miscanthus sacchariflorus,
M. sinensis varieties (deciduous)

You cannot have flowers all year long. The yellow tufts of Carex elata
'Aurea' will keep this yellow-schemed border looking good in winter too.

good all year round, or have two seasons of interest, are then invaluable. Good examples of the former are flowering evergreens such as the shrub *Viburnum tinus* and the perennial hellebores; indeed, these plants flower in midwinter and are thus invaluable on two counts. Small trees and shrubs which have attractive spring flowers and autumn colour or berries can likewise earn their place in the garden twice over. Cherries (*Prunus* species), crab apples (*Malus* species) and berberis are all immensely popular because of this characteristic.

Creating a garden or planting that looks interesting at all times is very much a balancing act; the trick is to have enough of interest and to have it well distributed, so that every month has some special feature without any particular part looking dull. Some plants, like bulbs, graciously retreat underground when their season is past; others stand wearing unfashionable clothes, like the rubus mentioned above. However, this will not matter so much if there is enough of interest around them or, better still, in front of them.

Achieving a really good all-year border is like conducting an orchestra, and just as much work, as it involves an awful lot of cutting back or removal of plants when they have finished flowering, putting new plants in the gaps or encouraging something else to move in. It also involves a lot of instruments: the full array of bulbs, hardy perennials, half-hardies, annuals, shrubs and climbers. If you are dedicated to creating a scheme of this kind, it is important to be good at keeping a gardener's diary, so that you can make a note of what performed when and how well for future reference.

It also helps to be ruthless: as your space and energy are limited, there is no room for plants that disappoint or are unreliable. In the winter, when all has quietened down, you can then replan the border, deciding what plants to take out and what to try instead. Constant retuning of a border like this will eventually result in a very fine spectacle indeed.

Such a border might be the envy of all the

AN ALL-YEAR BORDER

This series of cross-sections is designed to show how it is possible to achieve year-round interest in a border. For the purposes of explanation, this is shown as quite a wide border, but it would be possible to reduce the width by staggering the smaller plants on either side of the line represented by the cross-section, with no loss of overall effect. The sections at different times of year show how plants succeed each other in interest, with either flowers, foliage or seedheads.

Plants

1 *Buxus sempervirens* 'Suffruticosa'
2 *Scrophularia auriculata* 'Variegata'
3 *Miscanthus sinensis* 'Kleine Silberspinne'
4 *Tulipa* 'Margot Fonteyn'
5 *Viola* Icequeen Series
5a *Argyranthemum* 'Jamaica Primrose'
6 *Geranium* 'Johnson's Blue'
7 *Narcissus* 'Ice Follies'
8 *Crocus chrysanthus* hybrids
9 *Viburnum plicatum* 'Mariesii'
10 *Clematis* 'Etoile Violette'

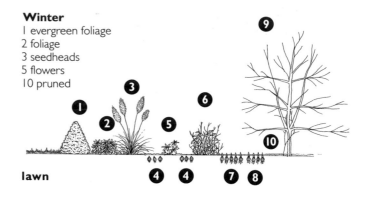

Winter

1 evergreen foliage
2 foliage
3 seedheads
5 flowers
10 pruned

lawn

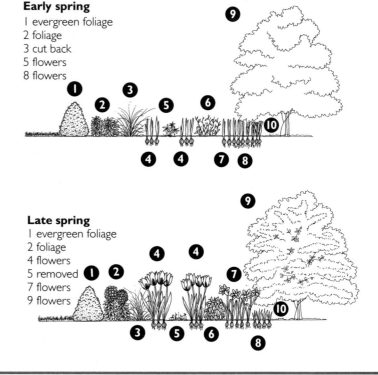

Early spring

1 evergreen foliage
2 foliage
3 cut back
5 flowers
8 flowers

Late spring

1 evergreen foliage
2 foliage
4 flowers
5 removed
7 flowers
9 flowers

neighbours (and, let's face it, this is an important part of gardening!), but it is too demanding for many. The best that most of us can hope for is a good distribution of colour and effect throughout the year, making the best use of the growing habits and lifecycles of plants to provide plenty of interest.

SPRING

Spring is many people's favourite time of year in the garden, the season when everything wakes up after the winter and seems really fresh and young. Many spring flowers are woodlanders by nature, so they flower and make as much growth as they can early in the season in order to take maximum advantage of the sunlight before the leaves grow on the trees. Consequently, many of them grow from bulbs or tubers – storage organs that allow them to put on a sudden burst of growth when the weather is still cold and the light poor. This means they are very conveniently packaged for the gardener, and makes bulb growing an easy and rewarding

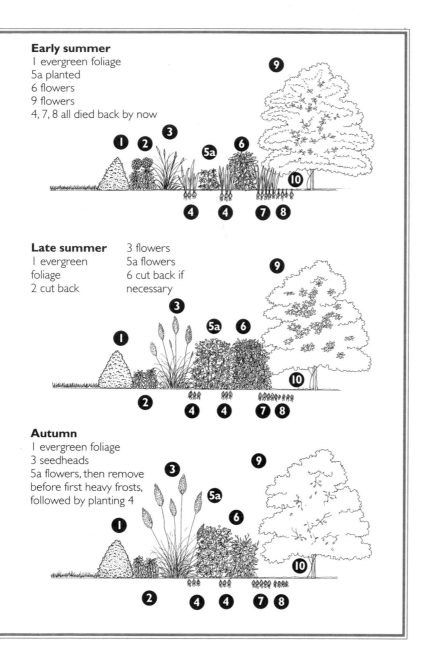

Early summer
1 evergreen foliage
5a planted
6 flowers
9 flowers
4, 7, 8 all died back by now

Late summer
1 evergreen foliage
2 cut back
3 flowers
5a flowers
6 cut back if necessary

Autumn
1 evergreen foliage
3 seedheads
5a flowers, then remove before first heavy frosts, followed by planting 4

experience for those who are new to gardening.

Shrubs are the other main source of spring colour; again, many are shade-tolerant woodlanders. Other spring-flowering plants include the dicentras, which are similar to bulbs in that they become dormant in the summer, primroses (*Primula vulgaris*), hellebores and pulmonarias. All are relatively low growing.

Since so many spring flowers are small and need or are tolerant of shade, they can be used underneath deciduous trees, shrubs and roses where they will be visible and colourful for the spring, but be shaded and largely out of sight for the summer. However, some evergreen perennials are too good to hide. Many of the pulmonarias have wonderful silver-splashed leaves that are useful for lighting up shady places at all times of year, and glossy hellebore foliage is a good foil for summer flowers in the border.

At a time of year when borders are rather featureless wastelands of cut-back stalks, leafless branches and the odd label, the possibilities offered by bulbs and other spring flowers are immense, and the whole border may be dotted with colour from plants grown between perennials or underneath shrubs. It is advisable, though, to keep a record (perhaps in the form of photographs) of where the bulbs are, as you do not want to disturb them later in the year.

Some bulbs and summer-dormant perennials are ideal for growing beneath trees; snowdrops, crocuses and anemones flourish in this position, often spreading slowly and intermingling. Further out from the base of the trunk, where the ground is not so heavily shaded, daffodils can be planted, preferably in a mixture of varieties to ensure a long season. All these bulbs may be naturalized in grass, but it is important that the grass is not cut until after the bulb foliage has died back completely, otherwise there will be no flowers the following year. It is also possible to grow primroses and polyanthus in shaded grass, so long as the blades of the mower are set higher than normal. Of course, cutting is suspended while they are in flower, and preferably until the early summer, which will give them a chance to self-seed and spread.

Bulbs and small perennials are the kinds of plants that can be tucked in more or less any-

THE BEST SPRING-FLOWERING SHRUBS

Plant	Height x spread
Amelanchier canadensis	5×3m (15×10ft)
Camellia × williamsii	3×3m (10×10ft)
Chaenomeles × superba	1.5×2m (5×6ft)
Cytisus × praecox	1×1.5m (3×5ft)
Daphne mezereum	1.2×1m (4×3ft)
Exchorda × macrantha 'The Bride'	1×1.5m (3×5ft)
Kerria japonica 'Pleniflora'	2×2.5m (6×8ft)
Kolkwitzia amabilis	3×3m (10×10ft)
Magnolia stellata	2×2m (6×6ft)
Olearia × macrodonta	2×2m (6×6ft)
Paeonia suffruticosa	2×2m (6×6ft)
Poncirus trifoliata	5×5m (15×15ft)
Rhododendron yakushimanum	1×1.5m (3×5ft)
Spiraea nipponica	2×2m (6×6ft)
Syringa	5×3m (15×10ft)
	(dwarf varieties
	also available)

where, making them very useful for putting in places where there is little room but they will still be visible. This is especially important in spring, when we want colour and nature close to us, not far away down a muddy garden. Most such spring flowers can be grown in windowboxes, troughs and pots, and in narrow borders fitted in around the house.

Flowering trees and shrubs are the other main attraction in the spring. Flowering currant (*Ribes sanguineum*), viburnums and berberis are among the best known among a very large number of shrubs, and the cherries (*Prunus* species) among the trees. It is all too easy, however, to get carried away on the first spring visit to the garden centre, and come away with something unsuitably large or which does not earn its keep later in the year. Many common trees and shrubs are now available in several varieties, and some of these are more compact than others. Among the flowering cherries, there is *Prunus* 'Spire', which is tall but relatively slim in shape, allowing it to fit into a narrow town garden.

If you have space for only one flowering tree it should be a dual-purpose one, such as an apple. The combined pink and white of apple blossom makes it far superior to many of the cherries, and later on you can eat the results.

GROWING LIME-HATING SHRUBS IN CONTAINERS

Lime-haters, such as rhododendrons, azaleas, pieris and camellias, may be grown in containers, where they can be given the type of compost they relish. Any multi-purpose compost not based on soil is suitable – not just the low-lime brands.

The shrubs' root systems are shallow so container culture suits them, but they have no tolerance of drought. Watering must therefore be consistent. In hot weather the plants should be kept out of the sun for at least part of the day. In a hard-water area, lime can build up rapidly in containers, so rainwater must be used, or even dregs from the teapot – these work well, as they also contain nutrients.

During winter root freezing can occur, so the container should be wrapped in bubble plastic or some other insulating material.

Key to seasons E=early spring M=mid-spring L= late spring

Flowers	Season	Aspect	Soil
profuse, white, star-like	M	part shade	most
pink, white, single or double	E	part shade	acid/neutral
pink, white, red	E	sun/part shade	avoid thin chalk
creamy yellow	E	sun/part shade	most
purple-red, scented	E	sun/part shade	most and thin chalk
white	L	sun	acid/neutral
yellow, double	M	sun/shade	most
pink/yellow	L	sun/part shade	most
white, star-like	E	sun/part shade	acid/neutral
white, daisy-like	L	sun/part shade	most
large white, pink, red	L	sun	most
white	L	sun/sheltered	most
white, pink	L	sun/ part shade	acid/neutral
white	L	sun/part shade	most
red, lilac, pink, white	L	sun/part shade	most

Camellias are, quite rightly, very popular flowering shrubs, but they need a moisture-retentive and preferably acidic soil. They are hardy enough, but the buds can easily be damaged by frost, although the varieties on sale are generally those selected for being tough and adaptable. For a touch of the exotic, they are unrivalled. In gardens where the soil is definitely acid or neutral, there is no shortage of rhododendron and azalea varieties for late winter onwards. The colour range is enormous, and the earlier-flowering kinds have an advantage in that they do not usually grow too big.

Spring-flowering climbers are few and far between. The delightfully scented honeysuckle *Lonicera fragrantissimum* and *Jasminum nudiflorum* flower in very early spring, but the former is not particularly colourful and both might be classed as wall shrubs rather thatn climbers. Later

Blue grape hyacinths (Muscari) *and paler puschkinias are a wonderful springtime contrast to the deep red of emerging peony shoots.*

Deep orange red-hot pokers (Kniphofia) *are quintessentially summer plants, and combine well with a wide variety of perennials*

on, the queen of spring climbers is undoubtedly the evergreen and vigorous *Clematis armandii*.

The predominant colours in spring seem to be yellow and blue among bulbs and perennials, and white, pink and yellow among trees and shrubs. The great thing about this time of year is the relatively soft light, in which colours work together more easily than they do in the summer: the yellows are not harsh and bright pinks do not shout nearly so loudly. It is thus possible to mix colours with gay abandon – how about blue scillas with

yellow daffodils, scarlet tulips and pink polyanthus?

SUMMER

Summer is the season when we use the garden most – when it really can become another room of the house. There is no shortage of flowering plants for this season and they come in an enormous range of colours, although pastel shades tend to predominate earlier in summer, with yellows and reds becoming more common later on. Herbaceous plants, annuals and bedding are all at their zenith in late summer, while shrubs dominate the early part of the season.

Whether your summer starts with rhododendrons or roses depends on your soil. The former tend to stand alone, rather overshadowing anything else planted with them, and their companion plants should be those that are destined to flower after the rhododendrons' season of glory. Roses are better suited to growing with other plants, both aesthetically and horticulturally; geraniums and many other herbaceous plants can be grown under and around them, and offer a perfect complement.

If your selection is restricted to the old-fashioned and shrub roses, the colour scheme will be very much dominated by pastel shades, with some deeper crimsons and perhaps the darker blues of herbaceous plants like campanulas. From midsummer on such a planting will begin to dull, requiring colour from later herbaceous plants or annuals to keep up the interest. Modern hybrid tea and floribunda roses flower for much longer and have a wider colour range, including yellows, oranges, scarlet and brighter pinks. Whether you plant bright annuals and bedding or more subtle pinks and silvers alongside them is a matter of personal taste, but they do look much better with companion plants of some kind.

There are other shrubs for early summer, too; the sumptuously scented philadelphus, for example, lilacs (*Syringa* varieties) and brilliant blue ceanothus. Many of these grow quite large, but dwarf varieties are often available and worth searching out. From midsummer on, the number of flowering shrubs decreases, although there are still plenty of buddleias, hydrangeas and hebes to come. The place of shrubs in the late-summer garden can be taken by large herbaceous plants and grasses.

The number of herbaceous plants in flower seems to increase steadily to a high point in midsummer, with plenty more still to flower in late summer and autumn. Herbaceous plants went out of fashion for many years, but their worth has now been recognized once again and there are plenty of different varieties available. They always look dreadful in pots in the garden centres, and many people buy them earlier in the season or by mail order in winter. Larger herbaceous plants provide temporary bulk in the late-summer garden, and

can be used to screen shrubs that have finished flowering earlier.

Climbers have an important role to play in the summer garden, especially those that are used for screening. If you use the garden for entertaining, the character of the surroundings is important and this is where climbers come into their own, not just for hiding the unsightly old garage or climbing over a trellis to obscure the neighbour's extension, but also, more subtly, to grow over archways and shrubs to help create a romantic atmosphere. There is no shortage of climbers to provide flowers right through the year.

In some ways, the classic summer flowers are annuals and bedding plants. Their speed of growth, adaptability and long flowering season make them ideal for use all around the garden, but especially where you want to create an impact: on patios, in front gardens or around the summerhouse. Nowadays they have been joined by the 'patio plants', which are as reliable as traditional bedding but have the advantage of making the garden look less like a public park.

The use of containers is most important in summer; hanging baskets and windowboxes can be used for the house, and pots and troughs for patios and other sitting areas. Keeping them watered is hard work, but well worth it for the cheerful impression they make. Traditional pelargoniums are among the best plants for containers (for one thing, they will survive the odd failure to water), together with various smaller annuals and half-hardy plants. The new generation of patio plants grow well with them and, on the whole, make splendid container plants in their own right.

Scent is a feature of the summer season. A garden may look colourful, but most of us feel cheated if nothing has a fragrance. Old-fashioned roses are especially valuable for scent, along with many of the plants associated with cottage gardens such as stocks (*Matthiola* varieties) and pinks (*Dianthus* varieties). Many white or pale yellow flowers have rich and exotic fragrances that are strongest in the evening – philadelphus and honeysuckle, for example. The role of aromatic foliage should not be forgotten either, especially as this scent has the advantage of being there all summer long, not just for the duration of the flowers. Herbs, lavender, salvias and some cistus are all potent sources, but perhaps the finest are the scented-leaved pelargoniums, whose varieties have an amazing range of aromas.

With all this scent and colour, it is easy to overlook the importance of foliage. Much of the best foliage is evergreen, but not all: hostas, ornamental rhubarb (*Rheum* species), rodgersias and the huge *Gunnera manicata* are all deciduous, and many grasses look much better at this time of year, when they are fresh and growing vigorously.

Water features, even just a damp patch of ground, come into their own when the weather is hot – the sight of water lilies and lush waterside vegetation can do much to make you feel cooler in the heat of the day. Particularly important in this respect are good-looking foliage plants, which can transform a small piece of water into an exciting jungle pool. Whether exotic or not, pools should be sited next to a seating area, as their cooling influence is vital for relaxation in the summer.

AUTUMN

Autumn is the time of year when the garden prepares itself for sleep, and it can have a rather tired look – but it can also be quite spectacular. Few of us have room for many trees, but good autumn colour is an important factor to bear in mind when making a selection. Shrubs with autumn colour

and berries are an essential part of a good autumn garden, as are the surprisingly large number of herbaceous plants, half-hardies and ornamental grasses that flower now.

There are a good many shrubs or smaller growing cultivars of large trees that are suitable for the average garden which can be used as a framework for a colourful autumn. Among the finest are the smaller cultivars of the japanese maple (*Acer palmatum*), many of which have foliage that looks very attractive for the rest of the year as well.

Climbers should not be forgotten in the search for autumn colour, and the familiar virginia creepers are among the best, although vines are also good: the mighty *Vitis coignetiae*, one of the largest of hardy climbers, is superb.

Berries can be amazingly colourful, especially in the last warm sunlight of the year. Many of the best berrying shrubs are on the large side, but there are good small ones too, such as pyracantha, which can be trained easily into a wall shrub or climber and hence is economical of space. On acid soils, the low-growing pernettyas treat us to berries in a wide range of colours, from deep red through shades of pink to pure white.

While the dying leaves and burgeoning berries are in russet shades of red, orange and yellow, the

AUTUMN FOLIAGE FOR SMALL GARDENS

Plant	Height x spread (10 years)	Autumn Colour	Shape
TREES			
Acer griseum	4x2m (12x6ft)	scarlet, crimson	upright
Pyrus calleryana 'Chanticleer'	5x3m (15x10ft)	orange/red	narrow
Sorbus aucuparia	6x3m (20x10ft)	yellow/orange	rounded
SHRUBS			
Amelanchier canadensis	5x3m (15x10ft)	yellow	suckering
Berberis thunbergii f. *atropurpurea*	1.5x1.5m (5x5ft)	orange/red	upright
Cornus kousa	7x4m (22x12ft)	orange/red	upright
Cotinus coggygria	2x2m (6x6ft)	orange/yellow	rounded
Cotoneaster bullatus	5x3m (15x10ft)	red	spreading
Disanthus cercidifolius	3x3m (10x10ft)	red, purple, orange, yellow	rounded
Euonymus alatus	1.2x1.5m (4x5ft)	red/pink	rounded
Fothergilla major Monticola Group	1.5x1.2m (5x4ft)	yellow/scarlet	spreading
Rhus typhina	3x2.4m (10x8ft)	orange/scarlet	spreading
Viburnum opulus	3x3m (10x10ft)	orange/red	spreading
CLIMBERS			
Parthenocissus henryana	10m (30ft)	red/orange	–
Vitis coignetiae	8m (25ft)	copper/purple	–

Vine leaves, rose hips and the flowerheads of Sedum spectabile *all contribute to this collection of characteristically russet autumn tones.*

Aspect	Soil	Notes
sun/part shade	most	attractive reddish-brown 'peeling' bark
sun	most	white flowers in spring
sun/part shade	most	bears orange/red berries in autumn
sun/part shade	acid/neutral	white flowers in spring
sun	moisture retentive	purple-red foliage needs full sun for best colour
sun/part shade	acid/neutral	large white flowers in early summer; needs some shelter
sun/part shade	most	pink plume-like flowers in late summer
sun	not wet	pink flowers in spring, red fruits in autumn
part shade	acid/neutral	red spidery flowers in autumn
sun/part shade	most	poisonous
sun/part shade	acid/neutral	fluffy white flower spikes in early summer
sun/part shade	most	poisonous; throws out suckers
sun/part shade	most	white flowers in late spring and summer
sun/part shade	most	self-clinging
sun	most	may be slow to establish

flowers of autumn offer different colours. Yellows are there too, but there are many rich violets and purples as well. This is a time when the larger members of the daisy family reign supreme, joined in increasing numbers by smaller cultivars bred for gardens. The michaelmas daisy of old (*Aster novi-belgii* cultivars), with their coating of mildew, and rank golden rods (*Solidago* species) have rather given these plants a bad name, but times are different now and many more varieties are available that make better garden plants. There is plenty of scope for vivid colour schemes based on yellow *Solidagos*, *Coreopsis* and chrysanthemums and purple asters and *Vernonias*. Backed by the warm colours of autumn leaves, the results can be absolutely spectacular.

Ornamental grasses are at their best at this time of year, varying in size from the majestic miscanthus varieties to many smaller ones. They com-bine well with late-flowering perennials to give a rich variety of texture and colour. Some, like *Panicum virgatum*, have excellent autumn leaf colour as well. When combined with the last herbacous plants and annuals of the year, and the seedheads of those that bloomed earlier, grasses can make a truly romantic, if at times somewhat untidy, end to the year.

Many annuals and bedding plants will flower well into the autumn, until the first hard frosts. Nasturtiums (*Tropaeolum majus*) and English marigolds (*Calendula officinalis*) are particularly good in this respect, and their rich golds and oranges echo autumn leaf colours. Unknown until a few years ago, many salvia species are now being grown to bring intense colours to late-summer and autumn borders. In many areas they have to be treated as bedding or half-hardy plants to be brought in over the winter, but they will flower

The white stems of Rubus cockburnianus *and mysterious green flowers of* Helleborus foetidus *typify the subtlety of winter colour.*

through a few light frosts. In terms of colour intensity, they are perhaps the brightest flowers for this time. Also worth remembering for autumn are dahlias, which will flower in a variety of showy shades and shapes until the first real frosts. Like salvias, they will need to be protected over the winter.

Lastly, autumn bulbs should not be forgotten; crocuses are ideal for areas of grass, the brilliant pink nerines and *Amaryllis belladonna* for hot spots near sunny walls, and colchicums for borders. Be warned, though, that colchicum foliage, which does not start to sprout until the spring, takes up a considerable amount of space.

WINTER

Winter is the time when most of us prefer to fantasize about gardening rather than actually doing it, or at the most peer out through the double glazing at the odd snowdrop. But there can be more to winter than this, although we have to try to change our aesthetic standards somewhat, looking for beauty in places where we would not normally expect it.

Many of autumn's berries will survive until the birds eat them, and so will many of the seedheads of grasses and perennials. The latter have a beauty all of their own, especially when lit by slanting winter sun or coated in hoar frost on a cold morning. Those with dense, sculptural seedheads, such as *Echinops* or teazel, are especially effective when they are silhouetted against their lighter-looking companions.

Bark and twigs are not features that we normally go out of our way to admire, but in winter their full beauty can be appreciated. Many trees have very attractive bark, especially the snakebark maples (*Acer pensylvanicum* and *A. capillipes*) and

The dead stems and seedheads of ornamental grasses and perennials can look very beautiful in soft winter light, so there is no rush to 'tidy up'.

CHEERFUL EVERGREENS

Plant	Height x spread	Foliage
Aucuba japonica 'Variegata'	3×3m (10×10ft)	glossy green, splashed yellow
Camellia × williamsii 'Golden Spangles'	3.6×3m (11×10ft)	glossy green, central yellow splash
Elaeagnus pungens 'Maculata'	1.8×1.8m (6×6ft)	glossy green, central yellow patch
Eucalyptus gunnii	10×5m (30×15ft)	blue-grey
Euonymus fortunei 'Silver Queen'	0.8×2.1m (32×86in)	green, creamy white margins; creamy yellow in spring
Fatsia japonica 'Variegata'	3×3m (10×10ft)	glossy green, tipped with cream
Hedera colchica 'Sulphur Heart'	3m (10ft)	pale green, central yellow splash
Ilex aquifolium 'Handsworth New Silver'	2.4×1.8m (8×6ft)	deep green, edged white
Phormium cookianum 'Tricolor'	1×1m (3×3ft)	green, white and cherry-red stripes
Photinia × fraseri 'Red Robin'	1.8×3m (6×10ft)	bright red shoots in spring
Pieris japonica 'Variegata'	0.5×1m (20×40in)	green, tipped with cream
Pittosporum tenuifolium 'Tom Thumb'	1×1m (3×3ft)	reddish-brown
Rhamnus alaternus 'Argenteovariegata'	3×3m (10×10ft)	grey-green, creamy margins
Thuja orientalis 'Aurea Nana'	1×0.5m (40×20in)	yellow-green
Yucca filamentosa 'Variegata'	1×1m (3×3ft)	green, cream and yellow stripes

birches. Twigs caught by the low winter sunlight can glow with an inner light; this is true of many willows (*Salix alba* varieties) and dogwoods (*Cornus stolonifera* 'Flaviramea' is a good cultivar). There are also willows with mysterious dark twigs, such as *Salix melanostachys*. These shrubs show their best winter colour when rigorously pruned every few years, as it is the younger growth which is the most attractive.

Winter is the time in the garden when the bare bones are most apparent, unclothed by foliage and flowers. The shapes of trees and shrubs are dominant, and anything evergreen is immediately obvious. Topiary and any other clipped shapes, such as hedges or cordon-grown fruit, become much more important at this time of the year. Their role in the overall structure of the garden becomes far more obvious, quite apart from their own intrinsic merits.

Evergreens are certainly appreciated in the winter, especially those in colours other than dark green. Silver foliage is valuable, although it can look pretty bedraggled, and gold even more so. Golden-variegated shrubs are really welcome at this time, bringing a ray of sunshine into the garden.

From midwinter onwards the first flowers of hellebores, snowdrops (*Galanthus* species) and aconites appear, their clear whites, greens and yellows standing out against the bare, dark earth. Hellebores are especially valuable, and not just the fashionable and expensive ones with dark-hued or spotted flowers: *Helleborus foetidus*, for example, is worth more for its stylish evergreen foliage than for its greenish flowers. Hellebores in general are useful and adaptable plants, thriving in shade as well as sun.

Perhaps the brightest winter flowers are those of the heather *Erica carnea* in pink, red and white, a plant that conveniently is tolerant of lime, unlike most heathers. Among the bulbs, the snowdrops and aconites are familiar favourites and can be used in all sorts of situations, including around the bases of trees or among dormant herbaceous plants in borders. They can be relied upon to increase steadily as the years go by. The dwarf cyclamen *Cyclamen coum* is less frequently seen in gardens, yet it is ideal for shady places and it is available in a variety of colours, including brilliant pink, which is a unique colour for the later months of the year.

Winter-flowering shrubs can be colourful, too; forsythia is well known, but is so scruffy for the rest of the year that it needs careful placing so as not to let down a summer border. *Chaenomeles japonica* has many varieties in reds, pinks and white, and it is a more attractive plant than the forsythia. Witch hazels (*Hamamelis* species) are unusual and beautiful shrubs for partly shaded conditions and where a dark backdrop will show off the yellow flowers. They are wonderfully scented, too.

Aspect	Soil	Notes
part/full shade	most	red berries only if male and female planted
part shade	acid/neutral	large pink flowers in early spring
sun/part shade	avoid thin chalk and heavy clay	scented white flowers in autumn
sun	most	prune hard to retain size and young foliage
sun/part shade	most	vigorous; can reach 3m (10ft) on a warm wall
part/full shade	most	shelter from cold winds
part shade	most	climber; leaves can reach 15cm (6in) across
sun/part shade	most	dark purple stems; orange-red berries in autumn
sun	most	shelter from cold winds
sun/part shade	avoid thin chalk and wet soils	shelter from cold winds
part shade	acid/neutral	white flowers sprays in spring; shelter from cold winds
sun/part shade	most	shelter from cold winds
part shade	most	shelter from cold winds
sun	most	turns bronze in winter
sun/part shade	most	large creamy flower spikes borne on mature plants

COLOUR

For many people, colour is the most important aspect of gardening. Its presence in the garden all through the year is regarded as a triumph of good design, for without it the garden seems dead. However much you try to point out the subtleties of winter colour, or the beauty of form and texture, most gardeners will still prefer the gay colours of spring and summer. There can be no doubt that a colourful garden satisfies a deep human need and its achievement is the most important thing the gardener can do.

In the following pages my aim is to encourage you to think about colour in the garden, and to be able to make up your own mind about what you want. Responses to colour are very personal – what is radiant beauty to one person is a psychedelic soup to another. What follows, therefore, is inevitably subjective, and contains some generalizations. The important thing is that you create what looks good to you.

COLOUR AND PSYCHOLOGY

Our responses to colour are emotional, but even though they may vary from one person to another, it is possible to perceive some general trends.

Most of us agree that red, yellow and orange are 'hot' colours and green, blue and white are 'cool'. Strong contrasts are generally felt to be lively, stimulating or restless, harmonies more mellow and romantic. It is an inevitable factor in human difference that some people prefer to be stimulated, whereas others want to be relaxed.

The colour wheel

However you use it – cautiously or outrageously – the colour wheel is a very useful way in which to analyse colour.

The inner circle of the colour wheel represents the three primary colours, and the nine colours made by mixing these primary colours. Harmonies can be created by putting together colours that are adjacent to each other in this circle. With more confidence, it is often possible to maintain harmony by bringing in more adjacent colours, up to five. More than this and most eyes will find the results less pleasing. Contrasts can be created by putting together complementary colours– those that are opposite each other in the circle. These rely for their effect on their power to startle.

The outer circle consists of the pastel colours obtained by adding white to the colours of the inner circle. They can be mixed with impunity, and the results rarely clash.

This is also a function of what we use the garden for – the busy executive with a dynamic modern painting on the office wall may feel very differently about their garden, which is a place for relaxation and forgetting about working life, and such a person is more likely to prefer a pastel border to a red and yellow one. Others may want to bring some colour and excitement into their lives, and their garden is a chance to express themselves, go wild and show off – with a brilliant formal bedding scheme as the result.

COLOUR COMBINATIONS, CONTRAST AND HARMONY

We may know what colours we like, but they still have to be put next to each other. The question of colour thus rapidly becomes one of colour combi-

Leaves should never be left out of the colour equation, as the juxtaposition of this blue-leaved Hosta sieboldiana *with* Primula viallii *illustrates.*

nation. This is a subject upon which vast quantities of dogmatic nonsense have been written – in my opinion, we just have to accept that everyone's taste is different.

Whatever your preferences, and however strongly you hold them, it will help your garden planning immensely if you have a good understanding of how colour works. The colour wheel is a very useful tool for this and, like any tool, it can be put to whatever use you choose to make of it, just as a spade can be used for planting a cabbage or a rose bed or a eucalyptus forest.

Using the colour wheel will help you to predict which colours will work for you, as it demonstrates which colours contrast with each other and which harmonize. Some people prefer to use harmonies in gardening; the results seem more restful and inherently more beautiful to them, but can appear a bit dull or tame to others. Proponents of colour harmony like to compare a border of theirs with a symphony by a composer like Schubert, something that inherently creates a sense of repose in the human mind. Plantings based on contrast, on the other hand, could be compared to a piece by a composer like Stravinsky, with some dissonant chords that may be stimulating but can also be restless.

Proponents of contrast in planting see their work as being more interesting and dynamic, believing that by juxtaposing different colours and forms it is possible to create a spark between them, a kind of creative tension. Undeniably this kind of planting is actually more difficult, but when done well it is truly stimulating.

RED

Danger, stop, revolution! these are among the dramatic connotations of the colour red, which is one of those strong colours that people are very cautious about using in the garden. It is true that it does rather demand attention – one red poppy in a border of pink immediately pulls the eye towards it. In the evening, the opposite happens: red becomes a very dark colour and is the first to disappear in the twilight. It is a colour, then, of two aspects.

There are several ways in which to make the most of red's drama and brightness. One is to use it in conjunction with yellows and oranges to make a crucible of visual heat; another is to dilute it with a

*Blue and yellow is a common springtime combination, and one that
works well:* Mertensia virginica *next to* Narcissus *'Sunburst'.*

kaleidoscope of other colours; a third is to be uncompromising and go for strong contrasts. The first solution is at least harmonious, as the colours are related to each other. the second works very well with wildflowers, where red poppies, for example, are dotted among many other colours, or in a riotous cottage border. The third solution, favoured by enthusiasts of nineteenth-century bedding who love combining red with blue and white, is very striking but also very unsubtle.

Adventurous designers have occasionally tried their hand at red borders, in particular combining red flowers with dark red or purple foliage. Personally, I feel that this highlights red's other quality – its darkness and oppressiveness – and these borders would work much better if they included some yellow to lighten them up.

One good way of lightening up or toning down the effect of red is to use it with green. The two are complementary colours and often look stunning together, particularly scarlet and a leafy mid-green; perhaps this is one reason why the scarlet pelargonium is such a universally popular plant.

Red is a colour that spans the seasons. Quince (*Chaenomeles*) is a very early-flowering shrub that is available in some excellent scarlet forms, and there are also fine scarlet tulips for late spring, both hybrids and species (I especially recommend the robust little *Tulipa praestans*). Various roses, poppy species, *Lobelia cardinalis*, *Monardas* and potentillas provide good hardy sources of red throughout the summer, but the choice is limited. It seems that red is much more a colour of the tropics, particularly as many tropical flowers are pollinated by birds, who are drawn to red. Perhaps the best time for red, especially pure red, is late summer and early autumn, with a selection of half-hardy or slightly tender plants including penstemons, salvias, cupheas, cannas and dahlias. These will, of course, need lifting or protecting for

Right: The soft oranges and yellows of an abutilon, petunias and pansies look warm without being aggressive.

Opposite: Too many colours of similar tone all together can look dull. A blue echinops 'lifts' a hot planting of a kniphofia, penstemon and Dahlia 'Bishop of Llandaff'.

the winter (see page 15). Fortunately, there are also a lot of yellow flowers for this time of year, so the potential for a high-temperature border is considerable.

YELLOW AND ORANGE

Yellow and orange are the colours of fire and the sun. They feel hotter to us than red, and they lack red's dark side. There are undoubtedly some warm oranges and soft yellows, but I find straight yellow the most difficult colour of all to use in a planting scheme, despite its cheerful, optimistic feel. Yellow usually looks dreadful with pink, which is one of the most common colours in the garden. Because of its strength, yellow tends to seize a lot of attention, and it is also affected considerably by sunlight, which is a very yellow light and therefore enhances it – a warm gold in early morning may become

harsh and brassy by midday. This, and the lightening effect of yellow, make it a better colour to use in light shade than full sun.

Although soft yellow is not a common flower colour, there are some very good ones around, including the creamy yellow of primroses (*Primula vulgaris*) and *Anthemis tinctoria* 'E. C. Buxton'. There are also the greeny yellows of the euphorbias. These are easy colours to place, and it is difficult to misuse them. They look especially refreshing in half shade or in the evening.

Yellows mix well with oranges, to create an array of subtle variations in strength, and with complementary blue or mauve. A good example for late spring is the greeny yellow *Euphorbia polychroma* with *Polemonium* 'Lambrook Mauve' or, later on, yellow climbing roses intertwined with blue ceanothus. Another good combination is paler yellows with grey foliage; mullein (*Verbascum olympicum*), which has yellow flowers and soft grey foliage, is a good example.

Yellows are available throughout the year, but it is the spring and autumn flowers that we seem to welcome most, perhaps because of the softer light at these times of year and our need for a reminder of the sun. For many gardeners, the year starts with forsythia and daffodils, and ends with golden rod and rudbeckia.

Orange is perhaps the warmest colour of all – hot, but lacking the harshness of yellow. Even so, it is far from relaxing – not a colour to sit next to with a martini at the end of a hard day in the office. Too much orange can be overpowering, so it needs to be used sparingly. Like yellow, it consorts well with blues and mauves – English marigolds spilling around *Salvia* x *sylvestris* 'Mainacht', for instance. Orange is very much a colour available for midsummer onwards, and is typical of annuals like Californian poppies (*Eschscholzia*), the various marigolds (*Calendula* and *Tagetes*), and perennials like heleniums and kniphofias.

Not all oranges are strong and fierce, and there are some intriguing shades where orange meets brown, particularly among the myriad varieties of hemerocallis. None are that 'hot', and when a mixture of these very adaptable summer-flowering plants is put together with one shade bleeding into another, the results are very attractive.

Finally, there are the reds, oranges and yellows of autumn foliage, which are not perhaps the easiest to introduce into a small garden, but which are worth bearing in mind. Although strong, they are never overpowering, and even if there is room for just a single maple or sumach in the garden, it is well worth the effort to celebrate the swan song of the garden year.

WHITE

Purity, cleanliness and light are values that come to mind in relation to white. White flowers have been used in many cultures to symbolize spiritual purity, and this may be one of the reasons why white gardens have become so fashionable. More cynically, perhaps, it is because with one relatively unvarying colour you do not have to worry about making mistakes with introducing clashing colours. Nevertheless, white is extremely useful in the garden, and its uses go far beyond the making of white borders.

White, or other very pale flowers, have the effect of bringing light to the place where they are planted – I always like to put white foxgloves or white *Campanula latifolia* var. *macrantha alba* under trees to bring light to the shade. However, white can also be used to create the opposite effect in areas of full sun, or among warm shades of colour. Here, white has a cooling and refreshing effect; think of how white cistus, for example, can refresh a hot, dry bank. White does not create a sense of depth in the way that blue, the other cooling colour, does. Instead, it tends to jump forward, and really pure white does this much more than does cream.

Putting white flowers next to coloured ones has the effect of enhancing their colour, so a white rose throws into relief the shades of its red and pink brethren. An effect I like is to mix the coloured varieties of a plant with their white counterparts, so that they are all identical except in colour.

Once you start looking in detail at 'white' flowers you realize that many of them are in fact cream, or very pale versions of other colours. There is something magical about pure white flowers but they can be rather dazzling, and the 'jumping forward' effect is not always welome. Off-white and cream-coloured flowers can come into their own in situations where you are worried that this might happen.

White flowers have the great advantage that they can be combined successfully with any other

Verbena bonariensis, Clematis *'Etoile Violette', an echinops and pink*
Malva moschata *form a powerful pastel-purple grouping.*

colour. As a consequence, it is possible to use white as a 'buffer' with strong and contrasting colours, because it keeps them separate: scarlet poppies and blue-mauve salvias together will tend to merge into a heavy purple, but if you place white oxeye daisies with them the colours will stay separate and clear. Variegated foliage may also be used to create this effect, and it has the advantage of having a longer season of interest than most flowers.

This use of white enables the bold gardener to combine strong colours. the results will still be pretty startling, but the charge of 'clashing colours' will not be a fair one. When white is used with gentle pinks and blues the effect is to keep them clear too, which can be useful as too many soft pastels together may get a bit muddy. I particularly like blue with white, which is a very refreshing combination.

Spring is the time when white flowers seem particularly special, with snowdrops, ivory-white daffodils and tulips all shining out against dark, bare earth. Summer is also well provided for, but autumn has relatively few white flowers.

PURPLE AND DARK RED

Purples and dark reds are receding colours, disappearing quickly at dusk and looking mysterious at the brightest of times. Really dark shades are rare, but there are plants that have flowers so dark that they are effectively black. Not everyone likes them, but they do have passionate admirers. Such exceptionally dark flowers also make great conversation pieces. There are black, or very dark, forms of hollyhocks (*Alcea rosea*), sweet peas (*Lathyrus odoratus*) and cornflowers (*Centaurea cyanus*), but perhaps the darkest of all are varieties of pansy and viola – *Viola* 'Molly Sanderson' is one superb example.

Like blues and mauves, dark purples are very useful for increasing depth and distance. This, together with their mysteriousness, allows them to

be used for enhancing a romantic atmosphere. The dark purple *Clematis* 'Jackmannii Superba' is especially useful in this respect, spilling over walls, fences and shrubs.

Being born from red and blue, purple is a colour that combines well with both, as well as with pink. When combined with pink and other pastels it provides depth, which can be lacking when there is a solid mass of paler colours. With reds and dark blues it can become rather dark and oppressive. Perhaps more than any other group of colours, these deep shades should not be grouped together, unless you want a corner of funereal darkness.

Having said this, there is one dramatic way to put together a high concentration of these colours, and that is to combine them with a lot of silver foliage. The contrast between the dark reds, purples and blacks and the grey and silver leaves is truly exciting – one of the most unusual plantings that can be made.

These dark very colours are found among perennials, climbers and annuals, but not among hardy shrubs, and nearly all of these are summer flowering. The darkest flowered shrubs are certain

rose varieties of rose and *Rosa* 'Souvenir du Docteur Jamain' is among the darkest, and it is wonderfully scented too.

PINK

Pink is the colour of warmth, softness and cosiness. It occurs in a wide variety of shades, from the coolness of a pink that is almost white to a fiery magenta. There are a great many, mostly summer-flowering, plants whose flowers are somewhere in the middle, giving the gardener plenty of choice in selecting appropriate plants for a variety of situations. Leaving aside the bright pinks and magentas, the colour is an easy one to live with and to use, at least in temperate climates. In warmer ones, the sunlight makes it look insipid and washed out.

Pinks have a natural affinity with reds, and some charming effects can be had by combining a wide variety of flowers of these two colours to create a myriad of different strengths and shades. Pinks consort more happily with purpley crimsons than with pure scarlets, which is one of the strong points of borders full of old-fashioned roses. Blues, mauves and purples mix well with pinks, and together they form the basis of many classic pastel

Opposite: The ball-shaped heads of Allium aflatunense *and pink pokers of* Persicaria bistorta *provide not only subtle colour contrast but also a contrast in form.*

Left: Colour combination can be controversial: red nasturtiums, yellow Bidens ferulifolia *and pink* Fuchsia 'Thalia'

borders. This mixing of pink and blue is enough of a contrast to be interesting, without compromising the restful, romantic feeling that both colours evoke. Grey is often a vital ingredient in these borders; pink and grey together (and dianthus, with their pink flowers and grey leaves, have them neatly together in one plant) is one of the most wonderfully mellow combinations.

Most people agree that pink and yellow look awful together. There are exceptions, but they usually involve a very pale yellow and a strong pink – primroses with pink polyanthus, for instance. However, in climates where the sun is intense these generalizations do not hold good, and bright pinks can consort happily with yellows and oranges: pink-flowered, purple-leaved *Iresine herbstii* next

Asters, roses, dahlias, a buddleia and a Clematis viticella *variety make for a warm pastel combination.*

to orange coleus looks stunning in Brazil, but I would never do it in England.

BRIGHT PINK AND MAGENTA

These shades scream at you for attention from the depths of wherever they are planted. On seeing a bright pink flower in isolation you may wonder how on earth you are to combine it with other colours, but once you know what to look for it can be done. Grey tones down magenta shades well: purple loosestrife (*Lythrum salicaria*) has deep pink flowers but looks fine with greyish-leaved *Macleaya cordata*. Adding some dark foliage to contrast with the grey will create a stunning combination.

Some of the most successful combinations of bright pink I have seen are with blues (especially pale ones) or greeny yellows. *Geranium psilostemon*, a large and uncompromising plant at the best of times, looks gorgeous next to *Geranium pratense* 'Mrs Kendall Clark', the very pale blue of the latter calming the magenta of the former.

In warm climates, magenta ceases to be a problem, and indeed comes into its own: a bougainvillea that sears the retina in an English conservatory merely looks a nice dark pink when seen on a house in Spain.

BLUE

The sea, the sky, vast depths and great distances – these are among the attributes of blue. On the whole, blue is a restful and cooling colour, and very useful for creating a feeling of depth. There are very few true blue flowers, and most of what we call blue is really mauve or purple. The true blues can be so electric that they are difficult to place. In contrast, mauvey blues are quite dark, retiring colours. They are also more affected by surrounding colours than perhaps any other colour. Accepting that 'blue' in gardening terms includes shades that also contain red and are therefore purplish in tone, there is a considerable variety to choose from, with summer the best time.

Too much blue together looks dark, and other colours are needed to lighten it. Red and blue can look startling, but it is a 'lively' combination, not a restful one. Blue and pink, we know, is a highly

successful association, a romantic one that works well in many summer gardens, especially those of a traditional bent (delphiniums and roses, for instance). Blue and complementary yellow and orange is often successful, but again is rather exuberant and restless. White adds a lightening element, overcoming the darkness of the blue to produce a delicious cool combination – white tulips and bluebells, for example – but it is still a vibrant one which appears to leap forward. My favourite is blue and lime-green, as with campanulas and *Alchemilla mollis*; here, the yellow-green of the alchemillas lightens the scene, but in a soothing way, and provides just enough contrast to bring out the exact tones of the blue.

Similar to the combination of blue with lime-green, and almost as successful, is blue with grey or variegated foliage. Again, the result is soothing and cool. This is a mix that can be applied very successfully to summer bedding, there being some very good intense blues among borderline hardy

plants such as salvias (for example, *Salvia patens* and the more hardy *S. uliginosa*) and the little daisy relatives, the felicias. This is an opportunity to combine blue flowers of a rare quality and depth with some very good greys. Among the grey foliage plants that can be used are half-hardy helichrysums and *Senecio cineraria*. Unlike most traditional summer bedding, which can become restless to the point of jarring, this combination is deliciously cooling and subtle.

MIXING COLOURS

Many gardeners suffer from sleepless nights over the business of mixing colours. This is not surprising, given that there are so many strong beliefs about colour, and so many rules about which colours 'go' with each other and which ones 'clash'. The important thing to realize about all this is that there is no right and wrong – all beliefs about colour are subjective. Certain colours and combinations are fashionable among different

groups of people and at different times in history. In the nineteenth century it was all the rage to mix strong and contrasting colours, whereas nowadays it is much more the done thing to create subtle harmonies. Quite apart from the different tastes to be found among different cultures, social classes and historical periods, everyone has their own likes and dislikes. It is important to have confidence in your own personal taste and decisions, and not to be swayed by what the garden magazines tell you, or what your family says, or for that matter what I say.

DISCOVERING WHAT YOU LIKE

The most important thing is to know what you like, and to work at finding out what you like. Even with a wide knowledge of plants and colour, it is not that easy to work out which colours will mix well. Books help a lot, and you may see a photograph that makes you think that you want to create something similar, but beware of the tricks that film can play on colour, especially on blues, which are often made to look more red than they really are. The best way to learn about colour is to visit plenty of gardens with your notebook in hand and record both the plants you like and the all-important combinations of plants and colours that appeal to you.

Personal experience is far more important than anything else when it comes to putting together good colour combinations. Friends may give you plants upon which they lavish great praise, you may order from nursery catalogue descriptions and select from books, and be sure that you have created a combination that works. But there is a good chance that it won't – it may well look horrible, or merely pedestrian. With experience you will find it easier to predict which plants will look good together, but the really stunning combinations are nearly always ones that you did not think of, but came across by chance.

One way to experiment with colour is to stand and look at a border, and then hold your hands up to your face to hide various plants and therefore colours. You will be surprised at how different the rest of the planting looks once one colour is taken away. When you start to think about putting colours together, perhaps by making a list of the colours and combinations you like, it will soon become apparent that some appear again and

Bluebells and a wallflower (Erysimum perofskianum) *have
flowers that are complementary – that is, they contrast
strongly but pleasingly.*

again. These are the ones that you are obviously drawn to, even though this might be subconscious, and it would be sensible to concentrate on these as the core of your new planting.

BUILDING A SCHEME FROM COLOUR COMBINATIONS

A season of garden visiting and looking at books may well result in a good list of plant combinations. Most will probably consist of two or three that look stunning together, and perhaps some additional plants that combine well with the core of the combination. The task now is to combine all these into a whole border or planting. Ideally, you should have some good combinations for different seasons, so that the risk of a clash is reduced and you have a good seasonal spread as well. Problems start when you have several combinations for the same season that seem incompatable at close quarters – a bright pink and blue scheme with an

orange and red one, for example. You will either have to choose between them, or try to separate them widely.

Having selected a number of more-or-less compatible combinations, it may well be possible to build up a whole planting around them. These core combinations may mesh together if the colours seem to you to work well, and the rest of the planting can then be built up around them using other compatible colours. It is worth bearing in mind that the most successful plantings are those that involve the repetition of groups of plants rather than lots of different ones.

APPROACHES TO MIXING COLOURS

Essentially, there are three approaches to colour mixing – harmony, contrast and 'avoiding the worst'! Some people are not so interested in colour, and it is the texture and form of plants that seize their interest. These gardeners are among the so-called 'plantsmen' who are primarily collectors of plants, or they are happy to build up plantings based on impulse buys. The main concern here is to arrange plantings based on factors other than colour, but to ensure that different colours are well distributed and that none 'clash'.

Finally, you do not have to be a great colourist to be a great garden designer – I would put some of the world's greatest in this category!

PLANTING IN HARMONY

As you might guess, harmonic planting is the safest way of combining colour and the most restful on the eye, especially in small spaces. The idea is to bring together colours that are next, or very close, to each other on the colour wheel (see page 153). These are colours that are related to each other, and thus do not contrast sharply. Such plantings rely for much of their interest on being able to compare and appreciate variations on related colours and the blends between them. Often this can be achieved by including several related plants, such as old-fashioned roses, which are all on a white/pink/red-pink/crimson-red spectrum, with none of the orangey scarlet or yellow of many modern roses to destroy the harmony.

Restricting the palette like this can, however, lead to a certain visual flatness, and the odd 'lift' is needed to provide some contrast: the old-fashioned rose border would benefit from the occasional mauve or blue geranium, or a catmint such as *Nepeta* x *faassenii*, or perhaps some silver foliage from *Artemisia ludoviciana*. Extending the idea of gentle contrast a little further, it is possible to continue to add unrelated colours if they do not contrast too much. More blues could be included in our rose border, for instance: pale ones would not clash, and darker ones would bring in a gentle level of contrast. The worst that would happen would be a rather heavy atmosphere between, for example, the dark violet-blue *Delphinum* 'Chelsea Star' and the deep-crimson *Rosa* 'Souvenir du Docteur Jamain', but this could be lightened by having paler pink roses alongside, with pale blue geraniums and campanulas.

CHANGING HARMONIES THROUGH THE SEASONS

With careful planning, it is possible to have more than one harmony in a year. A border could start off in spring with yellow and ivory narcissi combined with yellow and red polyanthus and tulips. Then, just as the latter finish, it becomes a pink and red border based on roses, poppies, potentillas and geraniums, ending with an autumnal feast of mauve, purple and violet asters.

Such a recipe requires minimal overlapping of the ingredients, although this will result in a series

---

A THEORY OF COLOUR MIXING

If the first colour chosen for a border is one of the three primaries (red, blue or yellow), then a second colour can be one of the three secondary colours derived from them (purple from red and blue, green from blue and yellow, or orange from yellow and red). A third colour can be added, but in order to work well with the first two it should be a pale version of the third primary colour – that is, the one not involved in the creation of the secondary colour.

For example, if red is the primary colour, then purple can be used as the secondary, as it is derived from red (and blue). Yellow has not been involved so far, so can be used as the third colour, but only as a pale version.

Of course, all this takes place against a background of green, but green itself can become part of the equation if a particularly vivid shade is used or large parts of the design are composed of green foliage.

Secondary colours

Primary colours

Pale primary colours

BLENDED PLANTING WITH PERENNIALS

This island bed is planted with a mixture of perennials and grasses, primarily for colour in early to midsummer, with a secondary season in late summer and early autumn. It is based on a yellow and blue-purple scheme.

The theme perennials (see page 80) are the tall grass *Stipa calamagrostis*, the verbascum, which looks best planted in groups so that its narrow flower spikes have more impact, and the dictamnus, which is planted in loose groups. The other perennials are scattered, some in very loose clumps, to create a mingled effect.

Gaps in the planting, and the areas underneath the grass, can be planted with spring bulbs.

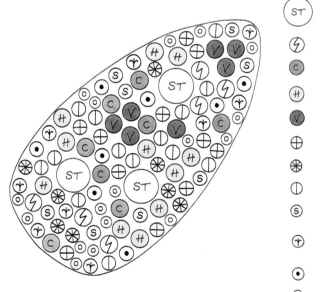

ST — *Stipa calamagrostis*, grass (late summer–winter)

Dictamnus albus, white (early summer)

C — *Achillea* 'Coronation Gold', gold (summer)

H — *Achillea* 'Hoffnung', pale yellow (summer)

V — *Verbascum phoeniceum*, purple (late summer)

⊕ — *Salvia* × *sylvestris* 'Mainacht', purple (early summer)

✳ — *Salvia* 'Blauhugel', blue-mauve (summer)

◐ — *Salvia nemorosa* 'Ostfriesland', blue-purple (summer)

S — *Sedum spectabile*, dusty pink (late summer–autumn)

— *Pennisetum alopecuroides*, indigo grass (late summer–autumn)

⊙ — *Origanum laevigatum* 'Herrenhausen'

◎ — *Nepeta* × *faassenii*, mauve (summer)

There are no colour clashes with wildflowers. The colours of Geranium sylvaticum *and buttercups are moderated by grass and white flowers.*

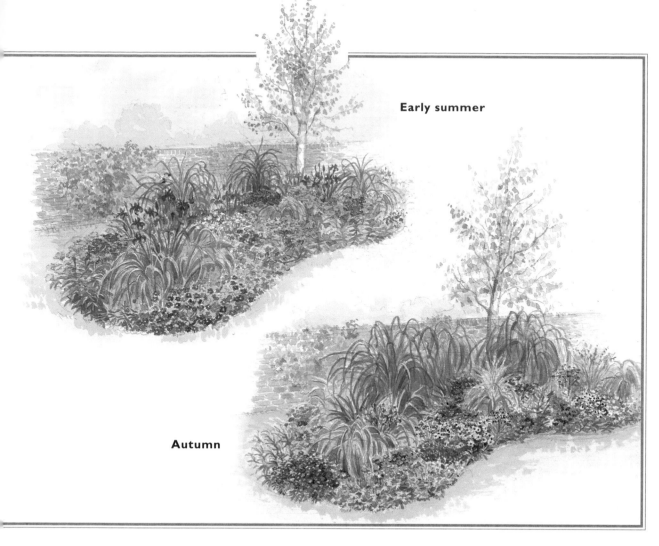

Early summer

Autumn

of flushes of interest, with relatively dull gaps of up to several weeks in between.

SINGLE-COLOUR BORDERS

The purest form of the harmonic approach is the currently fashionable single-colour border, where one colour is chosen and only variants on it are used. Much of the interest lies in the subtle variations on a theme, together with contrasts in leaf shape, habit and flower form. Indeed, these can become quite important as a source of variation and interest to the eye: for example, upright iris-type leaves to contrast with rounded shapes and small leaves in a blue border. Finding plants with the right flower colour may be difficult but can also be part of the fun, tracking down new variations to add to the border.

With borders of this kind, it is very important that the occasional plant of a contrasting colour (either flower or foliage) is added to provide relief for the eye, which otherwise can become very tired of too much harmony! A good example would be the occasional blue *Polemonium caeruleum* included in a yellow border.

WORKING WITH CONTRAST

There is no doubt that working with contrast involves more skill and care in the planning, but the effort is well worth it because the results are more visually stimulating than when working with harmonies alone. The bedding displays that so many regard as a cheerful and essential part o the summer garden are based on exploiting contrasts. Working with contrasting colours is more difficult than working with harmonies in a small space, but this should not put you off. The majority of gardeners are drawn to a variety of colours and do not want to restrict themselves too much, so the

Opposite: Hosta sieboldiana elegans *and* Polystichum setiferum *will form an attractive combination all summer long in a shady or moist spot.*

ability to work creatively with contrast is a necessary skill.

If you get carried away with impulse buys at garden centres or plants that you have fallen in love with somewhere and are determined to have, it is all too easy to end up with a garden that is a riot of discordant colours. It is better to concentrate on a few colours that you like, or that you know look good together. Indeed, it is this balancing of a limited number of colours that is the key to successful contrast planting. The colour wheel will give you some idea of which colours are complementary (this is, contrast vividly), but this is really only a theoretical guide. It is best to rely on your own experience of combinations that you have seen and like in order to build up a successful planting. Only you can tell what works for you.

There are various rules about how to use colour – rules in as much as they produce results that appeal to most people. One is to use two colours as the major elements in a design and introduce others only as subsidiaries. If the major colours are strong, then the minor ones should be paler, and preferably not too numerous; the minor colours can then be used to 'link' the major ones. For example, red poppies and blue delphiniums can look almost too vivid together, but add some lavender and the overall effect will be much calmer. The lavender links the red and blue because it contains elements of both colours.

Another way of applying this rule is by using strong colours to add a touch of brightness to pale plantings. A combination of pastels is very soft and hazy, but sometimes needs a lift; the occasional deep red – a rose or poppy perhaps – will help to liven it up a bit.

Buffer colours are very useful when combining strong hues, as they keep them apart and stop them from either seeming to clash or becoming too muddy. White is a very useful, but at times rather glaring, buffer colour. Grey foliage from plants like sage (*Salvia officinalis*), some of the artemisias or *Brachyglottis* 'Sunshine', can do a similar job. These have a tendency to darken the colours around them, but are often valuable border plants because of their long, and usually evergreen, season. Pale greeny yellows, as in the flowers of *Alchemilla mollis* or euphorbias, also make good buffers, although the yellow in them itself becomes a part of the colour equation.

COLOURS – TO SEPARATE OR BLEND?

We have looked at ways of choosing and combining colours in borders and other plantings, but this still leaves open the question of how they are to be distributed: in blocks of colour, as in a painting by Gaugin, or scattered in dots, as in a work by Seurat? The traditional herbaceous border puts plants in blocks so that the whole is made up of a

---

TEXTURED FOLIAGE

Glossy		Other
Asarum species	Filipendula species	Bupleurum fruticosum
Choisya ternata	Hosta sieboldiana	Ferns
Clematis armandii	Polygonatum campanulatum	Geranium macrorrhizum
Griselinia littoralis	Rhododendron, large-leaved species	Gunnera manicata
Magnolia grandiflora	Rodgersia species	Hebe, 'whipcord' species
Mahonia repens	Sorbus aria	(eg H. armstrongii)
	Veratrum species	Kerria japonica
Pleated or impressed veins	Viburnum davidii, V. plicatum,	Phlomis species
Carpinus betulus, C. japonica	V. rhytidophyllum	Salvia officinalis
Ceanothus impressus		Stachys byzantina
Crocosmia paniculata		

SILVER, GREY OR BLUISH FOLIAGE

Abies concolor 'Violacea'
Achillea × *taygetea*
Antennaria dioica
Anthemis cupaniana
Artemisia species
Ballota pseudodictamnus
Brachyglottis 'Sunshine'
Cedrus atlantica 'Glauca'
Centaurea cineraria
Cerastium tomentosum
Dianthus species
Elaeagnus commutata
Eucalyptus species
Euphorbia myrsinites

Festuca glauca
Hebe pinguifolia 'Pagei'
Helichrysum petiolare,
H. microphyllum
Juniperus horizontalis varieties
Juniperus virginiana varieties
Lavandula, most hardy species
Lotus bertholetii
Melianthus major
Olea europaea
Picea glauca 'Coerulea'
Pyrus salicifolia 'Pendula'
Romneya coulteri
Rosa glauca

Ruta graveolens
Salix alba var. *sericea*
Santolina chamaecyparissus
Sedum spathulifolium 'Capo Blanco'
Senecio cineraria
Tanacetum haradjanii
Verbascum bombyciferum,
V. thapsus

For shade
Hosta sieboldiana var. *elegans*
Lamium maculatum 'Silver Nancy'

pattern of patches of different colours, with more or less distinct boundaries between each one. Modern landscape practice follows the same guidelines, using blocks of the same variety (usually boring evergreen shrubs).

The cottage-garden style, which relies for much of its charm and appeal on a carefree look to the point of being almost disorderly, encourages more mixing of varieties and blending of colours. The modern continental style, characteristic of Germany and the Netherlands, rejects the old block style entirely, aiming to create a swirling blend of different but repeated colours and plant varieties. The result is not a total blend, but one where there are drifts of a particular variety, each concentration getting thinner towards the edges and more blended with another variety, before a concentration of another. This approach is inspired very much by the way in which wildflowers grow in nature. The wildflower meadow, of course, is almost entirely a blend of different points of colour on a background of green or yellow grass.

This naturalistic blended style is most applicable on a large scale, but is perfectly possible on a smaller one, especially if the plants used produce single, narrow flower spikes or clusters, rather than forming wide-spreading clumps. The continental and wildflower-meadow style both reject the concept of the traditional narrow border, preferring to cover a wide expanse. With the removal of the lawn, it thus becomes perfectly possible to create a miniature meadow or similar feature that distributes a number of different varieties across a broad area to create a blended effect.

The great advantage of the wildflower meadow as a garden feature is that it is very easy to colour scheme – have you ever seen a meadow with clashing colours? All colours, even bright ones, mix perfectly, because they are surrounded by the colours of the grass and by the buffering whites, creams and pale yellows of the many common, but less spectacular, wildflowers.

FOLIAGE COLOUR
Devising colour schemes for flowers may present its problems, but the task does not cause sleepless nights in quite the same way as interior design. This is partly because we do not live in our gardens, but also because colours are seen against a background of green, and the larger the proportion of green, the more daring can be the colour combinations. But the colour and texture of foliage can itself enter the equation, especially when considering the many plants that do not have uniformly green leaves.

TEXTURE
Some plants, especially those with grey foliage, have leaves with a distinctive texture, which has tactile as well as visual appeal. Perhaps the best

---

RED, BROWN AND PURPLE FOLIAGE

Reddish foliage

Atriplex hortensis 'Rubra'
Carex buchananii
Hebe 'Red Edge'
Photinia species
Pieris species
Uncinia rubra

Bronze or brown foliage

Acer palmatum varieties
Calluna vulgaris varieties
Carex comans bronze, *C. dipsacea*
Phormium 'Bronze Baby', *P. tenax*
'Purpureum'

Purple foliage

Acer palmatum varieties
Ajuga reptans varieties
Aster latifolius 'Prince'
Astilbe, many red-flowered varieties
Berberis thunbergii 'Atropurpurea'
Canna 'Wyoming'
Cordyline australis Purpurea Group
Cotinus coggygria, especially 'Royal
Purple'
Dahlia 'Bishop of Llandaff'
Fagus sylvatica 'Riversii'
Heuchera 'Palace Purple'
Ocimum basilicum, purple varieties
Perilla frutescens 'Atropurpurea'

Prunus cerasifera 'Nigra'
Rheum palmatum 'Atrosanguineum'
Ricinus communis 'Gibsonii'
Salvia officinalis 'Purpurascens'
Sambucus nigra 'Purpurea'
Sedum telephium ssp. *maximum*
'Atropurpureum'
Trifolium repens 'Purpurascens'
Viola labradorica
Vitis vinifera 'Purpurea'
Weigela florida 'Foliis Purpureis'

Black foliage

Ophiopogon planiscapus 'Nigrescens'

---

known is *Stachys byzantina*, an easy and vigorous low-growing perennial with very woolly grey leaves. Some of the mulleins, *Verbascum bombyciferum* for example, also have wonderfully woolly leaves, augmented by great fluffy spires of yellow flowers.

Common sage (*Salvia officinalis*) is an immensely useful plant in the border because of its interestingly textured leaves, which have a dense relief of 'hills and valleys'; *Geranium renardii* has a similar leaf. The visual effect of these plants is very soft, which is a perfect accompaniment to pastel-coloured flowers.

Surfaces that are matt absorb light, whereas glossy ones reflect it. This means that glossy leaves tend to stand out more – a worthwhile feature in itself, except that too much glossy foliage on a sunny day makes one want to reach for the anti-glare sunglasses. Like bright colours and large leaves, it also tends to pull plants forward visually, shortening the perspective.

BLUE, GREY AND SILVER

Plants with coloured foliage are invaluable in the garden, and those with blue, grey and silver tones especially so: for one thing, it seems almost impossible to go wrong with them. They work well with most colours, especially pastels, and old-fashioned roses alongside grey foliage is a great favourite with many gardeners. Grey has a slightly dulling

Variegated foliage: Ampelopis glandulosa var. brevipedunculata 'Elegans', a nasturtium and a phormium form a sophisticated grouping.

Ruby chard and young broccoli plants are a reminder that some vegetables have decorative value and are worthy of a place in the flower border.

effect on many colours, which can be a disadvantage, and a lot of people do not feel happy about combining it with yellow, even to the extent of cutting the flowers off the silver-grey, daisy-flowered shrub, *Brachyglottis* 'Sunshine'.

Most grey and silver foliage plants are native to hot, dry places, so schemes involving them are particularly appropriate for dry banks or gardens in areas with long, hot summers. Fortunately, this does not mean that they all need to be baked; many are perfectly happy in any well-drained soil in a sunny spot. For a Mediterranean-style garden there is a host of possibilities, including cistus, helianthemums, lavender or artemisias.

Lavenders are among the best known silver and grey foliage plants and, like most, are evergreen. They are useful not only in borders but also

for making low hedges. Artemisias are another valuable group, including some good low-growing species. The grey *A.* 'Powis Castle' is one of the best of the semi-shrubby ones, while the low-growing herbaceous *A. ludoviciana* looks particularly good among low perennials, such as geraniums.

Among plants that are not evergreen but that can be grown in shade, the hostas must rank supreme. The blue-grey of *H. sieboldiana* is wonderfully cooling, especially when combined with ferns and *Alchemilla mollis*.

Many grasses have splendid grey or blue leaves, especially those from rather harsh environments. The dwarf blue *Festuca glauca* thrives in poor, sandy soils and is evergreen. Taller grasses, such as *Elymus* species and *Helictotrichon sempervirens*, thrive in dry soils, and they can be

---

YELLOW AND VARIEGATED FOLIAGE

Yellow foliage	The best silver-variegated foliage	The best gold-variegated foliage
Calluna vulgaris, many varieties	*Arundo donax* 'Variegata'	*Carex oshimensis* 'Evergold',
Carex testacea	*Brunnera macrophylla* 'Hadspen Cream'	C. *siderosticha* 'Variegata'
Catalpa bignonioides 'Aurea'		*Cortaderia selloana* 'Gold Band'
Chamaecyparis, many including	*Buddleia davidii* 'Harlequin'	*Elaeagnus* × *ebbingei* 'Gilt Edge',
C. *obtusa* and C. *pisifera* varieties	*Cornus alba* 'Elegantissima',	E. *pungens* 'Maculata'
Erica carnea, many varieties	C. *controversa* 'Variegata'	*Euonymus fortunei* 'Emerald 'n' Gold',
Gleditsia triacanthos 'Sunburst'	*Euonymus fortunei* 'Variegatus'	E. *japonicus* 'Aureopictus'
Hakonechloa macra varieties	*Fuchsia magellanica* 'Variegata'	*Hosta*, many varieties
Humulus lupulus 'Aureus'	*Hedera*, many varieties	*Ilex* × *altaclerensis* 'Golden King',
Lonicera nitida 'Baggeson's Gold'	*Ilex* × *altaclerensis* 'Silver Sentinel',	I. *aquifolium* 'Golden King'
Milium effusum 'Aureum'	I. *aquifolium* 'Silver Queen'	*Miscanthus sinensis* 'Zebrinus'
Ptelia trifoliata 'Aurea'	*Iris pallida* 'Variegata'	*Pelargonium*, many varieties
Robinia pseudoacacia 'Frisia'	*Molinia caerulea* 'Variegata'	*Phormium cookianum* 'Tricolor'
Sambucus racemosa 'Plumosa Aurea'	*Nerium oleander* 'Variegatum'	*Salvia officinalis* 'Icterina'
Taxus baccata, many varieties	*Pulmonaria* varieties	*Sisyrinchium striatum* 'Aunt May'
Valeriana phu 'Aurea'	*Rhamnus alaternus* 'Argenteovariegata'	*Symphytum* 'Goldsmith'
	Scrophularia auriculata 'Variegata'	*Thymus* × *citriodorus* 'Aureus'
	Thymus × *citriodorus* 'Argenteus'	*Vinca minor* 'Aureovariegata'
	Vinca major 'Variegata',	*Yucca filamentosa* 'Variegata'
	V. *minor* 'Variegata'	

---

combined with grey-leaved nepetas and rich purple origanums for a colourful late-summer spectacle on the stoniest of ground.

RED, BROWN AND PURPLE

The selection of plants with leaves in red, brown and purple shades is more limited than those with silvery or grey leaves, which is a shame as they can be extremely useful. The main use of these plants is to provide a bit of variation among green foliage and as a counterpoint to certain colours. The well-known copper beech (*Fagus sylvatica* 'Purpurea') and flowering plum (*Prunus cerasifera*) give extra interest to the eye in many a park and garden; on a smaller scale, the smoke tree or Venetian sumach (*Cotinus coggygria*) is a welcome purple addition to a shrub planting, as are plants such as *Heuchera* 'Palace Purple' to perennial borders.

While it can provide an extra bit of interest, red and purple foliage can be quite darkening, especially in shade or when combined with deep flower colours such as red or purple. In my opinion, the same effect is the result when more than one dark-coloured foliage plant is placed in close proximity.

There are certain colour combinations with dark foliage that are absolute winners: for example, pale mauve asters with *Cotinus coggygria* 'Royal Purple' in early autumn or *Euphorbia dulcis* 'Chameleon' with soft yellow *Geum* 'Geogenburg'. Dark foliage also creates a stunning contrast when it is combined with silver – perhaps a bit too much for some tastes, but the combination is undeniably spectacular. Try the cotinus just mentioned alongside *Brachyglottis* 'Sunshine', or the annual *Atriplex hortensis* var. *rubra* with silver helichrysums.

There are several other annuals which provide good dark colours. Among these are the very dark forms of the herbs basil and perilla, which are compact and thus ideal for combining with bedding. However, the finest must surely be the vegetable known as ruby (or rhubarb) chard, whose stems glow in a shade of scarlet that is somehow startling and yet not dazzling.

Lilium regale *has one of the finest scents of any flower. next to it are the seedheads of an allium and* Hydrangea arborescens *'Annabelle'.*

Among shrubs, it is worth remembering the very dark-leaved *Pittosporum tenuifolium* 'Tom Thumb', which is most valuable for its compact shape. Among perennials, there is not a great deal of choice: many of the best dark leaves are to be had among the large moisture-loving rodgersias. The rhubarbs (*Rheum* species) will thrive in ordinary conditions, but gardeners on dry soils had better stick to silver coloured plants rather than these darker shades.

As with silver and grey foliage, it is the grasses – or, to be more precise, their close relatives the sedges, especially those from New Zealand – that give us some of the best dark leaves. Nearly all of these are evergreen, which is an added bonus. In combination with grey and silver foliage, especially with those other New Zealanders the hebes, they can provide some exceptionally good year-round foliage combinations. *Uncinia rubra*, with its unusual red-brown leaves, is a personal favourite,

as is *Carex testacea*, which comes in warm yellow-brown tufts.

YELLOW AND VARIEGATED FOLIAGE

Plants with variegated foliage are very popular with many gardeners, who enjoy the way that they bring an extra splash to the garden, lightening shady places or bringing warm tones to the winter months. Others are not so sure, seeing many of them as plants that look unnatural or diseased.

In winter, the golden tones of evergreen shrubs such as *Elaeagnus pungens* 'Maculata', or the yellows of conifers like the innumerable golden cypress varieties, are very welcome, but the same plants can be less attractive in summer if their tones interfere with pastel planting schemes. They can also look terribly suburban, and are thus inappropriate in natural settings. Placed well, however, they can be used in some wonderful combinations – the yellow-leaved tree *Robinia pseudoacacia*

FRAGRANT FLOWERS

Fragrant flowers for winter
Abeliophyllum distichum
Camellia sasanqua varieties
Chimonanthes praecox
Corylopsis species
Daphne species
Hamamelis species
Lonicera purpusii
Mahonia × media 'Charity'
Sarcococca species
Viburnum × bodnantense

Fragrant flowers for spring
Cornus mas
Daphne species
Euphorbia mellifera
Narcissus, especially jonquil and
paperwhite varieties
Osmanthus species
Primula, some polyanthus varieties
Ribes odoratum

**Fragrant shrubs and trees
for early summer**
Choisya ternata
Deutzia species
Pittosporum tenuifolium, P. tobira
Rhododendron × fragrantissimum,
R. hunnewellianum 'Lady Alice
Fitzwilliam'
'Ghent' hybrid azaleas, R. luteum
Syringa species
Tilia species
Viburnum carlesii, V. juddii,
V. carlcephalum

**Fragrant shrubs for mid- and
late summer**
Buddleia species
Cytisus battandieri
Magnolia species
Philadelphus species

Fragrant climbers
Jasminum species
Lonicera × americana, L. periclymenum,
L. japonicum
Mandevilla suavolens
Trachelospermum species

**Fragrant herbaceous and
bulbous plants**
Convallaria majalis
Dianthus species
Erysimum species
Hedychium species
Hedysarum coronarium
Hemerocallis species (not hybrids)
Hesperis matronalis
Lilium regale, L. candidum, L. longiflorum
and many others
Phlox paniculata varieties
Primula florindae

**Fragrant annuals and
half-hardy plants**
Calendula officinalis
Datura species
Heliotropium peruvianum
Lathyrus odoratus varities
Matthiola varieties
Reseda odorata

'Frisia' looks marvellous as a backdrop to purple and mauve flowers, for example.

Golden variegation can play a similar role, bringing a shaft of sunlight to a garden on a dark day, but the same caveats apply as for yellow-tinged foliage. Silver and cream variegation, however, is quite different in its effects and is much easier to use, as it rarely causes a colour clash. Indeed, in the same way as white or cream flowers, it can play a buffering role in plantings, separating strong colours and cooling down hot ones. It looks especially good in pastel colour schemes, setting off the more delicate shades nicely. White gardens also benefit from the presence of silver variegation, enhancing as it does the feeling of coolness and serenity.

All variegation is welcome in the shade, as it provides a long season of extra light. Variegated plants do vary in their tolerance of shade though, so it is as well to check this before planting. Many of the variegated ivies, for example, have an annoying habit of going green in deep shade, keeping their colour best in the sun, while a number of other plants are affected in reverse – *Philadelphus coronarius* 'Aureus', for example, tends to be scorched by day-long sun and benefits from the protection of light shade.

Variegation varies tremendously; it can come in the form of streaks, blotches, lines, stripes, chunks or dots, and it may be consistent or inconsistent. Some of the finest variegated plants are those that have lines of gold, cream or silver along the leaves, such as the lily-of-the-valley *Convallaria majalis* 'Variegata'. Those with fine dots of colour can look unhealthy, and are very much a matter of personal taste. Whatever you do with it, there seems to be one almost universally agreed rule: never put variegation next to variegation. For

---

HARDY PLANTS WITH AROMATIC FOLIAGE

Abies concolor
Artemisia species
Calamintha species
Cistus ladaniferus
Drimys aromatica
Eucalyptus species
Hyssopus officinalis
Illicium anisatum
Laurus nobilis
Lavandula species

Lindera benzoin
Melissa officinalis
Mentha species
Monarda species
Myrtus communis
Nepeta species
Origanum species
Perovskia abrotanifolius
Phlomis species
Rosa primula

Rosmarinus officinalis
Rubus odoratus
Salvia species

Half-hardy plants with aromatic foliage
Aloysia citriodora
Pelargonium species

---

some reason – maybe because it is overstimulating and 'fussy' – it never looks right.

FRAGRANCE

Scent is the most intangible aspect of the garden. we know when we like a scent, but find it difficult to recall or describe. The Victorians valued fragrance highly, but nowadays it is less treasured: plant breeders churn out new varieties that are strong on colour to the point of gaudiness, but they lack the scent of their wild ancestors or of older forms. Scent remains an especially important part of any garden with romantic leanings or one that aims to stimulate all the senses.

FRAGRANT FLOWERS

Flowers vary tremendously in their fragrance, not just from species to species but from variety to variety, as any sniff around a garden of old roses will soon tell you. It is a quality that cannot be featured in pictures, so do not expect catalogues or books to tell you much. More than with any other quality, it is necessary to assess plants for yourself – what is bliss for one, is stale cheese to another.

There is no doubt that roses are top of many people's lists of favourite fragrant plants, yet their scent varies from nothing to overwhelming, depending on the variety. The older varieties are undoubtedly the best; their colours are much more subtle as well, although many have a limited flowering season compared to the summer-long exuberance of modern varities. Shrubby plants have the advantage that their flowers are presented at a height that makes them easy to smell, and climbing plants, such as rambling roses and honeysuckle, can be trained so that their stems almost thrust blossom at us through open windows or hanging down from pergolas and archways.

Summer is the best season for scent, and the evening is often the best time to enjoy fragrant flowers, as many are moth pollinated. It stands to reason that they should be near the house, so that the fragrance can waft in through the open windows, or around areas where you are likely to entertain. Hardy plants in the ground can be augmented by exotic tender species such as daturas and jasmines in pots, conveniently portable to wherever they will be appreciated most.

Many spring flowers, including primulas, violets, lily-of-the-valley (*Convallaria majalis*) and many bulbs have beautiful sweet smells, but unless you are in the habit of crawling around on the ground they can be extremely difficult to appreciate. Being small, they can be grown in pots and put in a place where they may be picked up easily, or alternatively plants in the garden can be picked for early-season posies. Fortunately, there are some excellent winter and early-spring flowering shrubs that have surprisingly potent scents. The witch hazels (*Hamamelis* species) are among the finest, and can be a real treat on a cold winter's day.

AROMATIC FOLIAGE

Unlike the fleeting fragrance of flowers, aromatic leaves are with us for a longer season. Many herbs come in a multitude of varieties – mints and thymes, for instance – each with a distinct aroma. Rather than restricting such multi-purpose plants to the vegetable plot, they should be scattered

Regularly spaced clumps of yellow-green Alchemilla mollis *at
the base of this border generate a strong sense of rhythm, with*
Salvia x superba *at the front.*

about the whole garden, especially around sitting areas. Many of the best aromatic leaves are to be had on plants from Mediterranean climates such as lavenders, salvias, cistus and the myriad forms of half-hardy pelargoniums. A hot, dry bank is thus the obvious place for a collection of such plants, with the less hardy ones in containers, to be brought inside over the winter.

Collecting aromatic foliage plants can become an absorbing hobby in itself, and you may soon find youself crushing and smelling the leaves of any new plant that you come across. The results can be surprising, as many unlikely groups of plants seem to have the odd species or variety that is aromatic; the incense rose (*Rosa primula*) and *Ceanothus impressus* are good examples.

RHYTHM AND UNITY
Rhythm is one of the fundamental patterns that the mind recognizes and uses in order to make sense of the world. If something lacks rhythm, it is interpreted by the mind as lacking unity and wholeness. Many is the otherwise carefully planned planting that falls down on this score – a border may be packed with interesting plants and beautifully colour schemed, but lack any element of repetition to bind it together. Conversely, a sense of rhythm, of repeated elements, unifies a garden and gives it a common thread that becomes an important part of its personality.

Fortunately, rhythm is one of the easiest things to achieve in garden design. At the bottom line, it is possible to improve a border simply by buying a few small but distinctive plants, preferably evergreens (lavenders, for instance) and sticking them in at intervals, regularly or otherwise. The results can be quite transforming, as the border now has a trademark. To take things further, a particular grouping can be repeated a few times. To the lavender could be added the more-or-less evergreen bronze-leaved perennial *Heuchera micrantha*

ACHIEVING RHYTHM AND UNITY

The same border has been given structure by the planting of lavender and clipped box.

This informal perennial border may be very attractive, but it lacks a sense of unity.

A distinctive grass (*Calamagrostis* × *acutiflora* 'Karl Foerster') and a few repeated plants (*Rudbeckia fulgida* var. *sullivantii* 'Goldsturm' and *Aster cordifolius* 'Little Carlow') give a sense of unity to a double border in late summer.

A planting of low-growing heathers, dwarf conifers and New Zealand sedges is provided with a unifying element in the upright *Juniperus scopulorum* 'Skyrocket'.

'Palace Purple', perhaps with a long-flowering plant like *Geranium endressii*; the result will then be more powerful still.

Traditional formal gardens have a powerful sense of rhythm because of their subordination to the discipline of mathematical order. Yet even a fairly wild cottage garden can have its own formal element, which will give it a tremendous sense of structure and remind visitors that you did indeed plan the garden. A few small box shrubs, clipped into shape over a period of two to three years, will work wonders.

A garden composed of a number of disparate features can also be given unity by the repetition of one element – a particular plant for instance – which can then become a motif for your garden. To work effectively, this motif plant must be noticeable at all times; in other words, it should be evergreen or have a very strong and instantly recognizable form, and should not take up too much space or be too dominating visually. A very narrow cypress is a superb plant for this, taking up little space but being instantly recognizable. Other possibilities are the small, mound-forming Japanese maples such as *Acer palmatum* var. *dissectum*, which would be very suitable for woodland gardens, and hellebores, whose hand-shaped evergreen leaves always stand out.

A strong point of the modern continental style, which uses massed perennials and grasses, is its element of repetition, of achieving a powerful effect through using relatively few elements. Architectural plants, and especially grasses, play an important part in this, their height and distinctive form linking the whole planting, and indeed the whole of the garden if they are more widely planted.

We tend to think of our gardens in isolation, and yet they could contribute much more to the local environment if they were visually much more involved with it. The planting of a distinctive tree found locally will integrate the garden into the wider landscape, as does the planting of locally native species in country areas. Whole neighbourhoods could be given their own individual character if people carried out coordinated tree planting.

Chapter Eight

PRACTICALITIES

FOR THOSE WHO LOVE PLANTS and gardens, the most difficult part of the planning process can be working out what not to have! The true lover of plants will probably buy whatever they want regardless of how it fits in artistically with the rest of the garden, whereas the true artist will buy only what will suit the overall design. Most of us lie somewhere in between.

PLANNING CHECKLISTS

I find it useful to break down the decision-making process into several steps:

1 Make a list of plants that will thrive (or at least not be unhappy) in the given conditions; alternatively, it may be easier to do this the other way round by making a list of what to avoid.

2 Make a list of those plants that you feel are so exceptional that you absolutely must have them.

3 Choose some sort of overall scheme for the new planting, be it based on colour, foliage, ambience or some other factor, then check whether the plants you selected in step 2 are compatible with this. If not, you must either change the scheme or decide which of the 'musts' are not so essential after all; or you could decide to throw artistic principles to the wind and plant them anyway! As long as you adhere to basic horticultural principles so as to ensure plant health, then what may start out as a rather odd and incompatible mixture can turn out to be an idiosyncratic but successful scheme.

It is better to plant what you like with the courage of your own convictions than to feel constrained by what other people present as rules or 'good advice'.

4 Having decided on a basic scheme, you now need to select plants that will contribute to the scheme and that you like. This can then be treated as a shortlist.

5 Given that there will be less space for large plants such as trees, shrubs and climbers, it is advisable to select these first. With the help of a plan if necessary, decide how much space you have for them and where they are to go. It is also a good idea to consider what is going to give structure to the theme – shrubs only, or some architectural perennials and grasses as well.

Hellebores and crocus have been chosen for this site, as few other plants will flower beneath trees.

ACHIEVING A SEASONAL SPREAD

Listing the plant varieties for a planting and then charting their season of interest with coloured pens enables you to see at a glance whether there are any gaps in the year and to assess colour combinations for different seasons. Green indicates foliage interest.

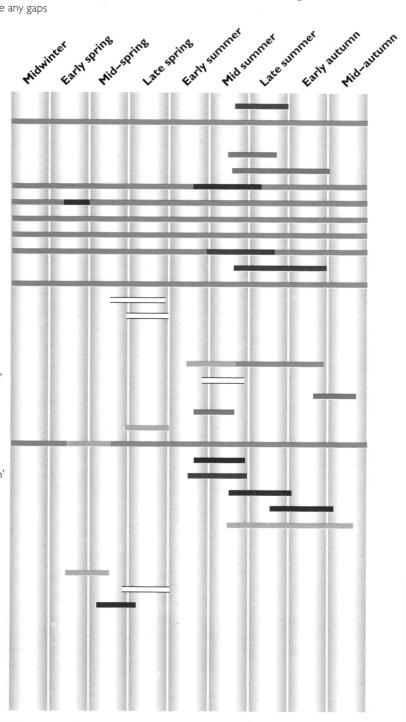

Shrubs

Buddleia davidii 'Black Knight'
Buxus sempervirens
Caryopteris × clandonensis 'Heavenly Blue'
Ceratostigma plumbaginoides
Cistus 'Silver Pink'
Erica carnea varieties
Hebe 'Red Edge'
Ilex aquifolium 'Argentea Marginata'
Lavandula 'Hidcote'
Perovskia atriplicifolia
Salvia officinalis
Spiraea nipponica 'Snowmound'
Viburnum × burkwoodii

Perennials

Alchemilla mollis
Anaphalis triplinervis 'Sommerschnee'
Aster cordifolius
Campanula persicifolia
Euphorbia polychroma
Euphorbia characias
Lychnis coronaria
Nepeta 'Souvenir d'André Chaudron'
Phygelius capensis 'Coccineus'
Sedum spectabile
Stipa gigantea

Bulbs

Crocus chrysanthus varieties
Narcissus 'Mount Hood'
Tulipa kaufmanniana varieties

Midwinter   Early spring   Mid–spring   Late spring   Early summer   Mid summer   Late summer   Early autumn   Mid–autumn

DRAWING PLANTING PLANS

This section of a planting plan for a courtyard garden shows how plants can be represented diagrammatically using symbols. The circumference of each circle should be to scale, so that the spread of plants can be illustrated exactly.

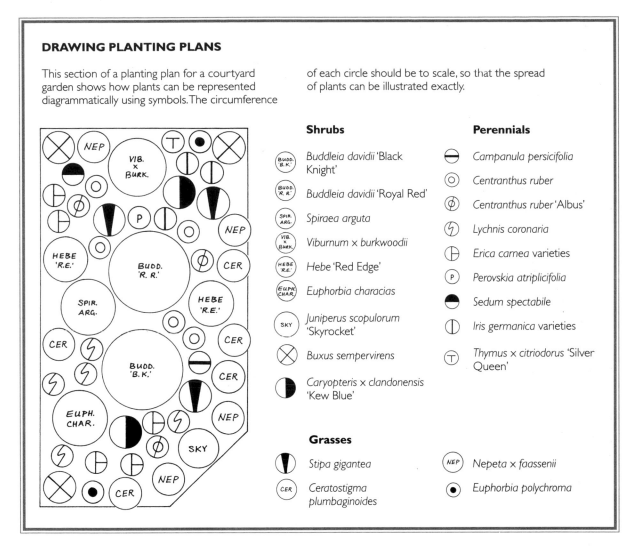

Shrubs

- (BUDD. 'B.K.') *Buddleia davidii* 'Black Knight'
- (BUDD. 'R.R.') *Buddleia davidii* 'Royal Red'
- (SPIR. ARG.) *Spiraea arguta*
- (VIB. x BURK.) *Viburnum x burkwoodii*
- (HEBE 'R.E.') *Hebe* 'Red Edge'
- (EUPH. CHAR.) *Euphorbia characias*
- (SKY) *Juniperus scopulorum* 'Skyrocket'
- ⊗ *Buxus sempervirens*
- ◖ *Caryopteris x clandonensis* 'Kew Blue'

Grasses

- ◣ *Stipa gigantea*
- (CER) *Ceratostigma plumbaginoides*

Perennials

- ⊖ *Campanula persicifolia*
- ⊙ *Centranthus ruber*
- ⊘ *Centranthus ruber* 'Albus'
- ⟰ *Lychnis coronaria*
- ⊞ *Erica carnea* varieties
- (P) *Perovskia atriplicifolia*
- ◐ *Sedum spectabile*
- ◫ *Iris germanica* varieties
- (T) *Thymus x citriodorus* 'Silver Queen'
- (NEP) *Nepeta x faassenii*
- ⦿ *Euphorbia polychroma*

6 Before proceeding with the selection of smaller plants such as bulbs, perennials and annuals, you should check on the seasonal spread of interest that your list of plants will cover. The table opposite illustrates how this can be done. If you make a similar table, you will be able to see at a glance how good your seasonal spread is going to be. Are any times of the year a bit bare? In winter this is only to be expected, but there is no excuse for a dull border in the middle of summer. On the other hand, you may have masses for early summer and little for later on. If you want a good seasonal spread, some of the earlier plants will have to go and others will need to be chosen for flowering later in the year. Remember that gaps in spring are easy to fill by planting bulbs around the bases of dormant herbaceous plants or leafless shrubs. Making a plan of your planting scheme (see above) is a great help, though by no means essential.

PLANTING PLANS

Not everyone is good with paper, pencil and ruler, but a plan drawn to scale is a great help in working out successful plantings. Once made, the plan does not have to be regarded as being cast in concrete and everyone, especially the world's great garden designers, makes lots of changes when it comes to the actual planting, if only because reality always looks different from any mental image.

Using a plan to decide on the format of a planting should involve the following steps:

1 Decide on the position of the major structural

A subtle yellow-pink combination of Allium aflatunense, Robinia
pseudoacacia *'Frisia' and forget-me-nots is the result of careful planning.*

elements – the shrubs, topiary, large grasses, climbers on pillars and sculpture or other ornaments. If you are repeating a structural element, consider whether you want to use it to create rhythm, in which case its distribution over the planting should be fairly even. It is helpful to regard these elements as the skeleton of the planting, with the rest built around them, although this does not mean that their position cannot be changed later on. Remember that tall, bulky plants will hide whatever is planted behind them. If you are planting a border with a backdrop, such as a fence, hedge or wall, these plants should be at the rear; if you are planting an island bed, they should be in the centre.

2 Now consider which plants or plant combinations are going to be the 'theme plants' for each season, the ones that will be visually dominant; for example, you may have some particularly powerful colour combinations that you want to include.

These can be put on the plan now; consider repeating them once or twice if there is space, to build up a good rhythm. It is a good idea to have seasonal interest well distributed through a planting rather than clumped unevenly

3 Now think about which plants are going to combine well with the theme plants and provide interest later in the year. Try to surround the theme plants with others that have compatible flowering seasons, but which will also look good at another time of year. Think, too, of how a plant in flower can be enhanced not only by the presence of other plants in their full glory around it, but also by the attractive foliage of something else nearby that has yet to flower. For example, the blotched leaves of *Geranium* x *monacense*, which used to be known as *Geranium punctatum*, are an attractive sight next to daffodils and bluebells.

4 By now much of the plan should be complete,

with only a few gaps left to fill. This is a good time to go back and check that all criteria are being fulfilled:

• Do you have a good seasonal spread, well distributed across the planting?

• Do you have a good spread of structural elements?

• Are the theme plants well distributed?

• Are there any plants next to each other that are going to look dreadful together?

• Does the spread of plants create a sense of rhythm through the planting?

• Are there discrepancies of height which may make it difficult to see parts of the planting?

5 Having made any changes necessary in answer to the questions raised above, it is time to consider gap filling. One good way of doing this is to put in some more of a plant already used in limited numbers, thus adding to the sense of unity; another is to fill the scheme with new plants that boost interest at the time of year when the planting will be at its weakest. Bulbs and small spring plants can be fitted in around larger ones, and can often be added last. It may also be an idea to leave some deliberate gaps, filling them in temporarily with annuals. These spaces can be kept for impulse buys, plants you have not yet been able to get hold of and for gift plants (in my experience, the latter never fit in with even the most flexible scheme, but that is life).

HOW MANY TO PLANT?

Having decided on which plants to acquire and how to arrange them next to each other, the final question before heading for the garden centre or nursery is 'how many?'. This is obviously not a difficult question to answer with single trees or shrubs, but it is an important one when planting massed shrubs, perennials or bulbs.

Many garden reference books give a plant's size in terms of its height and spread. The 'spread' figure can be used as a basis for how far apart to plant – remember that the figure represents the diameter of a circle with the plant in the centre;

ideally, the circles of neighbouring plants should touch but not overlap. The problem is that this figure represents the size of the plant at maturity, and in the case of a shrub it can take an awfully long time to reach this. The decision has to be taken whether to 'overplant' – that is, to plant more than is necessary, and then to thin out in future years – or to surround your shrubs with perennials as a temporary gap-filling measure (but at a distance of at least 50cm (20in) from the base). As the shrubs grow they will tend to crowd out the perennials anyway, and these can then be removed and used elsewhere in the garden.

When planting perennials, leaving gaps is not such a problem, and most will grow to maturity in two to three years. The plants can be packed in more tightly, or the gaps can be filled with hardy annuals, such as love-in-the-mist (*Nigella damascena*) or poppies. If the tight-planting option is taken, then some thinning out will be essential in three to four years if the plants are not to suffer from overcrowding, which can shorten the life of perennials.

Cost is a major factor in deciding how many plants to purchase for major plantings; areas that will be covered with ground-cover plants, for example, can work out very expensive. With species that establish quickly and are easily divided, such as geraniums or periwinkles you can buy a limited number and plant them far apart, covering the ground in between with a mulch. After a year the original plants can be split, and the divisions planted out over the whole area.

The planting of bulbs follows the same rules as for perennials, although if planted at the figure given for 'spread', the results can look rather sparse for several years; a more established look will be achieved if the bulbs are bunched in tighter clumps. The clumps should be not be too close together or they will become overcrowded in a matter of only a few years. In any case, after five years or so clumps of vigorous bulbs, like snowdrops, crocuses and narcissi, will need to be dug up and divided.

DIVIDING PERENNIALS

Many perennials make good ground-cover plants, although the cost of large-scale plantings can be prohibitive. A little patience can result in substantial savings: starter stock can be bought and then

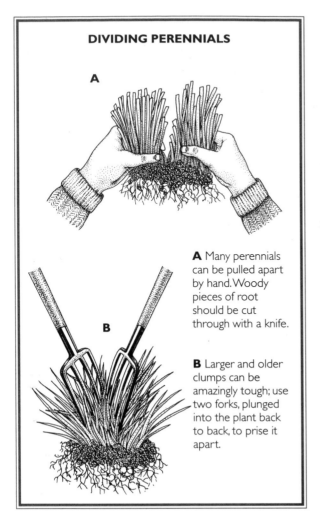

DIVIDING PERENNIALS

A

B

A Many perennials can be pulled apart by hand. Woody pieces of root should be cut through with a knife.

B Larger and older clumps can be amazingly tough; use two forks, plunged into the plant back to back, to prise it apart.

split into a good number of divisions after only a year or two in the ground. These plants can be divided into a greater number of small divisions or a lesser number of larger ones, depending on the condition of the area to be planted.

The key to dividing plants is to produce the maximum number of pieces that will make viable plants: anything with a shoot and a few roots will do. If the planting area is free from weeds and is unlikely to dry out, then it is practicable to use a large number of small divisions. A planting area less conducive to good growth should receive a smaller number of larger, more viable divisions.

The vast Gunnera manicata *is not something of which you buy a dozen! The smaller* Darmera peltata *and hosta may be, especially if you want quick results.*

A POND FOR WILDLIFE

Even a small pond in the city will attract aquatic insects and probably frogs, appearing as if out of nowhere and illustrating just how important ponds are as part of a strategy for turning a garden into a mini-nature reserve.

The planting around a wildlife pond must reflect the local flora, as many insect species are very specialized feeders. Most of the species illustrated here are from northwestern Europe and a few from North America, with an emphasis on those that can provide for a wide range of wildlife.

Inevitably, given that the needs of people and wildlife are different, the planting will be less colourful than for a strictly ornamental pond, but this should be made up for by the increased interest engendered by visiting birds, insects and amphibians.

With a wildlife pond it is important that there are areas of fairly dense vegetation right down to the water's edge and others where there is just a shallow grass slope, such diversity providing options for the needs of different animals.

MAINTENANCE – *Low*

As with any other pond, dead vegetation will need to be cleared out every year, but this should not be too rigorous, as seedheads will feed the birds and dead vegetation will often shelter insect populations during their hibernation period. Vigorous species can sometimes oust less vigorous ones, in which case some thinning out will be needed. This is most conveniently done in late spring (for one thing, the water is not so cold!).

SITE AND SEASON

The pond will need sunlight for most of the day, although a little shade over one end of it is very beneficial for many aquatic animal species during hot weather. Any reasonably fertile, moisture-holding soil will be suitable.

The main flowering will be in late summer.

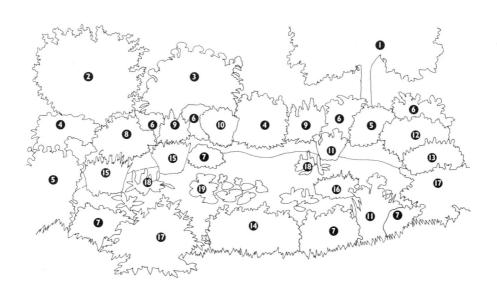

Shrubs

1 *Betula nigra*
2 *Amelanchier lamarckii*

Perennials

3 *Eupatorium purpureum*
4 *Eupatorium cannabinum*
5 *Sanguisorba officinalis*
6 *Filipendula ulmaria*
7 *Mentha aquatica*
8 *Hibiscus moscheutos*

9 *Lobelia cardinalis*
10 *Lythrum salicaria*
11 *Butomus umbellatus*
12 *Lysimachia vulgaris*
13 *Stachys palustris*
14 *Veronica beccabunga*

Grasses

15 *Typha minima*
16 *Schoenoplectus lacustris*
ssp. *tabernaemontani*

Ferns

17 *Osmunda regalis*

Aquatics

18 *Potamogeton nutans*
19 *Nymphoides aquatica*

A PRAIRIE GARDEN

THE AMERICAN PRAIRIE can be likened to a wildflower meadow on a huge scale, with an enormous and colourful variety of plant life, much of it majestic in scale, with some of the grasses and wildflowers growing to more than 2m (6ft) tall. Prairie gardens have been increasing in popularity, and not just in North America, because – like wildflower meadows – they require little maintenance once they are established. The vigour of prairie plants makes them especially suitable for areas where the soil is very fertile, because they can resist the encroachment of the strong-growing grasses that tend to make growing wildflowers difficult on these soils.

Prairie gardens are very wildlife friendly, providing good cover and a rich food resource for a wide variety of insects, birds and mammals. Late summer and early autumn are when prairie wildflowers are at their most colourful and most attractive to butterflies. If uncut, the seedheads of the grasses and perennials will help to feed birds throughout the winter.

MAINTENANCE – *Low to very low*

Once established, a prairie garden needs only an annual cut back, preferably in late winter, although if tidiness is important this can be done in late autumn. Over time, some species may come to dominate, in which case the more aggressive ones can be thinned out.

SITE AND SEASON

This garden requires full sun and any reasonably well-drained, fertile soil. It is especially suitable for rich terrain.

Late summer is the main flowering season, although a good mix of prairie wildflowers will provide colour from spring until late autumn.

Perennials

1 *Asclepias tuberosa*
2 *Baptisia leucantha*
3 *Desmodium canadense*
4 *Liatris aspera*
5 *Helianthus* × *laetiflorus*
6 *Ratabida pinnata*
7 *Rudbeckia subtomentosa*
8 *Silphium laciniatum*
9 *Solidago speciosa*
10 *Veronicastrum virginicum*
11 *Eupatorium purpureum*
ssp. *maculatum*
12 *Vernonia fasciculata*
13 *Euphorbia corollata*
14 *Filipendula rubra*
15 *Rudbeckia hirta*
16 *Eryngium yuccifolium*

Grasses

17 *Andropogon gerardii*
18 *Panicum virgatum*
19 *Sorghastrum nutans*
20 *Sporobolus heterolepis*

THREE WINDOWBOXES

WINDOWBOXES CAN MAKE all the difference to a house, whether you have a garden or not. Plants will need to be chosen carefully for the aspect: a sunny windowsill is ideal for a traditional mix of pelargoniums and annuals, but shade-tolerant alpines and ferns would be more appropriate for a window that receives no sun. Civic pride often demands a spectacular summer display of pelargoniums and other summer flowers, but this is quite hard work, as frequent watering and feeding are vital for success. Alpines are especially suitable for windowboxes, because of their small size and tolerance of climatic extremes; many also flower in early spring or even late winter. Using alpines and dwarf bulbs can mean that a windowbox is more or less permanent, as they will not outgrow the container for many years. Heathers and small hebes are also deservedly popular as permanent plantings, but need to be kept carefully pruned every year or they will begin to look straggly. If clipping is no problem, then the adventurous might even want to try their hand with a little miniature topiary; the dwarf box, *Buxus sempervirens* 'Suffruticosa' is ideal.

MAINENANCE – *Medium*

Like all containers, windowboxes need daily watering in dry conditions. Permanently planted boxes should be fed regularly throughout the growing season, and this is best done through the application of a slow-release fertilizer in spring. Summer windowboxes planted with annuals and half-hardy perennials benefit from generous and regular feeding; these are greedy plants and there will probably not be enough nutrients in the compost to keep them in good condition all summer. Dwarf shrubs like heathers should be cut back after flowering, but alpines require very little care.

SITE AND SEASON

Scheme 1 needs a well-drained, low-lime compost, scheme 2 a high-nutrient compost, and scheme 3 a gritty but not especially rich mixture.

Sun is required for most of the day for schemes 1 and 2. Scheme 3 should receive sun for no more than half the day.

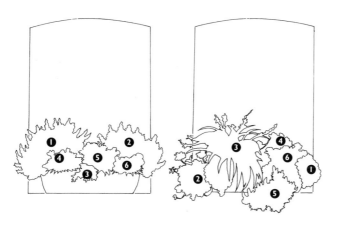
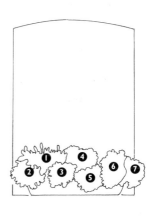

1 PERMANENT, SHOWN IN EARLY SPRING

Dwarf shrubs
1 *Calluna vulgaris* 'Aurea'
2 *Erica carnea* 'Springwood Pink'

Perennials
3 *Dianthus* 'Little Jock'

Bulbs
4 *Crocus chrysanthus* 'E.A. Bowles'
5 *Galanthus nivalis*
6 *Crocus chrysanthus* 'Blue Pearl'

2 SEASONAL, SHOWN IN SUMMER

Annual
1 *Lobularia maritima* 'Little Dorrit'

Half-hardy
2 *Pelargonium* 'Balcon Rouge'
3 *Chlorophytum comosum* 'Vittatum'
4 *Pelargonium* 'Balcon Rose'
5 *Lotus berthelotii*
6 *Nierembergia caerulea*

3 PERMANENT/ALPINE, SHOWN IN EARLY SPRING

Dwarf shrub
1 *Salix reticulata*

Perennials
2 *Campanula* 'Joe Elliott'
3 *Saxifraga* 'Jenkinsiae'
4 *Saxifraga* × *apiculata*
5 *Asperula suberosa*
6 *Saxifraga oppositifolia*
7 *Armeria juniperifolia*

FLOWERS AND FOLIAGE FOR WETLAND

THIS PLANTING is for an area of badly drained land, where low maintenance is a priority and vigorous perennials that can look after themselves are needed. It is designed to make the most of plants with attractive foliage as well as flowers.

Petasites is one of the largest leaved of all perennials, and looks magnificently exotic, as will the macleaya once it has had a chance to get established. They and the spartina are best used as background for the smaller and more colourful astilbes and primulas. Both of these plants are available in a great many colours and varieties, and on damp ground where there is no competition they will spread to form sizable clumps. The bulb camassia naturalizes easily, seeding itself around, and the ferns will naturalize too, although the blechnum is suitable only for areas that do not experience hard winters. It should be noted that the petasites and spartina are very invasive – ideal for the larger garden, but perhaps not so welcome in smaller ones!

MAINTENANCE – *Low to very low*

This is designed as a low-maintenance planting, with robust varieties that will spread with little intervention. However, it is important that the site is as weed free as possible before planting, and that it is kept this way during the first two years as the plants become established. Routine maintenance is restricted to an annual end-of-year clear-up of dead growth, but even this is not strictly necessary. In colder areas where the blechnum fern is not evergreen, it will appreciate a covering of straw or similar material as protection against hard frosts.

SITE AND SEASON

Midsummer, with flowering of many plants until early autumn and a long season of foliage interest.

Partial shade suits the majority of these plants best, full sun is suitable so long as the soil remains moist through the summer. The soil needs to be reasonably fertile.

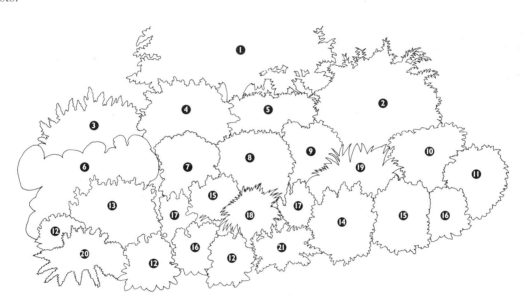

Trees

1 *Pterocarya fraxinifolia*
2 *Salix alba vitellina* 'Britzensis'

Shrubs

3 *Clethra alnifolia* 'Paniculata'
4 *Sorbaria arborea*
5 *Salix exigua*

Perennials

6 *Petasites japonicus* var. *giganteus*

7 *Thalictrum delavayi*
8 *Macleaya cordata*
9 *Filipendula purpurea*
10 *Aruncus dioicus* 'Kneiffii'
11 *Astilbe* 'Straussenfeder'
12 *Primula pulverulenta*
13 *Astilbe* 'Venus'
14 *Astilbe* 'Irrlicht'
15 *Astilbe* 'Fanal'
16 *Primula japonica* 'Postford White'

Bulbs

17 *Camassia esculenta*

Grasses

18 *Carex elata* 'Aurea'
19 *Spartina pectinata* 'Aureomarginata'

Ferns

20 *Blechnum chilense*
21 *Onoclea sensibilis*

A PLANTING FOR SPRING

FLOWERS ARE PERHAPS more important in spring than at any other time of year, for after the winter is when we appreciate them most, particularly when they are close to the house. This site is on the side of the house, where it receives light for half the day or less and there is little space for planting.

The narrow beds contain a selection of spring-flowering, shade-tolerant perennials, such as lily-of-the-valley (*Convallaria majalis*), and bulbs, plus tall plants like a bamboo and an early-flowering mahonia, to make the best use of the limited space. A small bed has been made in the middle of the paved area for spring-flowering shrubs and perennials, and pots of daffodils have been brought in for extra colour.

Shade-tolerant climbers are also included, all self-clinging varieties apart from the honeysuckle (*Lonicera japonica* 'Halliana') on the left, which clambers over a trellis concealing an oil tank.

MAINTENANCE – *Low*

Nearly all these plants require little maintenance, an annual clear-up of dead stems and leaves being all that is needed. The daffodils in pots are best planted out in the open ground when they have finished, and new bulbs bought for the following year's display. The camellia in a tub should be fed regularly throughout the growing season, and never allowed to dry out. During the winter, the container must be surronded with bubble plastic to prevent the roots from freezing.

SITE AND SEASON

This planting requires sun for only a few hours a day. Any reasonably fertile and well-drained soil is suitable – the soil around buildings is often full of rubble, which may mean that annual manuring and feeding is necessary in order to provide good growing conditions.

The main flowering is in mid-spring. Although there will be few flowers for the rest of the year, the foliage of all these plants is attractive in its own right. Annuals and half-hardy plants in containers could be brought in for the summer and stood in the lighter areas.

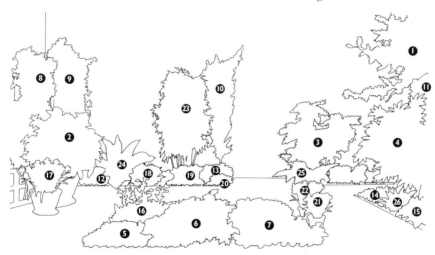

Trees
1 *Prunus* 'Pandora'

Shrubs
2 *Camellia* 'Anticipation'
3 *Mahonia* × *media* 'Charity'
4 *Fatsia japonica*
5 *Daphne* × *burkwoodii*
6 *Mahonia aquifolium*
7 *Rhododendron williamsianum*

Climbers
8 *Lonicera japonica* 'Halliana'
9 *Parthenocissus henryana*
10 *Hedera helix* 'Sagittifolia Variegata'

11 *Hedera canariensis* 'Variegata'

Perennials
12 *Brunnera macrophylla* 'Dawson's White'
13 *Pulmonaria saccharata* 'Leopard'
14 *Epimedium* × *rubrum*
15 *Convallaria majalis*
16 *Symphytum* × *uplandicum* 'Variegatum'

Bulbs
17 *Narcissus* 'Mount Hood'
18 *Narcissus* 'Portrush'
19 *Hyacinthoides hispanica*

20 *Cyclamen repandum*
21 *Narcissus* 'Actaea'
22 *Narcissus* 'Golden Harvest'

Grasses
23 *Phyllostachys nigra*

Ferns
24 *Polystichum munitum*
25 *Polystichum setiferum* 'Divisilobum Densum'
26 *Asplenium scolopendrium*

A PLANTING FOR AUTUMN

AUTUMN HAS TREMENDOUS potential, not just for the reds and yellows of trees and the wide range of colours that berries offer, but also for the number of flowers that are at their best at this time. It is difficult to fit many trees into a small garden, but there a several shrubs that are just as colourful, together with a number of climbers. The most valuable are those, like the amelanchier, sorbus and euonymus used here, which combine attractive fruit with good leaf colour.

The larger autumn flowers are nearly all members of the daisy family. The violet, purple and blue shades come from the asters, the yellow from *Solidago* 'Crown of Rays'. The best way to grow these plants is to mix them in with spring- and summer-flowering shrubs and perennials, so that they are not particularly noticeable until they flower. There are certain bulbs that bloom now: cyclamen will flourish in difficult places, such as deep shade in dry soil under trees, while colchicums make bold splashes of pink in borders or rough grass. Ornamental grasses are another special autumn feature, with the advantage that they will carry on looking good until well into the winter. Low winter light and hoar frost show them off to their best.

MAINTENANCE – *Low to Medium*

Most of these plants require little care and attention. The herbaceous flowering varieties can be cut down at any time from early to late winter, but the grasses are sufficiently ornamental to make them worth keeping until later on. Many of these grasses and late-flowering plants produce seed that helps feed bird populations through the winter, which is another reason to delay cutting back. The late-flowering members of the daisy family appreciate a good, fertile soil, so a mulch of well-rotted manure or garden compost is a good idea in spring, especially on poorer soils. The asters here require little maintenance, but will benefit from dividing and replanting every few years.

SITE AND SEASON

Any reasonably fertile, well-drained soil is suitable for this scheme. Choose a site that receives sun for most of the day.

The flowering season is from late summer to early winter, although autumn colour and flowers do depend a lot on the weather. Late flowering perennials are easy to combine with earlier flowering species and bulbs. Since they tend to look a bit untidy after flowering, put them behind the late flowering plants and grasses which, as they grow neatly through the summer, will help to hide them.

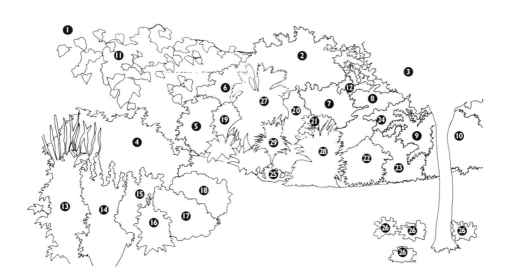

Trees
1 *Quercus coccinea* 'Splendens'
2 *Amelanchier canadensis*
3 *Malus tschonoskii*

Shrubs
4 *Acer palmatum* 'Osakazuki'
5 *Euonymus europaeus* 'Red Cascade'
6 *Sorbus vilmorinii*
7 *Pyracantha* 'Orange Glow'
8 *Cotoneaster horizontalis*

9 *Fuchsia magellanica* 'Riccartonii'
10 *Acer palmatum* var. *dissectum*

Climbers
11 *Vitis coignetiae*
12 *Parthenocissus quinquefolia*

Perennials
13 *Cimicifuga racemosa*
14 *Aconitum carmichaelii*
15 *Eupatorium rugosum*

16 *Serratula tinctoria*
17 *Aster × frikartii* 'Mönch'
18 *Aster ericoides* 'Blue Star'
19 *Vernonia crinita*
20 *Leucanthemum serotinum*
21 *Aster cordifolius* 'Little Carlow'
22 *Aster amellus* 'King George'
23 *Solidago* 'Crown of Rays'
24 *Aster* 'Climax'

Bulbs
25 *Colchicum agrippinum*
26 *Cyclamen hederifolium*

Grasses
27 *Miscanthus sinensis* 'Silberfeder'
28 *Panicum virgatum*
29 *Molinia caerulea* 'Variegata'

A WHITE BORDER

VITA SACKVILLE-WEST certainly started a fashion with her white garden at Sissinghurst. The great thing about white is its coolness, and the feeling of calm repose that it generates. As for choosing the plants, the task is relatively easy as so many coloured species have a white form (*alba* in Latin), although you will soon find that many so-called 'white' flowers (like 'white' walls) are really cream or very pale something else. I have restricted the selection here largely to pure whites, and the variegated and grey-leaved plants that combine so well with them.

Given the choice of plants, it is possible to create white gardens in a variety of different soils and situations, so this is a very flexible colour scheme. There should be no problems, either, in finding plants to keep the scheme going until autumn.

MAINTENANCE – *Medium to low*

The majority of these are easy and vigorous plants, so little maintenance is required, except for the usual autumn clear-up and perhaps a mulching with well-rotted manure or garden compost. With the exception of the shrub roses, which must be pruned in late winter, the shrubs should be pruned after flowering if they need it.

SITE AND SEASON

Any reasonably fertile soil and a site that receives sun for most of the day will be suitable.

The main flowering season is midsummer, although there are so many white flowers available that there is no problem extending the season. Bulbs, such as snowdrops and ivory-white daffodils, are especially easy to interplant between the shrubs and perennials. White asters and other daisy relatives can be planted for autumn.

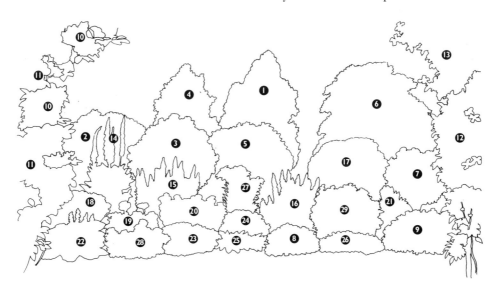

Trees
1 *Eucryphia* × *nymansensis* 'Nymansay'

Shrubs
2 *Rubus* 'Benenden'
3 *Rosa* 'Boule de Neige'
4 *Abutilon vitifolium* var. *album*
5 *Choisya ternata*
6 *Cornus alternifolia* 'Variegata'
7 *Rosa* 'Iceberg'
8 *Hebe pinguifolia* 'Pagei'
9 *Cistus corbariensis*

Climbers
10 *Solanum jasminoides* 'Album'

11 *Rosa* 'Long John Silver'
12 *Jasminum officinale*
13 *Clematis* 'Alba Luxurians'

Perennials
14 *Digitalis purpurea* f. *albiflorum*
15 *Epilobium angustifolium album*
16 *Dictamnus albus*
17 *Crambe cordifolia*
18 *Achillea ptarmica* 'The Pearl'
19 *Papaver orientale* 'Perry's White'
20 *Anaphalis margaritacea*
21 *Libertia grandiflora*
22 *Hosta sieboldiana*

23 *Geranium clarkei* 'Kashmir White'
24 *Geranium renardii*
25 *Pulmonaria officinalis* 'Sissinghurst White'
26 *Lamium maculatum* 'White Nancy'

Bulbs
27 *Lilium* 'Sterling Silver'

Half-hardy
28 *Osteospermum* 'Whirligig'
29 *Argyranthemum frutescens*

A PASTEL BORDER

IDEAL FOR CLIMATES with grey skies, where every subtle nuance of tint and hue can be appreciated, and also for those gardeners new to border planning, it is almost impossible to go wrong with pastel combinations. There is a huge variety of plants with flowers in shades of blue, mauve and pink, and plenty too of the silver- and purple-leaved species that set them off so well. A limited number of pale yellow flowers can also be blended in; deep yellow and orange would destroy the effect of romantic softness.One or two scarlet flowers are possibly permissible, but dark crimson fits in better. Many of these flowers are fragrant, especially the roses. Old-fashioned and shrub roses are the most appropriate for this kind of planting, their flowers coming in a huge variety of shades of pink, setting the tone for the rest of the border.

Given the large number of plants that may be fitted into this colour scheme, there is no shortage of varieties that can carry it through the summer until early autumn.

MAINTENANCE – Medium to low

As it consists mainly of robust perennials and shrubs, this border requires little care. The roses are not the kind that need annual pruning, but if they begin to get untidy or too large they should be pruned in late winter. The other shrubs should be pruned after flowering. The lavatera is notorious for becoming very big very quickly, so make sure it is given plenty of space and be prepared to cut it back, preferably in late winter.

An annual tidy-up will be needed in autumn, and a mulch with well-rotted manure or garden compost will help maintain fertility, especially if the soil is at all poor. The roses and peony will certainly appreciate this

SITE AND SEASON

This scheme is suitable for any reasonably fertile soil that receives sun for most of the day.

The main period of flower is in early summer.

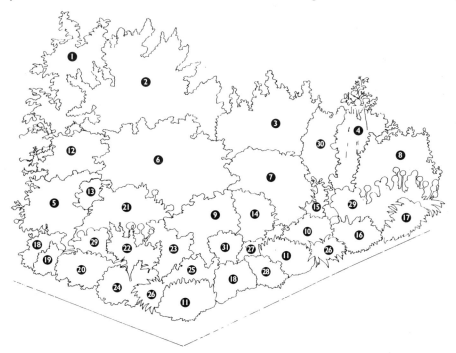

Trees
1 *Prunus* 'Spire'
2 *Cercis siliquastrum*

Shrubs
3 *Lavatera* 'Barnsley'
4 *Rosa* 'Reine Victoria'
5 *Rosa* 'Souvenir de la Malmaison'
6 *Ceanothus impressus*
7 *Syringa microphylla* 'Superba'
8 *Cotinus coggygria* 'Royal Purple'
9 *Cistus ladanifer*

10 *Rosa* 'The Fairy'
11 *Lavandula angustifolia* 'Munstead'

Climbers
12 *Clematis montana* 'Elizabeth'

Perennials
13 *Thalictrum aquilegifolium*
14 *Hesperis matronalis*
15 *Symphytum* × *uplandicum*
16 *Dicentra* 'Boothman's Variety'
17 *Polemonium folio-sissimum*

18 *Geranium* 'Johnson's Blue'
19 *Lamium maculatum album*
20 *Geranium* × *oxonianum* 'Wargrave Pink'
21 *Paeonia lactiflora* 'Sarah Bernhardt'
22 *Campanula persicifolia*
23 *Anthemis tinctoria* 'E.C. Buxton'
24 *Alchemilla alpina*
25 *Campanula* 'Burghaltii'
26 *Ophiopogon planiscapus* 'Nigrescens'
27 *Artemisia ludoviciana*
28 *Dianthus* 'Doris'

Bulbs
29 *Allium aflatunense*

Annuals/biennials
30 *Lathyrus odoratus* 'Selana'

Half-hardy
31 *Argyranthemum* 'Mary Wootton'

A HOT BORDER

REDS AND YELLOWS are not colours for the fainthearted or those unsure of their skill at combining different shades. These are not relaxing colours, and they can be overpowering in a small garden. For those brave enough to try their hand, however, the results can glow magnificently.

Too much red can be quite oppressive, and too much bright yellow harsh and glaring. The trick is to mix them, so that they flicker together in a multiplicity of shades, and to be aware of the possibilities offered by dark purple and yellow foliage, and by good fresh greens that will complement the scarlet.

When selecting plants you will find that a lot of the best reds are half-hardy – many salvias, pelargoniums and cupheas (the cigar plant), for example – but they make up for this by being very long flowering, and flowering towards the end of the season, which many gardeners find a difficult time to make interesting. The exotic aspects of 'hot' planting should be played up, perhaps with some large foliage plants, like the castor oil plant, *Ricinus communis.* Such a planting is an exciting alternative to the traditional bedding that is often the mainstay of late summer. Hot-coloured flowers are not generally noted for their fragrance, but *Salvia rutilans* has wonderfully scented leaves.

MAINTENANCE – *Medium*

The dahlia, cuphea and chrysanthemum are definitely half-hardy and will need to be lifted and taken inside for the winter in most areas. The cuphea and chrysanthemum should be kept in a greenhouse or on a light windowsill, but the dahlias die back to convenient tubers. The salvia and erythrina are tender, but will survive the winter outside if the roots are well insulated. The annual perilla has to be started off indoors from seed, but the nasturtium (*Tropaeolum majus*) can be sown where it is to flower. The herbaceous plants will simply need their dead stems cut back in late autumn.

SITE AND SEASON

This border needs a sheltered corner which receives sun nearly all day, but with the right-hand side in sun for only half the day. Any reasonably fertile soil will be suitable.

The main flowering is in late summer, with many varieties looking good until well into the autumn. The main red and yellow season may be late summer, but there is not too much problem in extending it. Spring is easy, with all those yellow daffodils, tulips and polyanthus in almost any strong colour you want.

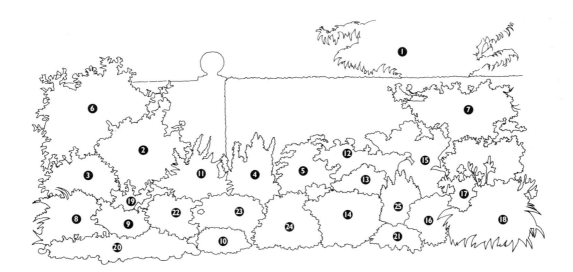

Trees
1 *Eucalyptus gunnii*

Shrubs
2 *Fremontodendron californicum*
3 *Euonymus japonicus* 'Aureopictus'
4 *Phygelius capensis coccineus*
5 *Berberis thunbergii* f. *atropurpurea*

Climbers
6 *Campsis* × *tagliabuana* 'Madame Galen'
7 *Tropaeolum speciosum*

Perennials
8 *Crocosmia* 'Lucifer'
9 *Oenothera fruticosa* 'Fireworks'
10 *Potentilla atrosanguinea*
11 *Erythrina crista-galli*
12 *Helenium* 'Wyndley'
13 *Monarda* 'Squaw'

14 *Coreopsis verticillata*
15 *Ligularia dentata* 'Desdemona'
16 *Rudbeckia fulgida* 'Goldsturm'
17 *Hemerocallis* 'Stafford'
18 *Hemerocallis* 'Golden Chimes'

Bulbs
19 *Lilium* 'Lady Bowes Lyon'

Annuals/biennials
20 *Tropaeolum majus*
21 *Perilla frutescens*

Half-hardy
22 *Dahlia* 'Bishop of Llandaff'
23 *Argyranthemum frutescens* 'Jamaica Primrose'
24 *Cuphea ignea*
25 *Salvia rutilans*

A TACTILE AND FRAGRANT GARDEN

THIS PLANTING IS DESIGNED primarily with the partially sighted in mind, but it should serve to remind all of us of the importance of stimulating senses other than sight in the garden.

There is a considerable variety of plants with scented flowers for a wide range of seasons, together with several species that have aromatic foliage, such as the scented-leaved pelargoniums and lemon verbena (*Aloysia triphylla*). It is quite a good idea to place such plants around a seating area; some are potent enough to release their scent on being brushed against, and all can be a stimulus to conversation.

Touch is an underrated element in the garden; leaf shapes and textures vary enormously, from the smoothness of Magnolia grandiflora 'Exmouth' to the roughness of witch hazel (*Hamamelis* x *intermedia* 'Pallida'). Many plants have tactile seed-heads, too, such as honesty (*Lunaria annua*) and the quaking grass (*Briza maxima*), and flowers, like bleeding heart (*Dicentra spectabilis*).

MAINTENANCE – *Medium*

Most of the plants here are shrubs or perennials which require little attention. The annuals and biennials, though, will need to be sown every year, although honesty usually manages to do this for itself.

The plants in containers, and the pelargoniums, will have to be kept in the house or in a greenhouse over the winter, ideally above freezing point, or above -4°C (25°F) if they are kept dry.

SITE AND SEASON

Any reasonably fertile, well-drained soil is suitable for this garden. The wall facing the patio also faces the sun, with the plants immediately against it appreciating good summer heat. Those on the far left are the most shade tolerant.

The main flowering is in early summer

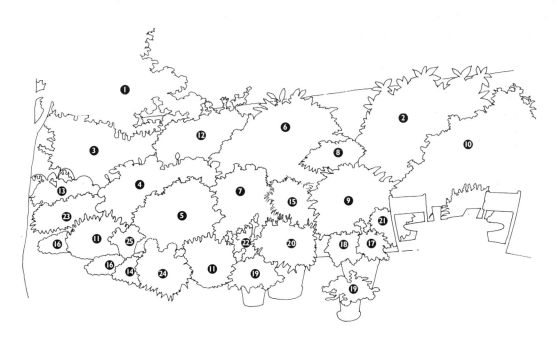

Trees
1 *Populus* × *candicans*
2 *Magnolia grandiflora* 'Exmouth'

Shrubs
3 *Hamamelis* × *intermedia* 'Pallida'
4 *Rosa* 'Madame Isaac Pereire'
5 *Choisya ternata*
6 *Cytisus battandieri*
7 *Viburnum* × *carlcephalum*
8 *Euphorbia mellifera*
9 *Syringa* × *persica*

10 *Philadelphus* 'Belle Etoile'
11 *Lavandula stoechas* 'Pedunculata'

Climbers
12 *Lonicera caprifolium*

Perennials
13 *Dicentra spectabilis*
14 *Mentha suaveolens* 'Variegata'
15 *Foeniculum vulgare*
16 *Thymus* × *citriodorus* 'Aureus'

Half-hardy
17 *Pelargonium* 'Chocolate Peppermint'
18 *Pelargonium odoratissimum*
19 *Pelargonium* 'Royal Oak'
20 *Aloysia citriodora*

Annuals/biennials
21 *Matthiola* 'Giant Imperial'
22 *Lathyrus odoratus* 'Knee Hi'
23 *Lunaria annua*
24 *Dianthus barbatus* Monarch Series
25 *Briza maxima*

Part Four

PLANT CARE

*M*OST GARDEN PLANTS *will give pleasure for many years. Spending time and effort on preparing the ground before planting is thus well worth the effort, and can even mean the difference between success and failure. Just as important is the establishment phase, the year or two it takes plants to settle into their new homes. Spotting problems during this time can save a great deal of trouble and money.*

Chapter Nine

BUYING AND PLANTING

SURVEYS SHOW that 80 per cent of plant sales are impulse buys! This is not the best way to a well-planned and coherent garden, but is one that even the most strictly organized gardener will fall for at some stage.

If you are planning your garden carefully, then you will probably have a 'wants list' of plants you have seen in other people's gardens and would like to grow. If a plant is at all rare, obtaining it can require some determination. So how do you go about finding the plants you want?

BUYING HEALTHY PLANTS

Garden centres are the supermarkets of the gardening business, with all the advantages and disadvantages that implies. If you want anything out of the ordinary you will have to shop around, and it is probably best to telephone first because, unlike supermarkets, one garden centre's stock is never the same as another's. If a plant is not in stock and you cannot rely on the centre to get it for you, it is better to look elsewhere.

The number of specialist nurseries is now very much on the increase, and these will sell plants that the garden centres regard as uneconomic. The owners are invariably enthusiastic and expert, and you will learn a great deal from them.

Nurseries can be found by looking up plants in one of the directories that are now becoming an important part of the horticulture business. Spending a day driving around these small enterprises is immense fun, but remember to telephone first to check opening times and availability, both of which can be erratic.

Many nurseries run a mail-order service and this can be a very good way of buying plants, especially if you live a long way from the nearest source. It is especially useful for fruit trees and bushes, as even the best garden centres carry only a limited selection and it is very important to buy fruit from reliable growers. Accidents do happen – packages are opened to reveal mushy leaves and broken stems – but this is rare and plants usually travel surprisingly well. In any case, most nurseries will replace plants damaged in the post. As you might imagine, the service is generally a winter one, for this is the time when most plants are dormant.

Flower shows are perhaps the most enjoyable sources of plants. They usually have displays

Tulips and wallflowers usually have to be replanted every year for good results, but the effort is worthwhile for their bright early colour.

THE ULTIMATE PLANTING GUIDE

which give you some idea of what the shoot in the pot on the sales table will look like when fully grown.

SOIL PREPARATION

The traditional approach to gardening emphasizes the need for heavy digging to maintain a high level of soil fertility. While it is certainly nice to have that 'good loam' that old gardeners wax lyrical about, it is not a necessity. Much depends on what you want to do with your garden: fruit and vegetables, traditional herbaceous borders, bedding and many annuals make great demands on the soil and also need a lot of cultivation, but less labour-intensive plantings – shrubs, modern perennial borders and wildflowers – require nothing like the level of soil improvement of traditional gardening.

My philosophy – at least for growing ornamental plants – is to work within the prevailing conditions, which means choosing plants that naturally grow well in your garden. Working within the natural constraints means that you can minimize wholesale soil improvement, and need worry only about the preparation of specific planting sites.

If you do want to grow vegetables, or would like a lush border full of labour-intensive plants like delphinims, you will have to put the work in. You will need to make as much of your own compost from garden waste as possible, and it would be good to make friends with your local stable owner

to arrange regular deliveries of manure. The proverbial 'good loam' will need relatively little improvement, but a light, sandy soil or a heavy clay can absorb enormous quantities of such material or other soil additives, over many years.

The other situation where I would recommend wholesale soil improvement is when builders have ruined the soil around a house, especially in situations where there is heavy shading – there are plenty of lovely plants that thrive in rubble in sun but hardly any for rubble in shade! It is worth adding lots of garden compost, composted bark or manure to any bed where shade-tolerant plants are to flourish, the reason being that shade plants grow naturally in woodland, where their roots are always in cool, moist leafmould.

PLANTING

Bare-rooted plants should be put in the ground in autumn. Container-grown plants can, in theory, be planted all year round, but you must take your soil conditions into account. Frost, drought or water-logging will stress a new plant beyond its endurance, so wait until conditions are more favourable. A good indication that the soil has warmed up enough to plant is the emergence of weed seedlings in the border!

Conifers and evergreens should be planted in spring. If they are planted in autumn, their roots will not have time to establish before the cold,

SOIL IMPROVERS

Material	Uses	Application rate
Lime	reduces acidity; improves clay soils	0.5 kg/sq m (1lb/sq yd)
Gypsum	improves clay soils	0.5 kg/sq m (1lb/sq yd)
Bark compost (from garden waste)	improves drainage; improves water- and nutrient-holding capacity; some effect on clay soils	15l/sq m (sq yd)
Cow manure	improves water- and nutrient-holding capacity; improves sandy soils	15l/sq m (sq yd)
Horse manure	improves water- and nutrient-holding capacity; improves clay soils	15l/sq m (sq yd)
Seaweed	improves water- and nutrient-holding capacity	15l/sq m (sq yd)
Mushroom compost	improves water- and nutrient-holding capacity; improves sandy soils	15l/sq m (sq yd)
Leafmould	improves water- and nutrient-holding capacity; acidifies limy soil	15l/sq m (sq yd)
Green manures	improves water- and nutrient-holding capacity; improves sandy soils; improves clay soils	15l/sq m (sq yd)

The materials listed here may be dug into the soil to create conditions that are more congenial for growing a wide range of plants. They are not fertilizers, although all (except lime and gypsum) contain some nutrients. Their main purpose is to improve the nutrient-retaining capacity of the soil, or to make those nutrients available for plant growth.

Geranium sylvaticum, white-flowered Galium odoratum and the fern Dryopteris felix-mas will thrive in semi-shade on a fertile soil, forming good ground cover.

drying winds of winter drive the moisture from their foliage, mimicking the effects of summer drought. Early spring is also the best time for planting in cold, wet regions. That way, roots do not have to languish in hostile soil throughout the winter.

Most soils benefit from some sort of improvement, but try to improve the soil over the whole planting area rather than just in the planting hole. Only if your soil is very sandy and free draining, or exceptionally stony and poor, will adding compost to the hole help in establishing a new plant. Water is the most vital ingredient that you can supply to your newly planted specimens, so water heavily and regularly. The plant will rely on you to provide it with water until its roots are established and can go off in search of water for themselves. A good soaking twice a week is more beneficial than a light sprinkling every day.

TREES AND SHRUBS

Soak the compost a few hours before removing the plant from its pot. Bare-rooted plants will benefit from soaking in a bucket of water. Prune back quick-growing shrubs to one-third of their height. Dig a hole at least three or four times the size of the rootball; the roots will then need good, friable soil to spread into. Grafts on fruit trees should be planted above the soil level. All other grafted plants should be planted with the graft below the soil level to prevent the rootstock from throwing out suckers.

Do not add compost or fertilizer to the planting hole – trees and shrubs establish much more quickly without it as the roots are forced to spread out further in search of nutrients, thereby stabilizing the plant more quickly. Much more important in establishing new trees and shrubs is firm planting and the application of a mulch to keep down

PLANTING A TREE

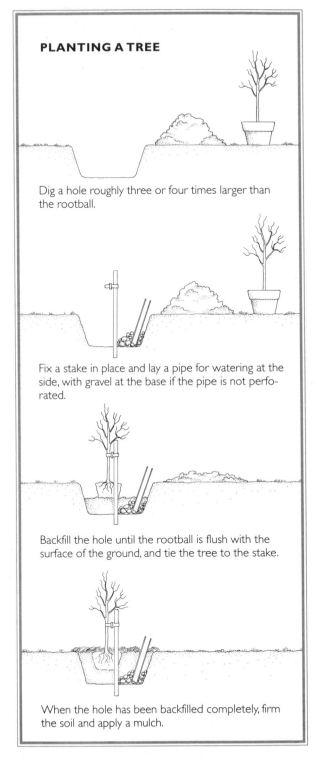

Dig a hole roughly three or four times larger than the rootball.

Fix a stake in place and lay a pipe for watering at the side, with gravel at the base if the pipe is not perforated.

Backfill the hole until the rootball is flush with the surface of the ground, and tie the tree to the stake.

When the hole has been backfilled completely, firm the soil and apply a mulch.

at least 75cm (30in) of their length is below ground. The stake should be positioned on the windward side of the tree so that the tree will be blown away from the stake, not on to it, thus preventing damage to the bark. Attach a tree tie to the top of the stake and to the stem of the tree.

A 30cm (12in) perforated pipe sunk vertically next to a tree will enable you to get water directly down to the roots. Alternatively, a length of unperforated pipe can be used, with a handful of gravel at the bottom to prevent it from becoming blocked with soil. This is useful for watering when getting the tree established and in times of drought. The pipe can be filled using a hosepipe or watering can, and none of the water goes to waste.

Make sure that you water the rootball particularly well. Moisture is lost at a faster rate from the rootball – just where it is needed most.

CLIMBERS

If you are planting a climber at the foot of a wall, fence or hedge, the soil will almost certainly need to be improved with organic matter to increase its water-holding capacity. Climbing is thirsty work and few climbers thrive in dry soil. If you are using a trellis or support fixed to a wall, put it in place before planting.

Dig a hole at least twice the size of the rootball and no less than 45cm (18in) away from the wall or tree. Angle the plant in the hole and use short canes to guide it toward the support. When the plant has been firmed in, mulch for a distance of 30cm (12in) around the stem and water well. Many climbers like their tops in sun but their roots cooler, so provide some shade for these with large stones or other plants. Plant on the windward side of any support so that the climber is blown on to it, rather than straining away from it.

HERBACEOUS PERENNIALS

For this group of plants, dig a wide hole rather than a deep one as most perennials have shallow, spreading roots. Exceptions are peonies and any others that have deep tap roots and consequently need deep holes.

Water the plant and the hole thoroughly, filling the hole with water and letting it drain before placing the plant in position. Plant 2.5cm (1in) deeper than the plant was in the pot, as perennials have a habit of lifting themselves out of the soil.

competitive weeds. Apply it for a good 30cm (12in) around, but not touching, the stem.

Stabilize trees with short stakes inserted so that

Many will need protection from slugs and snails while young. Provide this with thinly scattered pellets or plastic guard rings cut from bottles placed as a collar around each individual plant.

Perennials can also be planted in grass by removing a circle of turf and planting into the soil that has been exposed.

BEDDING

Make sure bedding plants are hardened off before setting them out. Soak the plants in their pots a few hours before planting them.

Dig small holes with a trowel or dibber and fill with dilute liquid fertilizer. Always handle young plants by the rootball or the leaves, never the stem – they only have one and if that is damaged you might as well throw the plant away. Carefully drop the plants into the holes before the liquid drains away. Young plants that are 'puddled in' in this way get off to a flying start. Gently backfill the hole with soil.

Use pellets or plastic rings to protect the plants from slugs and snails, and cover them with fleece or netting if late frost is threatened.

BULBS

Many bulbs need an open, sunny position so that the sun can ripen them ready for next year's display. Early bulbs, such as snowdrops and daffodils, exploit the spring sunshine under trees before the leaves develop and are thus ideal for woodland planting. Later in the season, when the trees are in full leaf, very little will bloom in their shade.

Spring bulbs, particularly daffodils, need to have their foliage left until early summer before cutting it down, so think twice before planting them in a lawn. When planting in borders, make sure you know where the bulbs are so that you don't dig them up later in the season. Plant them next to a path or wall, near steps, beside a large rock or at the base of shrubs.

Wet, stagnant soil is the main enemy of bulbs. Dig over the whole area if possible, and add some grit for drainage if the soil is prone to waterlogging. Dig a hole wide enough for the bulb to fit in and three times as deep. The exceptions are the rhizomes of bearded irises (*Iris germanica* varieties), which should be only half buried so that the summer sun can bake their tops. Do not put sand in the base of the hole: it does not assist drainage and acts

as a sump, drawing all surrounding water to it. And do not just push bulbs into the soil – they invariably bruise, and this provides an ideal site for infection to set in.

PLANTING PERENNIALS IN GRASS

This technique can be used for planting wildflowers in turf to create a small wildflower meadow, or for naturalizing robust perennials such as geraniums, hemerocallis or achilleas in grass, for a wild-garden look.

Kill off a circle of grass about 40cm (16in) across using a glyphosate-based weedkiller.

Take out a small circle of turf about 20cm (8in) across and dig a planting hole.

Plant the perennial and backfill the hole.

Cut up the dead turf and arrange it around the plant. This helps to prevent buried weed seed from becoming exposed and germinating. A mulch could also be applied now to save water and help prevent weed seed germination. The grass must be prevented from encroaching for the first year at least.

Chapter Ten

AFTERCARE

IF PLANTED PROPERLY, most plants are not greatly demanding of your attention in their first year. A mulch is vital for conserving moisture and keeping down weeds, although additional watering and weeding are usually necessary. Take care not to let new plants dry out: they will not have had time to develop a root system that can sustain them and will rely on you for the first few weeks at least.

WEEDING AND STAKING

It is very important to weed around new plants and to keep grass away from the stems of trees and shrubs planted in lawns for at least the first three years. Weed and grass roots are a major source of competition and will slow down the establishment of young woody plants considerably. Be careful when weeding around newly established plants because it is very easy to dislodge them. Most weeds will not survive if chopped off at ground level – this is best done with a hoe or V-shaped weeder to minimize disturbance. Perennial and deep-rooted weeds, such as bindweed and nettles, should really be dug out before planting is attempted. If they do rear their heads it is best to

finish them off with a touch-weeder stick so that you do not affect your new plants. Some tall plants will need staking as they grow, although for perennials in particular just pushing a few twiggy pea sticks around the perimeter of the clump will usually suffice. It is always worth checking tree ties after a high wind or heavy storm to make sure that they are still doing their job.

People often think that if their plants don't romp away in the first season they must be going to die. Many plants will secure themselves a good root system before they even attempt to put on top growth and this is especially true of trees and evergreens, which may take two or three years to settle in. Another common misapprehension with evergreens is that dried-out leaves mean no water at the roots. While this might be the case in some instances, it is more likely to be the effect of a cold, drying wind desiccating the leaves. In this event, a windbreak will be more effective than a watering can.

MULCHING

Mulching is a very successful way of conserving soil moisture and helping to prevent the growth of

A mulch of chipped bark conserves moisture and suppresses weeds. It also makes a good path.

weed seedlings (although only plastic has any effect on perennial weeds). The mulch should be applied, or reapplied, in spring, while the ground is still damp and must be kept away for plant stems. Chipped bark, the most popular form of mulch, lasts for several years and looks good around established plants, but it is inadvisable to use it where the soil will need to be disturbed, as it removes nitrogen from the soil if buried. Straw, mushroom compost, corn hulls and other agricultural wastes are often available locally, but usually last only a season before decaying. Gravel makes an attractive permanent mulch and is useful in dry climates for its ability to condense dew and cool the roots of nearby plants.

PRUNING

Training and pruning trees and shrubs during their early lives are essential tasks if you want to secure healthy, shapely and productive specimens. Pruning is one of the major plant maintenance jobs that you will have to undertake; it is not only about cutting back overgrown plants, but also about stimulating new growth and encouraging the production of fruit and flowers.

Trees and shrubs often take a year or two to settle in before they put on any top growth, so it is best to train them while they are young. If you train a young plant to do what you want it to do, you can save yourself an awful lot of hard work in future years. The removal of a bud usually stimulates those left behind into action. For example, removing a dormant leader will encourage the stems below it into growth, so that the plant becomes bushier as a result and its continued upward growth is halted.

The time of year that you prune also affects growth. Winter pruning stimulates copious spring growth. Spring pruning may cut out dormant flowerbuds and result in spindly growth. Summer pruning may stimulate the plant into putting on new growth that is likely to be damaged by early frosts. Most trees and shrubs should be hard pruned when first planted and will then require no further pruning for two to three years. Some, however, will need to be pruned the following spring – buddleias, ceanothus, hardy fuchsias, spiraeas and willows all fall into this category. Prune all the first season's growth back to the first bud above the old wood.

Most trees will not need pruning until two or three winters after planting. Winter pruning, done when the plant is dormant, is ideal for most. Some, such as cherries and plums, must be pruned in summer to minimize the risk of silver-leaf disease. Walnuts also need to be pruned in summer to prevent the sap from bleeding.

If you have prepared the soil well and staked the tree properly, you should be able to remove the tie after about 18 months. Very large trees may need to be supported for another season. Remove the tie and flex the stem gently. If the base of the tree seems loose it is too early to remove the tie, so replace it. If the tree has still not anchored itself after three years there is probably something wrong with it, or with what it is growing in. You will need to establish the cause (waterlogged soil is the most common problem) and remedy it. If the tree has established well, remove the tie in spring at the start of the growing season. It should then be quite secure by the time the winter winds arrive.

PROBLEMS

So, if you have done everything right, why do some plants still turn up their toes and die? The most obvious answer to this is that they were half-way dead when you bought them. It is surprising how many gardeners blame themselves, when in fact they have been sold a duff plant. If, despite all your best efforts, a plant dies, it is worth digging it up, taking it back to where you bought it and asking for a refund.

However, the problem may be a cultural one. The wrong plant in the wrong place is an obvious and all-too-common mistake. Plants can rarely struggle and win if the odds are that much against them, so take time to get to know your soil and local conditions; then you will have a better idea of what is likely to thrive and what is not worth bothering with. A common sight are the yellowing leaves of acid-loving plants, such as rhododendrons and camellias, languishing in limy soil, so make sure you choose the right plant in the first place or be prepared to do a lot of work to change the condition of your soil. Drooping leaves and stems are usually an indication that the soil is too dry or that wind is drying out the leaves. Drought-lovers will rot and die in cold, wet soils; likewise, damp-shade lovers will dry up in poor soil. The sun may be too

MULCHING MATERIALS

Material	Pros	Cons
Black polythene	good weed control	moist conditions beneath attract slugs; not very attractive – cover with gravel or bark for better effect; expensive
Chipped bark 5cm (2in) thick	good for conserving moisture	
Coco shells 7.5cm (3in) thick	good for conserving moisture and suppressing weeds	expensive
Garden compost or shredded material 5cm (2in) thick	free	may contain weed seeds
Grass clippings 10cm (4in) thick	good for suppressing weeds; free	
Gravel 5cm (2in) thick	keeps roots cool; attractive	poor weed control; expensive
Mushroom compost 5cm (2in) thick	cheap if you have a local source	may raise pH to unacceptable levels as contains a lot of lime
Straw 12cm (5in) thick		thick layer needed; blows around in the wind; may contain herbicide residues and weed seeds

Mulches help to suppress weeds (although only plastic has any effect on buried perennial weeds) and conserve moisture. All mulches should be kept away from plant stems.

bright for some delicate foliage and may cause brown scorching on the leaves, while lack of flowers may mean that the plant is not getting enough sun. In either case, the only remedy is to dig up the plant and move it to a more favourable position.

Poor planting is another possible cause of decline. The plants often start off well but begin to deteriorate when they should be thriving. Plants need to have their roots spread out in the planting hole. This is particularly true of container-grown trees and shrubs whose roots may have started to coil around the pot. Unless you tease them out in a more natural direction, they will stay coiled and be of no use to the plant at all. If this is the case, you will need to lift the plant and soak it in a bucket of water until you can manipulate the roots out of their coil.

It is surprising how many plants are left to decline just for the want of a bit of food. Many gardeners, while happy pruning and digging, will often forget to feed their plants and then wonder why they refuse to thrive. Small leaves, sparse growth and lack of flowers are all indications that the plant is crying out for a good feed. Most borders need a good feed in early spring; plants in containers may require feeding once a week during the growing season. Even old, well-established plants will benefit from an influx of nutrients.

Pests and diseases love lush new spring growth.

This is when plants are at their most vulnerable. Young plants suffer more than larger ones, partly because they are more vulnerable before they are established and partly because they are smaller and have fewer reserves. The top five most common problems are:

1 SLUGS AND SNAILS
Slugs and snails are impossible to eradicate from a garden, so it is best to concentrate on protecting individual plants with pellets or guard rings. They are a particular menace to seedlings and herbaceous plants in early spring, when lots of nice juicy shoots are growing, especially in species with fleshy foliage which lacks deterrent hairs or bristles to discourage slugs and snails.

2 APHIDS
Aphids can appear very early in the year when you least expect them, so keep a sharp eye out. They can breed at a fearsome rate and do a lot of damage to young shoots. Greenfly, blackfly and the like can be zapped with chemicals, but this often kills off most of their predators as well. The best way of controlling these pests is to squash them between your fingers before the colonies get too big, or practise a little biological control by moving ladybirds to infested plants. These can munch their way through hundreds of aphids every day.

3 LEAFSPOT

Many plants can be attacked by leaf-spotting fungi and there are hundreds of these fungi to choose from! They are rarely detrimental to the overall health of the plant although some, such as rose blackspot, can cause severe defoliation. The only way to control this disease is by spraying with a systemic fungicide – one that gets into the plant's system and fights the fungi from within. It is often the case that some varieties of a particular plant are more susceptible than others, so careful research before choosing a plant may repay with less trouble later.

4 MILDEW AND MOULD

Mildew and mould are caused by bacteria that attack an already stressed plant. Mildew is usually caused by damp, overcrowded conditions, so space out the plants more to encourage good air circulation around them. Mould is usually caused by the combination of damp and cold, so make more effort to protect vulnerable plants by improving conditions.

5 CATERPILLARS

From the maggots that infect apples and pears, to the cabbage whites that munch their way through brassicas and the leaf-rolling caterpillars that make their homes in pelargoniums, caterpillars are the bane of every gardener, not least because they are so difficult to control. To protect fruit trees you can tie grease bands around the trunk, which will prevent the adults crawling up and laying their eggs, or you can hang pheromone 'sex traps' in the branches of the tree to break their reproductive cycle. Contact insecticides can be used nearer the ground, but you have to score a direct hit on the caterpillar for them to be effective. Hand-picking and then placing the caterpillars on the bird table is time-consuming but acceptable to those who do not like to use chemicals. A safe biological, bacterial control has yet to be developed.

Bibliography

Brickell, Christopher (Ed). *The RHS Gardeners' Encyclopedia of Plants & Flowers* (Dorling Kindersley, London, 1989).
Very useful and comprehensive, but can be difficult to use and surprisingly inaccurate information is given in places.

Davis, Brian. *The Gardener's Illustrated Encyclopedia of Trees & Shrubs* (Viking, London, 1987) and *The Gardener's Illustrated Encyclopedia of Climbers & Wall Shrubs* (Viking, London, 1990). Two excellent books, packed with information.

The Hillier Manual of Trees & Shrubs (David & Charles, Newton Abbot).
Periodically updated, and the most comprehensive book on the subject, of use mostly to the more adventurous gardener. The illustrated version is more novice-friendly.

Rice, Tim. *Perennials* (Mitchell Beazley, London, 1995).
Very good general introduction.

Thomas, Graham Stuart. *Perennial Garden Plants* (Dent, London 1990).
Splendid, readable reference work by one of the most experienced gardeners of our times.

Thomas, Graham Stuart. *Ornamental Shrubs, Climbers annd Bamboos* (John Murray, London 1992).
Another most useful book by the above author. The only weakness of both is the paucity of illustrations.

Acknowledgements

This book is the product of years of garden visiting in many countries and innumerable discussions with other gardeners and designers. I am very grateful to those people who have generously allowed me access to their gardens and taken the time to discuss them with me. It is quite impossible to list them all, but the following I think deserve special thanks for teaching me, inspiring me, offering me hospitality or unlocking the doors of secret gardens to me: in Brazil, Conrad Hamerman and the late Roberto Burle Marx; in Germany, Urs Walser and Hans Simon; in The Netherlands, Piet and Anja Oudolf, Leo den Dulk and Rob Leopold; and in Britain, Nori and Sandra Pope of Hadspen House and Guy Acloques of Alderley Grange, and, for their frequent hospitality in London, Helen and Johnathan Barnes. I would also like to say thank you to Sharron Long, who read the manuscript and helped with research, to my wonderful agent Fiona Lindsay, and to my partner Jo Eliot, for her constant love and support.

Photographic acknowledgements

Jacket:
Left: **Clive Nichols** (Mrs Frank, Steeple Aston, Oxon)
Right: **Andrew Lawson**.

Jerry Harpur 7 (Mr & Mrs Royle, Home Farm, Balscote), 63 (Quiteways, Cumbria), 128 (Fudlers Hall, Mashbury nr. Chelmsford), 217 (Iden Croft Herbs, Kent/Designer: Simon Hopkinson); **Andrew Lawson** 2 (Ashtree Cottage, Wilts), 8 (Designer: Thomasina Tarling), 13 (Hadspen Gardens, Somerset), 17 (Marwood Hill, Devon), 19, 22 (Knightshayes, Devon), 27, 29, 30–31 (Alderley Grange, Glos), 32, (The Priory, Kemerton, Worcs), 58–9 (Barnsley House, Glos), 61, 65, 67 (Exbury Gardens, Hamps), 69 (Vann, Hambledon, Surrey) 73, 77 (The Priory, Kemerton, Worcs), 79 (Waterperry Gardens, Oxon), 81, 83, 85, 88 (Bourton House, Glos), 91 (Barnsley House, Glos), 109, 112–13 (Ashtree Cottage, Wilts), 118 (The Manor House, Upton Grey, Wilts), 121 left, 121 right, 124 (Beth Chatto Gardens, Essex), 125 (Eastgrove Cottage, Worcs), 130 (Hadspen Gardens, Somerset), 132, 136, 141 (The Priory, Kemerton, Worcs), 145, 146 (The Priory, Kemerton, Worcs), 149, 150, 154 (Brooklands, Dumfries), 155 (Designer: Lynden Miller, New York), 156 (Bourton House, Glos), 157 (Wollerton Old Hall, Salop), 159 (The Priory, Kemerton, Worcs), 160, 161 (Powis Castle, Powys), 162 (The Priory, Kemerton, Worcs), 164, 169 (Ashtree Cottage, Wilts), 171, 172 (Designer: Mary Keen, Berks), 174 (Designer: Rupert Golby, Oxon), 177 (Waterperry Gardens, Oxon), 181, 184 (Gothic House, Oxon), 187 (Hadspen Gardens, Somerset), 208 (Tintinhull, Somerset), 211 (Chenies Manor, Bucks); **Noël Kingsbury** 11 (Würzburg Botanical Gardens), 16, 25 (Frau Bahlo, Fürth im Odenwald), 89 (Josef Becherer, Dillingen), 106–107, 117 (Westpark, Munich/Designer: Rosemary Weisse), 127 (Westpark, Munich/Designer: Rosemary Weisse), 213 (Hermanshoff, Weinheim/Designer: Urs Walser), 166; **Nick Macer** 76; **Piet Oudolf** 122–3, 138–9, 151.

Index